THE
Petit Lenormand
—ORACLE—

A Comprehensive Manual For The 21st Century Card Reader

LISA YOUNG-SUTTON

DEDICATION PAGE

I lovingly dedicate this book to my best friend and husband, Padraic Sutton. You are the anchor that keeps me from drifting out to sea. Beidh grá agam duit go deo.

"If you have knowledge, let others light their candles in it."

-Margaret Fuller

ACKNOWLEDGEMENTS

Special thanks go to Bjorn Meuris – because you never forget your first. Thank you for introducing me to the world of Lenormand; to Toni Puhle for showing me the value of studying a system; to Susan Branch, whose own story gave me the confidence to share my words with the world; to my caring and supportive husband, Padraic Sutton, without whom this book wouldn't exist; to my late father, Ray, who forever reminded me to take a break from learning once in a while and teach; to Serge Pirotte, who always had an answer; and a special thank you to Camelia Elias, for giving me the permission I needed to be myself and do it my way. And, finally, to my muse, Beaker. My little Beagle-Cocker mix. The steadfast heartbeat at my feet. Thank you for waiting patiently for your walks when I suddenly started sitting a lot more than usual, staring at the electronic box and tapping my fingers furiously on the plastic board.

CONTENTS

A LENORMAND STORY TO
WHET YOUR APPETITE

Picture this, if you will. You're sitting at your desk on a lovely Friday after-noon in June playing with your cards. A woman approaches and says, "Oh, I didn't know you read cards!" excitedly. You reply that you're only learn-ing. She proceeds to tell you that her Persian kitten, Irina, got out of the house a couple days prior and asks you to see what the cards have to say about the kitten returning home. You remind her that you're new to the cards and are a little nervous about asking such an important question. She assures you that she will take what you say with a grain of salt. Ok. The pressure's off. You begin to shuffle your deck while concentrating on this question, "Show me if Irina will return home by the end of the week." You lay out three cards. They are, Cross-Sun-House. You look at the cards for only a second or two and say, "After church on Sunday, she'll return home". No sooner do the words leave your mouth that you begin to second-guess yourself and you start to make excuses, reminding her that you really don't know how to read these cards yet. Once again, she assures you that it's fine and thanks you before leaving. As soon as she's gone you start rethinking what you'd just told her. No wait, maybe Irina is in distress (Cross) and she's stuck in the sun or a very hot place (Sun) and the House card could be someone else's house. Maybe it's a yellow house and she's hot because they have no AC (Sun). What if that woman doesn't even go to church (Cross)? Oh no! Maybe I spoke too soon and should've pondered over the cards longer. Interpreting these cards can't be that easy. What did I do! You put your cards away and remind yourself that she wasn't going to take what you said seriously anyway. Upon returning to work the following Monday, you receive an amazing phone call. It's the woman with the kitten. She tells you that the day before (Sunday), Irina was waiting for her on her patio when she returned from church. Everyone lives happily ever after and a new Lenormand reader is born.

This is the magic of Lenormand. While you were amazed and relieved to find you were correct, it wasn't a fluke. These simple images can trigger an immediate response from your right brain. Consider that your left brain is in charge of letter recognition, the recall of memorized facts and prefers to dissect and analyze whereas your right brain is in charge of recognizing shapes, colors, similarities and patterns and immediately wants to see the whole picture. You'll soon see that Lenormand is amenable to both sides of your brain. Read on, my friends.

(This is a true story of my very first Lenormand reading)

WHO THE HELL AM I, ANYWAY?

If you'd asked me only five years ago if I believed in psychics, I would've said something like, "Well, I think some people have a gift, but most of them are fake!" I'd never been to a psychic, a Tarot reader, a fortune teller, or an astrologer. I definitely didn't believe in phone psychics or the daily horoscopes in the paper.

So, what happened? Well, it all started when my husband gave me an Amazon Echo for Christmas, 2016. (I had started receiving number signs about a year prior but made no connection).

I wondered what to do with this device. Other than listening to music, I assumed it must perform some other tasks. Ok, it can tell me the weather, but so can the TV and my phone. Then, by chance, I saw an advertisement for Audible.com on the Internet, and it hit me! The Echo could read me audio books! Now we're talkin'!

So, Audible offered a free trial and you got a free book – which you could return if you didn't like it, so no pressure! I began sifting through all the available books. This was no easy task as I'd been reading nothing but non-fiction related to dog training and nutrition and scent detection for years! At that moment I wondered how I'd become such a boring person! As I continued searching there was one book that just kept showing up – as if it was haunting me! I kept dismissing it as I had no interest in the subject at all. But it persisted. Then, finally, I thought why not buy the stupid thing. I can listen for a few minutes and then return it, so it would leave me alone. That, my friends, is where it all started. The book was The Universe Has Your Back by Gabrielle Bernstein.

As planned, I started listening to it that evening as I prepared the dogs' dinner. I was busy so I let it continue playing even though I was thinking how stupid it was the entire time. Then, there was something she said that stopped me cold. I wish I could remember what it was, but honestly, it probably wouldn't faze me now so even if I listened to it again I don't think I'd find it. Whatever she said made me stop and take notice. I stopped the book and told myself that I'd start it over that night when I could give it my full attention. That's exactly what I did. In fact, I listened to that book in its entirety, three times! Suddenly, a whole new world was opening up for me. I was hooked. It was bringing out thoughts and feelings I hadn't experienced since childhood.

So, what came next was a mad reading frenzy! In my quest to not drain my bank account, I decided to start with books that I could find at the local public library. So I started with Angels 101 by Doreen Virtue, which I devoured in a couple days. Next was The Angel Therapy Handbook by the same author. As luck would have it, I had a snow day that enabled me to work through most of the book. I worked through each exercise, not having a clue what I was doing. I always thought that mediation was something that only some people could do. And even if I could do it, I thought it would be such a huge waste of time. After all, I was a book-reader, a studier, a learner. As far back as I can remember, I've been a bibliophile. My family still jokes about the danger of giving me a book at a Christmas gathering or at my birthday party because I will get lost in it immediately and tune everyone out. I can't resist reading. There is so much to learn and we're on this planet for such a short time. How, on earth, can I possibly fit it all in? I couldn't imagine wasting my precious free time sitting cross-legged on the floor with my eyes closed! But I was being sucked-into this new world like a dog hair under a vacuum!

Then, one night, I was reading the mediumship chapter in one of Doreen's books where it asked you to close your eyes and try to sense a deceased loved-one and feel where they are in relation to your body. I did so and focused on my Mom. I first imagined she was at my right side and we were walking arm in arm. But suddenly, my left arm raised and I physically felt her at my left side just above my shoulder. It was an eerie feeling for me. I opened my eyes and turned the page to a diagram that shows where your mother appears and low and behold, it was on your left side just above your shoulder! I was petrified that I'd crossed some evil line and was entering a forbidden world. I threw down the book and vowed to forget all this ridiculousness. I planned to return the book to the library in the morning and get back to my "normal" life. That night, I awakened as usual to use the bathroom (if you're young – just wait – you'll get there too!) and something made me look at my digital watch. It was 4:44:44! Still groggy, I wondered what the odds were of looking at my watch at that exact second. And suddenly my eyes opened wide and I remembered reading about the Angel number 444. I told myself that I'd look it up again before I returned the book in the morning. Then, I returned to bed.

Morning came and all was forgotten. My dogs were anxious for their morning run through the fields of a friends farm that I drove to every morning. As far as I was concerned, life was about to return to normal. I grabbed the book on the way out the door so I could drop it off at the library on my way home. But, of course, it didn't happen that way. On the way to the library, the book sat next to me in the passenger seat. I was lost in thought about dog training and the day ahead when I realized that the car in front of me was sitting at the stop sign for an unusually long time. I looked up and saw that the car was a restored 1970s model that looked like it just rolled off the assembly line. In it sat two small white-haired women, close together on the big bench seat, their heads barely clearing the seat's back. I was debating tapping the horn to wake them up when I happened to notice their license plate. I have head to toe chills right now as I recount that moment. It said Angel444. Ok, here come the tears. I can't even recount that moment without being overcome by awe at the magic of it all! Needless to say, the book returned home with me and I finished it that night. I'd outgrown the library at this point and started searching online, though I wasn't exactly sure what I was searching for. I found Hay House and bought several books by Louise Hay, Wayne Dyer, and Sonia Choquette. I now had both feet in the pool! But, being the hard-sell that I am, I once again began to think it was all my imagination and tried to walk away from it and return to my non-believing life full of logic and facts. Enter: The Crows.

I've always been a nature-lover and have three bird feeding stations on my property so when I awakened one morning to a yard full of crows I thought it was odd but certainly not impossible. They were everywhere – all over the grass, in the trees, on the shed and the house. They were so loud! I didn't think too much about it and went about my day. As I left the house a couple crows swooped down at me, making me duck. What was their problem? I wished they'd move on. Throughout the day I was asking people if they'd noticed all the crows and no one seemed to know what I was referring to. It continued day after day. They were flying alongside my van as I drove and swooping down at me as I entered the post office. My sister and I attended a dog training conference in Connecticut and they followed me there too. After the conference, we decided to head up to the Beach house on Cape Cod for a few days and, you guessed it, the crows followed. The first morning there, I sat on the couch sipping my tea and watching the crows in the trees outside the window when my sister awakened and came out to say, "What's with all these crows? We never have crows here!" Their squawking had awakened her. I told her they were with me and began to tell her my story. I believe she said something like, "You always were a little odd," and we laughed and got on with our day though I intended to research this phenomenon when I got home. The following week, I was talking to a client in my grooming shop and she told me about a group mediumship reading at the New Age shop in town. I had to go! I sat in that seat like a child waiting for Santa to come through the door. I could've exploded. I was so excited. His name was Matt Kamont, the Lehigh Valley Medium, and he was amazing! After the session, we spoke and I asked him about the crows. Finally! Someone understood!

He said the same thing happened to him when he discovered that he was a medium but had no intention of using his gift. "The crows were relentless," he said. He told me they'd leave me alone as soon as I committed to pursuing my own gifts. He was correct. There was no turning back now. I was in the club. Meditation became a daily practice.

Suddenly, I was remembering things about myself that had been long forgotten. As a young child I was a mystic. My mother was always waving her hand in front of my face as I sat glassy-eyed, performing a thousand mile stare. She named it "fog island." I seemed to know that there was a spirit world coinciding with our own and I felt an overwhelming need to connect with it. I was a lucid dreamer and growing up above a funeral home (my father was an undertaker), I always felt that spirit was trying to connect with me too. I truly wanted to know why we were here – What was our purpose?

I remember sneaking into the Catholic Church across from our home because I felt Spirit was there. My Presbyterian parents were less than thrilled – especially when the priest called my father to ask him to keep me away from mass because I was receiving communion (which non-Catholics are forbidden to do)! The clincher was when I ran into the house one day and told my mother that I'd just seen the Virgin Mary above the pond behind our home! My parents were desperate to distract me so they bought me my first horse. Their plan worked. I switched my focus to speaking to my horse and any animal I could find. Finally, someone understood me!

But as kids do, I grew up, pushed all of that "spiritual nonsense" to the back of my brain, and got on with life in a human body. Fast forward about thirty years. For reasons I may never know, I started receiving number signs – specifically my birthdate. I was seeing it everywhere – license plates, billboards, number of emails I received each day, etc. But it was when the totals at stores were coming up as my birthdate that I finally had to research what it meant. I performed an online search and found that numerology and Angel numbers were a "real thing"! A book-reading frenzy began, followed by local and online courses in everything from remote viewing to mediumship and from psychometry to animal communication. I immediately found that I had a real gift for animal communication and began practicing it in online forums as well as in my grooming salon and training business.

I was happy enough with the information I was receiving but felt like there must be a way to get even more. I began searching for a better way to channel messages and information. I hired a Shaman to give me a reading on where I should focus my energy. She was a lovely woman, half Native American. She started by retrieving my totem animals and told me that my first birth totem animal was a bobcat. The cat's large paws told her that my talents could be best accessed via something I held in my hands and she suggested psychometry and scrying. I attempted psychometry with some success, but I knew it wasn't what I was looking for. I then tried crystal ball and water gazing and again, it was no better than simply closing my eyes and using no tools at all. Next, I tried automatic writing and was getting closer. But then, I ordered my first deck of oracle cards and BINGO! I found my niche!

I was avoiding tarot because I thought it was evil. My Christian upbringing was preventing me from going down that road, but before I knew it, I couldn't resist and ordered my first tarot deck. I simply removed the devil and death and thought I'd be fine. LOL! I knew there were plenty of books on the subject of tarot and card reading, but somehow I resisted buying any. Being the book-addict that I am, I still can't believe I was that strong! But, I didn't want to use the cards the way anyone else was using them and I never thought I'd be reading for humans. No, I simply wanted to use them for my animal readings. I wanted to use the symbols on the cards to develop a common language with Spirit. I'd already started a symbols journal, which I'd learned to do through my mediumship classes, and I already knew I could "see" things with my eyes open and looking at a piece of paper in front of me through my remote viewing courses. So I was trying to piece it all together. By using cards as the things I'd hold in my hands (as the Shaman had predicted), I was able to let my eyes move to whatever symbols they were drawn to and it was exactly what I was searching for.

Next stop, Lenormand! I continued to buy as many oracle and tarot decks as I was drawn to. I mean, seriously, can we card readers ever have enough? Then, one day, I was looking through an email regarding a deck sale (I don't recall from which company), and I saw an interesting oracle deck. It was so cute I had to have it. It was Liz Dean's Fairy Tale Fortune Cards. Because she doesn't call them Lenormand cards, I still didn't know what I had. I read the LWB, which has a brief history of the origins of the cards and was fascinated by the story of Mlle LeNormand. I was so intrigued that I did an online search of her name and well, you can guess what came next. Oh my! Another card system? I thought there were only two flavors! Of course, I had to learn more about it because by this point I was already becoming a cardophile! While I was still only using the cards in my own way to read animals, I began my first study of a card system and Lenormand was the big winner! Other than the Grand Jeu Lenormand – my "other" Lenormand system, I now rarely use anything else.

And, as they say, the rest is history. Here I am, Lisa the Lenormand Lady, who used to be called Lisa the dog lady. I'm liking the Lenormand title better! So, it only took me fifty plus years to discover this passion but as I believe that everything happens in its own time, I know that it was meant to happen the way it did. My sincere wish in writing this book is that someone – even one person – will read it and become inspired and realize that anyone, even someone who has no family connection to anything psychic and wasn't born a Gypsy can read Lenormand cards and read them with amazing accuracy. So, read on my friends and enjoy the journey.

HOW TO USE THIS BOOK?

I wanted to include in this book everything that a new reader would need to become successful with this deck. Because I began writing this book while I was still learning how to read cards, it's truly a greenhorn's journey! My intention from the start was to write as I learned so that the language and approach of the book would come from the viewpoint of a rookie, making it more approachable and effective for other learners. All the examples in the book are taken from actual readings that I journaled, or in some cases, I asked the question and drew the cards at the time I was writing – asking the cards to provide me with the best example for those who will read my book. To keep things authentic, no cards were changed. I hope that the examples are clear and helpful.

What you won't find here is a history of Marie Anne Adelaide Lenormand. She didn't develop this deck, probably never used it, and it was named after her for marketing purposes only. If you wish, you can read all about her in other books. You also won't find combination lists here. I've never studied nor practiced them and quite frankly, I've never seen the point in wasting my time with them. Because I want the cards to paint me a picture or tell me a story. Unless I'm asking a simple yes/no question, I minimally use three cards. Any 2-card pair can say different things depending on the question, context, proximity to the significator, surrounding cards, and the intended mode of reading (that is, narrative or descriptive). If I didn't want to pigeon-hole the cards' meanings, I likewise didn't want to pigeonhole combinations.

The Chapter, The 36 Cards And Their Meanings, is a compilation of information regarding each card. These are my meanings, which are based on the original game rules and the Philippe Lenormand sheet that accompanied all early decks. I even considered the Coffee Card verses that the deck was no doubt based on. I understand that there are other ways to interpret these cards based on regional differences or personal preferences. My advice is to choose the meanings that resonate with you and don't stray from them. For instance, if you want to use the Fox as your primary work card because it's what you're already accustomed to, that's fine. There's no reason to change that. Choose your meanings and adhere to them consistently and you'll have no problems. Remember that these cards are the words in a language. A language that you'll use to communicate with Spirit. Once your language is in place, it will be understood and communication will take place.

Each card section contains the following information:

1. The name and number of each card: All Lenormand cards are numbered the same – no exceptions. Card 1 is always the Rider and Card 36 is always the Cross. A few names can vary slightly, so I've included all that are popular.

2. The Playing Card Inset: Because there are several ways to read playing cards and there's no need to combine cartomancy with Lenormand, I have no cartomantic meanings included here outside of the court card insets, which readers may choose to represent people in a reading. (See the section: Playing Card Insets)

3. The Primary Vibe: This is the core essence or base meaning of each card. Being a tree-hugging hippie from the sixties, I chose the word "vibe" to describe this. The primary vibe should be the first thing you think of in any reading. It's the building block for each card from which you'll form sentences.

4. Energy: This relates to the "charge" of each card. Whether it's positive, negative, or somewhere in between. For me, this is of the utmost impor-

tance in a reading. For example, if I'm performing a reading for someone with Cancer and I ask about the outcome of a treatment and draw several favorable cards, one of which is the Stars, would that indicate that it's spreading? NO! It would indicate healing, success, and a new direction. Mice is my card for a spreading of something negative such as a disease. Mice spread disease and are thieves and bring loss, and what is disease but the loss of good health! If you understand that my question is about the success of a treatment and not the progression of the cancer, then this should make perfect sense. (See the section on questions)

5. **Influence:** This gives you the general impact a card will have on the reading. Such as, does it bring it up or down or is it fast or slow.

6. **The Theme Group:** This simply gives you an idea of the general category each card fits well into and what themes you'll most likely find certain cards showing up in.

7. **Base Keywords:** These are the primary keywords from which you'll derive your interpretations. They're the words that will immediately come to mind when you first look at a spread.

8. **The Basic Concept:** This simply explains why the primary vibe is what it is and how the base keywords were chosen based on the card's original emblem meaning. This is where I explain the core meaning of each card.

9. **The Broader Concept:** This is based on the cards' emblems as well as their symbolic meanings. We use these meanings in a secondary fashion for general readings, and to answer specific theme questions such as spiritual, animal readings, missing objects, or to describe characteristics, locations, or for time references. You'll find my Chakra associations here also. I believe that Chakras are very important and open and close them every day. I got involved in spirituality and divination as a non-believing skeptic, so any practice that had a perceptible concrete effect on me turned me into a believer. Chakras fall into that category! If you don't work on your Chakras already, I recommend searching for

some online meditations to get started. You'll find many on Youtube. What you won't find here are any associations to astrology as that is built into the Grand Jeu Lenormand deck, which is my "other" standard Lenormand system. I provide a brief example for using each card in a spiritual and relationship reading to give you some ideas. They are not intended to be all-inclusive statements as each reading will be unique. You'll also find my directions here, which are based on my location on the Earth. I live in the Northern hemisphere on the East Coast, so those directions apply to my position on the planet. You can use them or develop your own based on where you live.

10. Descriptive Words: These are the symbolic keywords that we use in describing physical and personality traits as well as occupations.

11. Advice: Not everyone uses the cards for advice readings but it's one of my most popular reading requests so I've included some of my advice meanings for each card. Even if you don't use them yourself, I hope that they'll inspire you to think more broadly and creatively when using this little deck!

12. Directional Cues: These are optional but come from some of the oldest reading traditions. Once I discovered directional reading, there was no going back for me so I hope you find these useful.

13. The PLOT: This gives you the original meanings that were included with the deck once it was repurposed and marketed for divination rather than simply as a game (even though the original game mentions that the cards can be used for a "fun divination game"). While Philippe Lenormand was simply a fictitious character invented for the marketing of this system, the meanings are valid nonetheless.

14. Game of Hope: I've included the game directions to give you a broader perspective on how the card meanings were derived and which cards were considered favorable or detrimental.

15. The Method of Distance: This is the original divination reading method for this deck as all early readings were performed using a grand tableau and it was the distance from the client's card that impacted the other card's meanings.

16. Compare To: I included this section to help differentiate between similar cards that tend to confuse new readers.

17. Emblem's Meaning: This section tells you why the card's pictures were chosen and what they originally meant to the readers of the period.

18. House Meaning: These are based on the standard Lenormand card meanings. Some readers may choose to use the Master Method, which I have studied but prefer not to use as it appears to be based on the playing card insets rather than the actual Lenormand cards. You can read about the Master Method in Andy Boroveshengra's book as well as Caitlin Mathew's.

19. Timing: I include the most common timing associations here for convenience. There is also a chapter on using this deck for timing.

20. Well-being: Lastly, I've included the most common health associations for each card for those of you who wish to perform health readings. Keep in mind that health readings are subject to the laws of your country. They may also leave the reader open to legal actions should you give someone the wrong advice. If you choose to read for health, please include a disclaimer on your website or in any literature you share with your clients freeing you of any responsibility.

Abbreviations:

1. GT = Grand Tableau
2. PT = Petite Tableau
3. PSC = Primary Significator Card
4. SC = Significator or life-area Card
5. MOD = Method of Distance

6. PLOT = Philippe Lenormand original translation

7. CC = Coffee Cards

8. C/H = Card and House

9. AC = Animal Communication

START HERE

L et's begin at the beginning. What is Lenormand? It's a cartomantic oracle, which can be used for fortune telling as well as divination. Allow me to explain those terms. While cartomancy is a word that's generally applied to the use of playing cards, its literal definition is the use of any cards for divination or fortune telling purposes. Tarot, Sibilla, and Lenormand are all cartomantic tools.

What is an oracle? If you search for oracle cards, you'll find everything from Angel cards to crystals to spirit animals – everything but tarot and Lenormand, but the fact is that an oracle is defined as any person or thing serving as an agency of divine communication. This makes the Lenormand deck a cartomantic oracle.

What's the difference between fortune telling and divination? Fortune telling is simply seeing the future while divination is asking for divine guidance. It's the difference between being told something and being inspired. Lenormand has a reputation of being a fortune telling deck, but it's equally useful for divination. While I sometimes use the deck strictly for fortune telling, as in, "Will I receive my package today?" I'm more inclined to use it for divination. In fact, even when clients come to me with straightforward, everyday questions to lend themselves perfectly to fortune telling, I still connect to the divine and include a little divination in the reading. I'm all about inspiration. It's why I got into card reading in the first place! Throughout this book, you'll see me refer to connecting to Spirit. This is what I call the

Divine. What am I referring to? The Divine is defined as universal forces that transcend mortal capacities. So all the steps I take to connect with the Divine are for the purposes of divination. This brings me to the topic of intuition.

Many people come to Lenormand with a background in tarot and others are drawn to this deck because of its reputation for not requiring the use of intuition. In my opinion, this is a lot of hooey. But I realize why this amazing deck got that reputation. Lenormand just may be the most straightforward, cut-to-the-chase, no nonsense card system available! I'm absolutely obsessed with this adorable little deck and I hope that, if you're not already, you will be too after reading this book.

I use a combination of a learned system and intuition when I read. Why do I need both? Simply put, because one involves my left brain and the other, my right. If we see our left brains (generally our more dominant side) as being the part of our brains that stores the information of the learned card meanings and the learned card system, then it's our right brains where our intuition resides and actually does the interpreting. Trying to use one without the other is problematic. For those who only want to use keywords and system rules, the readings can be general, vague and lacking in nuance. They can also be wrong! Many spreads can be interpreted in more than one way, no matter how many rules you memorize. Your intuition will be the tie-breaker. Let me explain what I'm referring to when I talk about intuition and card systems.

What is a card system?

A card system gives us standardized card meanings and general rules and guidelines for how to interpret the cards. In the Lenormand system, we have guidelines for how we'll interpret the cards. For example, reading a line from left to right as a story will make the first card the beginning of the story and the last card the end of the story. Using a center card as the focus card will make it the theme or answer card while the cards on either side will describe it. Always seeing cards above as weighing down on those below thereby giving it more power is a system rule. Seeing the cards closest to any theme or significator cards as carrying more weight than those further away is a system rule. Using knighting is a system rule. By learning and adhering to a system, our readings will become "systematic", getting our left brains out of the way and allowing our intuitions the freedom to express themselves. We won't have to stop and think about what we're doing, which halts intuition in its tracks. Our readings will become fluid and we'll quickly see what we need to see in the cards.

What is intuition?

Most sources describe it as a gut feeling. Some call it your inner voice or guide. I like to describe intuition as an awareness of your inner energy. It's so quiet and subtle that it mostly goes unnoticed. Another problem is that we often confuse our emotions, intense desires or fears, and even our own beliefs and biases with intuition. I'd like to categorize intuition as a right-brain skill while logic resides in the left-brain.

I believe that no one can become a successful card reader without using it and every human on the planet is born with it, the issue seems to be learning to trust it! This, I can help you with.

I always start a reading from a calm, neutral and centered place. Your frame of mind and purpose in drawing cards on any given day will be directly related to your success as a card reader, regardless of the card system you choose. Lack of focus or ill-intent can cause you to draw "gibberish" cards that aren't related to your question, to not seeing anything in the cards, or can simply lead to misinterpretations.

To start developing your intuition, there are many fun games you can play such as guessing who's calling before you look at your caller ID, guessing who the next person to walk into the room will be, drawing a face-down Lenormand or tarot card and "feeling" it to see if you can determine which it is or at least if it's positive or negative, and playing "guess what color I'm thinking of" with a friend. With your Lenormand deck, daily draws will be a great way to hone your intuitive skills. Start journaling daily draws of three cards where you simply ask to be shown something from your day. It's essential that you don't take this too seriously. The Coffin can be a box that's delivered, the Scythe can be a lawnmower or a paper cut, and the Cross may relate to an encounter with a religious person in your travels or having an aha moment in your car while it's stopped at a red light in front of a church! Write down all of your thoughts and at the end of the day, see if anything came to pass. If you play intuition games separately from learning your card system, you'll give each your full attention and ultimately you'll be able to combine them effortlessly.

Other than working your intuitive muscle with games, there are other ways of tapping into it. If you meditate, then you're already connecting to your intuition. For those of you who don't think you can or have never wanted to meditate, read on anyway as well.

I enter a semi-meditative state every time I read cards. Meditation doesn't have to involve sitting on the floor cross-legged with your eyes closed, fingers clenched in a Mudra as you chant "om" for an hour. It can take place while you're walking silently in nature. It can happen while you're washing the dishes or even while zoning out in front of the TV. It's nothing more than moving to a deeper state of awareness within yourself. It involves tuning out the world and connecting to Source. Source can be described as your higher-self, Angels, Spirit Guides, God, the Divine, the collective unconscious or the Universe. I typically call it Spirit. There's an easy way of getting there and it only involves a few steps, which you'll find below. I call it going to Alpha, and it's in Alpha state where we connect to our Mojo. I'm including the other rituals that I perform regularly to keep myself centered, protected and my vibration high. These include: Grounding or earthing, clearing and raising your vibration, mindful breathing, protection, setting intentions, reaching Alpha, and closing.

1. Grounding/Earthing:

Anyone who's had a dog with thunderstorm phobia may understand this concept. Grounding is when we connect to the earth's electrical charges to make an exchange. We release our own and absorb the earth's. Dogs will try to get in the bathtub or behind the toilet, under the sink, or into the basement or laundry room in an effort to connect to the earth via the plumbing. All the pipes in your house connect to the earth.

The Earth has a negative charge and we, living rather artificial lives inside and in front of computers, cell phones and TV's, pick up a positive charge. So basically, we're all buzzed-up. Therefore, we need to release the positive charge into the earth or water.

The easiest way to ground is to simply remove our shoes and step onto the earth where there is soil or grass. You can also use water via drinking it, soaking in it, even washing your hands.

Touching trees and plants outside and hugging trees will also ground you. Yes, I'm a bit of a tree hugging hippie from the sixties. Lying on the ground and swimming are excellent. I often soak my feet in water with sea salt before or after readings. When the weather prohibits this, I place my hands in the soil of my houseplants and touch their leaves.

Grounding studies show benefits to our hearts, depression and anxiety disorders, chronic pain, and sleep disorders, so I urge you all to practice it every day.

2. Clearing and Raising your Vibration:

This is an important step if you perform a lot of readings for others – even if it's just reading others' cards in the online practice groups – you're still taking in others' energies. Let's face it, with all that's going on in the world today, even if you don't read cards, you need this.

I simply start with smudging, which for those of you who don't know about it is the burning of dried plants, wood, or resins. It's an ancient practice and the belief is that the negative energies (with your intention) attach themselves to the smoke, which you then fan out of an open window or door.

But, once again, there is science behind smudging.

While it's impossible to scientifically prove that negative energy is attaching to the smoke, what studies do show is that it releases negative ions, thereby neutralizing positive ions such as pollution, dust, mold, and pet dander. So, just as with grounding practices, here again, we have neutralization positive ions. Remember that negative is good and positive is bad – unlike cards.

The herbs or woods traditionally used have been proven to have healing effects also. I use palo santo which is a natural remedy for colds and flu. It's also known to relieve asthma, headaches, anxiety, depression, and it reduces inflammation. White sage has both antimicrobial and antibacterial properties and it repels insects.

I have two rituals that I perform with smudging. The first is for my home, or at least my office where I perform readings. I do it once a week or whenever I feel a build-up. I walk through the house and get in all the corner as I chant the following:

"Smoke of air and fire and earth. Cleanse and bless and bring rebirth. Chase away all harm and fear. Only good may enter here."

I then banish the energies from my home. I have always been able to feel a difference in the house afterwards. Additionally, I love the way it smells.

The other ritual is for myself and I do this after I clear the house. As the smoke is rising, I cup it in my hands and wash it over the top of my head saying, I cleanse my mind that I may think clearly. Over my eyes, that I may see the truth. Over my throat, that I may speak the truth. Over my heart, that my heart may be open to the truth.

3. Mindful Breathing:

Breathing is where it all begins. Breath and Spirit come from the same Latin word, spirare (verb) or spiritus (noun). Spiritus is translated as spirit or breath. Spirare is breathing. How many Catholics here have heard the mass in Latin. Spiritus Sanctus is the Holy Spirit. So, if Spiritus means both breath and spirit, then deep and focused breathing is your first step in connecting to the world of spirit.

There is also science behind controlled breathing.

Deep breathing is actually a form of meditation, which dates back several thousand years. Research shows that meditation can reduce anxiety, sharpen memory, treat symptoms of depression, promote more restful sleep, and even improve heart health.

Controlled breathing has been shown to reduce stress, increase alertness and boost your immune system. For centuries yogis have used breath control, or pranayama, to promote concentration and improve vitality. Buddha advocated breath-meditation as a way to reach enlightenment.

Studies show that when you take slow, steady breaths, your brain gets the message that all is well and activates the parasympathetic response. When you take shallow rapid breaths or hold your breath, which is what you naturally do when you're stressed, the sympathetic response is activated. If you breathe correctly, your mind will calm down. Do it at the first sign of stress – before your chest tightens up, which makes it hard to breathe deeply.

Dr. Chris Streeter, an associate professor of psychiatry and neurology at Boston University, recently completed a small study in which she measured the effect of daily yoga and breathing on people with diagnoses of major depressive disorder. After twelve weeks of daily yoga and coherent breathing, the subjects' depressive symptoms significantly decreased and their levels of gamma-aminobutyric acid, a brain chemical that has calming and anti-anxiety effects, had increased.

There are several different breathing techniques that you can try, but I primarily use equal and abdominal. They're the easiest to learn and remember, so I'll walk you through them now.

A. Equal breathing is simply slow and steady in and out with a count of four. Let's try it now. I can't talk and do it at the same time so I'll walk you through it. Exhale and then slowly inhale through your nose to a steady count of four and exhale through your mouth to the same count of four. If you practice this every day, you'll be able to naturally do it during readings without giving it much thought.

B. Abdominal breathing is what I practice before readings and it's the first step to achieving Alpha state. Abdominal breathing is very powerful in reducing stress. When you're first practicing it, you may want to place a hand on your chest and the other on your abdomen so you can focus on where the breath is going. I do it to a count of five, focusing on filling my abdomen – not my chest. Inhale through your nose for a count of five, Hold for a count of five, and exhale through your mouth to a count of five. I perform this from one to three times before heading to Alpha. Do it as many times as it takes to relax. You'll know when you're there – you'll definitely feel the difference.

4. Connecting to Alpha:

These steps are based on my remote viewing training.

What exactly is remote viewing? The term was coined by physicist and parapsychologist, Russell Targ when working at the Stanford Research Institute in the seventies. He was researching ESP, which is nothing more than using your Clairs –primarily clairvoyance.

The US military got involved and spent $20 million on the research and found that anyone could do it with some training. In all their studies, they were measuring brain waves using an EEG (electroencephalogram) and the results are measured in frequency bands called Hertz, which are cycles per second and abbreviated capital H, small z.

How many of you have seen three numbers followed by Hz when searching for meditation music on Youtube? They're called Solfeggio tones or frequencies, binaural beats, or Gamma, Beta, Alpha, Theta, Delta waves. But you need to know what these mean because some of them can have an opposite effect of what you're going for.

The fastest are Gamma waves – measure 35 to 100Hz. Scientists and mathematicians solving difficult problems may operate at this level. I can't stand to listen to these waves – it's like nails on a blackboard for me. This probably isn't what you want for meditation of divination, but because everyone is unique you may give them a try and see how they make you feel.

Beta is the next level down and where our brains normally function and measures 13 to 30 hertz. You're already here. Why would you want to listen to that? Well, it's still soothing and makes nice white noise. I occasionally listen to this when I write.

Gamma and Beta are both considered left-brain dominant states.

Finally, we have Alpha, which is 8 to 12 Hz. This is the optimum state for performing all mediumship and psychic activities as well as creative endeavors. Artists and creative geniuses often work at this level. This is the first right-brain dominant state.

Below Alpha, there is Theta, which is what you experience right before you fall asleep. It measures 4 to 8 Hz and is perfect for putting you into a deep meditative state.

Lastly, we have Delta, which is below 4 Hz and is only experienced during sleep.

Now we know about brainwave states. How do they relate to Left and right brain thinking?

Your left brain is linear, logical, sequential, analytical, objective.

Your right brain is holistic, creative, emotional, intuitive, subjective.

So, why do we want to bring our brains to Alpha? Because it's where all the Clairs reside! It's where our intuition and creativity exist. It's the place where there's no fear, anxiety, jealousy, or insecurity. Alpha is where your Mojo lives!

Why do some people think they aren't clairvoyant or psychic? Because they don't know how to get to Alpha! Yes, everyone has psychic abilities to some extent. Just as with anything else such as musical abilities, affinities for speaking foreign languages, or a beautiful singing voice, abilities vary. But, yes, you do possess all the Clairs, you do have intuition, and you can perform divination with cards. Period.

Getting back to the topic of brainwave states, let's see what studies tell us about them:

Music tuned to 396 Hz helps remove fears, worries, and anxiety. It also helps to eliminate feelings of guilt and subconscious negative beliefs blocking the path to achieving personal goals. Perfect for when you want to feel more uplifted and secure. Excellent to listen to before readings or during sleep or meditation. The 417 Hz are for facilitating change and undoing situations. I don't resonate with this one, but check it out.

432 Hz is a frequency that fills the mind with feelings of peace and well-being, making it perfect for yoga, meditation, or sleep. Studies have shown that it slows the heart rate. This can also be perfect before or during readings.

The 528 Hz for miracles and transformations like DNA repair. Early research indicates that it has the ability to heal and repair the body. For divination, I do some of my best work at this frequency. A 2018 study from Japan discovered that music tuned to the frequency of 528 Hz significantly reduced stress in the endocrine systems and autonomic nervous system, even after a mere five minutes of listening. And in a study published in the Journal of Addiction Research & Therapy, the frequency of 528 Hz reduced the toxic effects of ethanol, the principle ingredient found in alcoholic drinks, on cells. Even more astounding was that this frequency also increased cell life by about 20 percent.

639 Hz is for relationships and reconnecting. It helps balance emotions and elevate the mood. It also promotes communication, love, understanding. This one is ideal if you find yourself comparing yourself to others or feeling envious of others' abilities or successes. 741 Hz helps with problem-solving, cleansing the body, and self-expression. It also helps to awaken intuition. It's ideal if you're struggling with expressing yourself creatively, or speaking

your truth. It is another great one for before or during readings. The 852 Hz frequency helps to replace negative thoughts with positive ones, making it ideal when nervousness or anxiety is bringing you down. It also aids in awakening intuition and inner strength. Try them all and see which ones resonate with you. This may vary over time or even from day to day, so save them in a folder. Sometimes, one will be your favorite for weeks, and then suddenly it will grate against your nerves and you'll listen to another and it'll be perfect. It depends on what you need at that moment.

Other than listening to these frequencies, you can program your mind to reach Alpha state in a matter of seconds by repeating a meditation daily for at least a month, followed by once a week for another month. If you commit to that, you'll be able to bring yourself to Alpha state in a few seconds whenever you want. Start conditioning your mind and body to work with you by adopting consistent practices and performing them regularly. In animal training, we call this "placing a behavior on stimulus control," which is simply pairing a stimulus with a behavior repeatedly until it becomes involuntary. If you remember Pavlov's dog study, then you'll understand what I'm referring to. You want to be able to run through a few steps and be in the right frame of mind to read cards in a few seconds. To begin, you'll need to find your mental screen. It's not the inside of your eyelids, but is found in the same place in your mind where you imagine or visualize things. You want to imagine a movie screen while your eyes are closed and looking up about 20 degrees. It's also been found to work best when facing south. We start with physical relaxation and connect that to the number 3. So, you visualize the number 3 several times and then proceed to go through your entire body from head to toes, tensing and relaxing. You then want to imagine yourself floating out of your body, so you're no longer hindered by it. Next, we want to relax mentally and we connect that to the number 2. We visualize the number 2 several times while visualizing pleasant, relaxing scenes. Anything that makes you happy and relaxed. Walking alone on the beach, through the woods, a field of flowers. Include all details like fragrances, clouds passing by, birds singing, colors, etc. If it makes you smile, it's perfect! Lastly, is Alpha level and we connect that to the number 1. Here, we visualize the number one several times and begin a countdown from 100, 50, 20, or 10 to 1, depending on how long it will take you to completely let go and relax. When I get to 1, I visualize myself entering my sacred place. Think about where you want to go. This is where you'll go to perform all readings. Nothing can hurt you here. All is calm and beautiful. You can meet your guides here. You'll invite the one for whom you're performing a reading (the querent) to join you here. This is where the magic happens. For me, I go down to this level in an elevator located in a huge oak tree. I found this place during my Shamanic studies and I've been going there daily ever since. It is different for everyone. Allow your imagination to paint a picture for you. You'll know when it feels right. When I'm finished, I thank my spirit team. Then, I release the querent and cut ties. Thereafter, I get back into my elevator and I see the numbers rising from 1 to 5. At 5, I'm back on the earth plane in the here and now. If this is all new to you, it may seem like it would take forever. When I was first learning, it probably took me thirty minutes or so to reach Alpha. It now takes me literally three seconds.

5. Protection:

I learned early on of the importance of protection. I'll tell you a quick story. I came home from my first group medium reading. It was during the very beginning of my spiritual awakening and I knew nothing about mediumship. I was amazed by the reading! Afterward, the medium spoke to me and told me that he sensed I had mediumship abilities. Of course, I was very excited. When I got home, I got right on the computer and started doing research. But, suddenly, my old doubts and skepticism hit me and I shouted, "Ok, Spirits, here I am. If you're real, come and talk to me! I was alone." My hubby was away and my two Dutch Shepherds laid at my feet. Suddenly, there was a loud knocking from the adjacent room that was dark. My younger Dutchie rose to his feet, hackles raised, staring into that room growling. My heart started pounding! I turned on the light and saw nothing but my dogs were slinking around the room growling and staring into the corners and doorways. The only thing I knew was what I'd just read online and I shouted, "No! Go to the light! You're not welcome here! I take back my invitation!" And suddenly, as fast as it started, there was calm and my dogs settled down. That didn't matter because I was so shaken. I couldn't sleep for two nights and was petrified to be in my own home alone! I started reading about protection right away and have consistently practiced it since!

Protection starts with an intention and a prayer or invocation. Ask and thou shalt receive! This starts with visualization. Call down the light of spirit to enter your crown, full your entire body, shooting out of your fingertips and toes. It forms a bubble of light around you. Ask that it protect you from all energies that might harm or confuse you. This bubble is your aura. When you connect to others for readings, you expand your aura and welcome them into it.

Next, call upon the archangels, your guardian angels, and your guides to stand guard as you're about to open yourself up to connecting with spirit and/or the collective unconscious, which is still something outside of yourself. Even if you don't believe in angels or guides, or dragons and unicorns, if you believe in the collective unconscious, then you are still opening yourself up to connecting to energies outside of yourself. You need to protect yourself and don't wait for an attachment to make you believe. You may want to recite the Lord's prayer. Believe it or not, spirit rescuers swear by this prayer! "Our Father, who art in Heaven…" I'm sure there are equivalent prayers for other religions. There are many protection prayers on the Internet or make up your own. One example is:

"Spirits of Love and Light; come to the Gateway of my soul and protect me from all that is evil."

6. Setting your Intention:

I think this is often overlooked. We set our intentions before laying the cards as to how many cards we'll lay, what our question is, and how we'll be interpreting the spread, but we should also be stating a clear intention before we even pick up the cards.

I took a class with psychic detective, Pam Coronado, and I learned about the value of this practice. It's as simple as this:

State your intention clearly. Psychic detective Pam Coronado says, "I'm a clear and accurate channel. I'm receiving only divine truth." Be sure to ask clearly and specifically for the information that you need and nothing else. Also, set your intention to only receive information from your target (person or animal). Right before the reading, say, "I set my intention to receive only information about this case and set aside all my beliefs, fears, and doubts and perceive only divine truth, no matter what it is." Before any reading, reinforce your successes in your mind. This will lead to more of the same. Focus on them often and not on your failures. Remember the best card readings you've ever done, some great feedback you received, or the day that you realized you could do this!

7.Closing:

Closing it simply disconnecting from whomever you were reading for and thanking and disconnecting from your spirit team. Closing is extremely important. If you don't, you're leaving yourself open to unwanted spirits popping in and draining you of your energy. This is how attachments are formed. Don't take chances!

Close your eyes and send out thoughts of love and gratitude to your spirit team and thank them for their help and protection.

Ask that all energies that have built up during the session be dissipated into the Universe or sent into the earth for transmutation. Energies never die – they always exist – they only change form. This is a basic law of physics. You can also ask that these strong energies be sent to healing those in most need of them.

Now imagine that huge bubble of light that you formed at the onset shrinks back to only surround your body. Visualize a cutting of all cords that you formed in connecting to people – living or in spirit – or animals. Send them away with love and gratitude.

Stand, stretch, and drink water.

KILLING YOUR MOJO

How many of you have seen the Austin Powers movies? If you have, then you've heard the term, "mojo" and probably have an idea of what it really means. Mojo is defined as a magic charm or amulet, or more broadly, a magical power. Austin was powerless when he lost his. Interestingly, the entire movie was built around the theme of mojo and Austin's last name was Powers! When it comes to card reading, we're attempting to see the unseen and to understand what others can't. It's not easy to prove what we see until it actually happens or comes to light. It takes confidence. It takes guts. It takes mojo!

When we lose our mojo, we'll second-guess everything we see or worse, we won't see anything at all. It's important to go to Alpha and connect with your mojo before every reading. By following the steps in the Start Here section, you'll get there. But, there are some buzzkills out there that I'd like you to be aware of that will diminish or destroy your mojo. Here are some:

1. Insecurity – The "I can't" syndrome.

2. Being told you're wrong. Don't walk, but run from anyone who tries to tell you that you're doing it the wrong way and of course, they're way is no doubt the only right way. There's a lid for every pot. Your way is your way for a reason.

3. Inexperience. Don't be in a hurry. For example, only move on to reading five cards once you feel confident with three.

4. Lack of knowledge. Did you buy your first deck and decide to just use it your way without learning the system as I originally did? You can certainly do this, but you'll have no foundation in place to support you when a reading makes no sense or you receive feedback that you were wrong.

5. Disorganization. Forming a regular routine before readings will put you in the right frame of mind and your mind will be focused on the task at hand. If you have a million things on your brain and just grab your cards to ask questions, you won't get very far.

6. Drugs and alcohol. Yeah, I know, some of you swear that you can't read without them. Everyone is different and some people are wound so tightly that a glass of wine or beer, or a bit of weed may be exactly what you need to wake up your right brain. For others, you won't be able to focus at all or simply won't care enough about what you're doing to feel any empathy for your client.

7. Caffeine. Same as above. Some need a little boost to wake the brain up!

8. Too busy. You need to be in a calm state to be able to center yourself.

9. Not enough sleep. When I'm tired, I can't do anything well. I very often start a reading at night and stare at the cards as if I'd never seen them before. If I leave them on the table and look at them again after a good night's sleep, they speak volumes! Any time you're stuck, you might need to just wake-up a bit. Get up and walk outside for some fresh air if possible. Jump on the exercise bike for a moment. Take the dog for a walk. When you return, you'll be fresh and the cards will come to life again.

10. Not entering Alpha and finding your mojo from the start. Once you get in a regular practice of doing this, it will only take a few seconds. It literally takes me three seconds to get there.

SHUFFLING AND DRAWING CARDS 101

I'd read about and tried several methods when I was starting out in card divination. When I discovered the best methods for me, they became my standard and I never waiver. You'll do the same, so try them all out if you're just starting and you'll quickly discover what feels right for you. Keep in mind that it really doesn't matter how you do it. If you question five different card readers, you may get five different opinions on how it should be done. It doesn't matter a lick.

Standard shuffling methods:

1. Riffle – I could try to describe this but a picture is worth a thousand words in this case. Also known as casino, faro, weave, or dovetail shuffling. You can see pictures and videos of this method demonstrated online.

2. Hand over hand – Holding the deck in your non-dominant hand, you grasp a section of the deck with your other hand, hold it above the other section, and allow cards to fall to the front and back of the section below. You can also slide them into the middle. This is my standard method that you can see in my videos.

3. Swoosh – You don't have to shuffle at all and instead can schmear the deck all over the table or floor and swoosh them around. You then draw

33

any card you're led. I use this method when I have a deck of a large size, an extended deck with a lot of cards, or two decks mixed together. Basically, whenever I can't easily hold all the cards in my hands without dropping them.

Drawing methods:

1. Drawing from the top – After shuffling, you leave the cards in a single stack and draw the top cards.

2. Cutting the deck into piles and taking the top card from each.

3. Taking the top card and then cutting the deck and taking the two bottom cards for a line of three or two bottom cards from each stack to give you a line of five.

4. Fanning out the deck and randomly choosing the cards.

5. Setting your intention to search for a charged card (See the section My Signature Spreads). After shuffling well, you turn the deck over and search for that card, taking the card in front and behind for a 3-card spread or the two cards in front and behind for a 5-card spread. If you're at the end of the stack and need another card, you consider the other end of the stack to be the next card. You can use this method for any descriptive/focus card line.

There are other ways of drawing cards and you can let your imagination lead you. I almost always draw random cards from a hand over hand shuffle, though I may start with a few riffles – especially if it's a new deck in which case I start with at least three riffles and as many as seven if I feel the cards are "sticky".

Just as with shuffling, the important thing to understand is that this is entirely up to you. You can be as creative as you'd like as long as you're clear in your intention. You can devise a method of counting the cards such as drawing every ninth card from the pile for a box spread. The key is that you need to establish in your mind how you'll do it beforehand and stick to it. So, as you're shuffling, you'll decide exactly how you'll draw the cards. This will allow the cards to fall as they need to in order to ensure that the cards that are meant for you will be in the correct positions. As far as which hand to use, again, that's up to you. You may hear that some suggest that you always draw with your left hand as it's closer to your heart, while others will suggest that you only draw with your non-dominant hand as it's not as influenced by the left-brain. For me, that refers to my left hand in both instances. I tried for many months to adopt the practice of drawing with my left hand but it felt so awkward that I eventually gave up. There was no difference in my readings. Use whichever hand you'd like. Use something other than a hand. You could schmear the cards out and use a pendulum or a wand to point to the right cards. You could use your foot if you'd like! Seriously. If your intention is clear and you're taking it seriously, you can use any method that seems appropriate at the time.

SYSTEMS? WE DON'T NEED NO STINKING SYSTEMS! OR DO WE?

I t's common these days to hear card readers discussing the difference between a card system and reading intuitively. While I never use one without the other, many claim they do, though I don't believe they truly are. I believe that intuitive card readers develop some sort of system and system readers use their intuitions, albeit in a way that feels safe for them. I thought I'd dig deep and examine exactly what the difference is between the two. I then want to discuss systems and how to develop your own.

So, what exactly is a card system and where does our intuition or psychic ability come into play?

Let's start by considering that cards are but one of the many divination tools one can use. We have scrying, runes, bone or charm casting, channeling, and psychometry just to name a few. So we can say that cards are a divination tool. There are many different categories or genres of cards at our disposal. A genre is a class or division of things regarded as having particular shared characteristics. So, some of the more popular genres include Tarot, Sibilla, Kipper, Petit Lenormand, Grand Jeu Lenormand, Gypsy, and Gypsy Witch. Each genre will include at least one system that has been developed and is widely accepted as the standard for using that particular genre.

A system can be defined as a set of principles or procedures by which something is done. It is an organized scheme or method. A system contains a structure and guidelines. Yes, you can call them rules, but many object to this word because they think that rules will prevent them from accessing their intuition. I know because I used to be one of those people! But, read on and you will learn that nothing could be further from the truth!

Now we know what a system is. At the other end of the spectrum, we have oracle reading. What do I mean by "reading oracularly"? I'm using this term to refer to the free use of our creativity – our psychic abilities – our intuition. Oracle decks were designed for this very purpose. Outside of the guidebooks that give us the deck creator's interpretations, we are free to study each card and search for its meaning. There are no guidelines and no structure. Images, numbers, and colors will all be taken into account and individual readers will all come to their own conclusions. Each time we draw an oracle card, we may get a different message. So, cards are just one divination method. Different types of cards are genres, and how we use each genre is its system. Now, let's delve deeper into what systems are. Card divination is both a science and an art. Let's define these two words before we proceed. Science can be defined as a systematically organized body of knowledge on a particular subject. Art can be defined as the expression or application of human creative skill and imagination. We can then say that card reading is based on using a system (the science), to which we then apply our intuition (the art).

In learning a system, once the left brain has the science under control, it frees up the right brain to create the art. While most readers agree that Tarot has a system, actually several, as well as Kipper, Sibilla, and the other long-established card genres, Lenormand, being the new kid on the block, seems to be causing some confusion due to the fact that the deck didn't come with a complete set of instructions and it hasn't existed in the English-speaking world long enough to have established one primary agreed-upon system that trumps all others. But, if we consider that card reading is nothing more than learning a common language with which to communicate to Spirit, regular use will inadvertently lead to the development of a specific method or system whether we realize it or not. Yes, even those who claim they use no system are actually using a system! For example, if every time they see a circle they think of something continuous, something cycling, something that encloses, and they consistently interpret that every time, then that is a system.

Some modern Lenormand readers want to forgo any system because they think it will interfere with their intuition – their creative expression – their oracular reading – their art. This couldn't be further from the truth. Without a system in place, many Lenormand readers are relying on extensive lists of keywords and never-ending lists of possible card combinations, which leave them virtually unable to perform the simplest reading without relying on their reference materials. Or, worse, they are relying solely on what they think is their intuition, which sometimes is nothing more than their personal thoughts, feelings, or past experiences forming a bias. To sum up, they're making it a lot harder than it should be! Because the Lenormand deck contains cards with a single image, they can be viewed symbolically or used as emblems. We want to start by establishing a system based on giving each image one primary meaning, thus creating emblems rather than symbols.

What exactly is the difference between emblems and symbols? Simply put, an emblem is a picture chosen to represent one specific thing or idea. The picture of the red cross is an emblem that represents the Red Cross organization. It won't represent anything else such as Christianity. A symbol, on the other hand, is open to individual interpretation, though they are generally chosen because they are universally seen in a particular way. For example, tarot uses symbols from archetypal energies, numerology, astrology, Kabbalah, spiritual symbols, colors, and more. With that in mind, Lenormand differs in that we assign one primary meaning to each card so that we can read them as specific words or ideas. This is why they need to be read in combination with each other. It's no different than putting together a sentence where you minimally need a subject and predicate and often include an object. There are, however, times when we can read the cards more symbolically such as when we use them to describe a person or thing, but we need to establish an emblem meaning first and foremost.

Is there one correct system? No! Anyone can create a system for the deck as long as it is well thought out and balanced. What I want you to consider is that the deck actually did come with a balanced core system. While the Philippe Lenormand instructions that accompanied all early decks is vague and its wording outdated, it truly covers all life areas and is a balanced system once we examine its deeper meanings. We can gain more insight from the instructions for the original Game of Hope, from which the Lenormand deck comes. Lastly, we can look at the meanings of the early Coffee Cards, which apparently inspired the conception of our Lenormand deck to gain even more understanding.

We can also blame some discrepancies in card meanings on flawed translations from the original German to English. Let's take #15, the Bear card for example. The Philippe Lenormand meaning for this card is translated using the words, prosperity and good fortune. This has led many to believe that this card relates only to our finances but this isn't the case. The phrase, good fortune, is defined as an auspicious state resulting from favorable outcomes. Likewise, the word prosperity refers to the state of flourishing and thriving. It can refer to affluence and success as much as comfort, security, and well-being. So, this card is not referring to your income, but rather how you manage and protect all that you have, and that's not just the money. It's how you make your money and resources work for you. Don't think "money" when you see the Bear, think "resources" and having a need to protect them. The Bear is a very "take charge" kind of card. It's a card of power, strength, protection, and control. It also reminds you to control and protect what you have from those who may want it (envy) or simply don't want you to have it (jealousy). This relates to the classic story of the haves versus the have-nots and we can connect this via the Fox and Bear cards to the Reynard the Fox tale, which was widely popular during the period in Germany. Its reference to leadership, management, and being the boss follows the same line of thinking – that of controlling and managing what you have and what you're in charge of. Once we've decided what each card means to us, we need to establish a method for using the cards. Because Lenormand only hit the

Anglosphere about ten years ago, most readers are coming from Tarot and are, unfortunately, bringing some Tarot baggage with them. Some tarotisize the Lenormand cards by attempting to pigeonhole each card into a specific meaning rather than using the intended system, which relies upon tableau reading in order to view the constellations and clusters of cards. A cluster is a group of connected cards, that is, cards that belong to the same theme group. A constellation is a grouping of cards related only by proximity. The Lenormand system relies on themed groups and core energies rather than individual card meanings. By understanding the core energy or what I call the primary vibe of each card and using only a few keywords for each, a reader can easily apply those meanings to any theme, that is, work, relationships, family, health, etc., without the need to refer to a keyword or combination list. This is why the deck came without a specific work card, sex card, family card, etc. What we have instead are clusters or themed groups of cards, the combinations of which give us the meanings. For example, the relationship cluster contains the Ring, Anchor, and Heart, but also includes cards such as the Lily and Whip. With only 36 cards in this small deck, all the cards will perform double-duty and will fit neatly into other themed groups. For example, one can argue over which card should be the primary work card, but the fact is that the Anchor, Moon, Bear, Fish, Tower, House, Fox and Ship all belong in this group. The most important thing to consider is that Lenormand was designed for tableau-style reading, not interpretation by single cards. Therefore, the cards rely on interaction with the other cards to give us answers. It's the connections among the 36 cards that provide a world of interpretations.

LAYERS OF MEANING
AND HOW DO YOU DECIDE
WHICH TO CHOOSE?

Because of the simplicity of the deck, determining exactly what information you want to receive is of the utmost importance and will determine how you'll lay the cards and how you'll read them. In Lenormand, context is everything! (Please read the section on questions)

Choosing the right spread and determining how you'll interpret it needs to be established before you lay the cards. (See the section on spreads) For example, are you going to lay a simple line of three cards to answer a simple question? If so, be sure to determine first whether you'll be interpreting that line as a sequence/narrative where you'll read it across as a sentence or will you use the center or first card as a focal point, thereby allowing the other two cards to further describe it.

Do you want to describe something? How does he feel about me? What will the weather be like for our vacation? How will my blind date look? What will her personality be like? In this case, you can lay all cards as descriptors or preselect a "focus" card and place it in the center of the spread. The surrounding cards will describe it. For example, if you ask what your blind date will be like, you can choose #28 or #29 for your center card and lay a 5-card line setting your intention that the cards to the left will describe personality and the cards to the right will describe physical appearance. You're in charge here. Spirit wants to communicate with you, so establish a clear mode of communication and off you go!

Do you want to tell a story? What will happen after I say yes? How will the meeting turn out for me? What will the outcome of the election lead to? These are all sequential spreads to be read as a sentence or story. They start with the first card and follow a succession or progression of events and actions, leading to a final answer or outcome.

I think what you really need to take away from this is that the very simple nature of the cards require some organization for ease of interpretation. Your system is like the recipe you follow when you cook. Your intuition is that extra special something that makes what you're cooking unique and special. Once you have all the pieces in place, there will be no stopping you!

Following is the method I employ every time I use the cards.

1. I start with the primary vibe/core essence for each card. I can then quickly and effortlessly run through the line or group of cards that I'm considering and give each a single primary meaning. I have a starting sentence or phrase.

2. Next, I consider my base keywords. These are the keywords that are derived from the primary vibe.

3. I now look at the type of reading I'm performing. Is it a narrative or a descriptive reading? If it's a narrative, I'll be starting with the basic concept of the cards. I may also consider their broader concepts based on the context and any theme correlations I see in the spread. For example, are three out of the five cards all from the same theme group such as relationships? If that's the case, I already know my main theme and can dig into a broader concept for the way the cards are connecting to each other (see directional reading) as well as any connecting cards that are between or around the themed cards.

4. Example: Your question is, "What is the most significant thing that will happen to me at tonight's party?" You draw: Garden-Child-Heart-Rider-Bouquet. You can immediately see a theme among these cards and that is primarily with the Heart, Rider, and Bouquet, which indicate a new love interest. We can add the Child to this theme as well. The Garden card showed up as reference to the social event itself, but that doesn't mean it has no message. It also indicates an opening-up and connecting with others. Add the Child to that, and we can already see that we're going to make a new connection. What kind of connection? Heart and Rider comes next. This clearly narrows it down to a new love interest. The final card being the Bouquet indicates an invitation.

5. If I'm performing a descriptive reading such as asking about someone's appearance, I'll be using my descriptive words, which are symbolic and derived from the picture on the cards. For example, if I asked, "What will my next date look like?" and I draw Lily-Bear-Tower, I will not read these cards using their base keywords, but instead, will use my descriptive or symbolic keywords. The Lily tells me that he'll be older than me and possibly have silver or white hair. The Bear says he'll be muscular or stocky, maybe a little heavy, and have a lot of hair. And finally, the Tower says he'll be tall and again, we have a reference to older age. Because two of the three cards relate to older age, I would bank on that fact. We also have a cross-over with the Bear and the Tower as they both relate to a larger physique.

6. Lastly, the theme of the reading itself will tell you what meanings to use. Are you performing a well-being/health reading? An advice reading? A spiritual reading? All of these put a slightly different spin on the cards. For example, my primary vibe for the Moon is impression/social success/career. This is the first thing I think of when I see the Moon in a spread. But, if I'm performing a spiritual reading, the Moon is now also my intuition card.

LENORMAND: THE GAME OF LIFE

Have you ever played the game called Life by Milton Bradley? It was one of my favorites as a child and when I first laid out the Lenormand cards in order from 1 to 36, I saw it as a progression through life, much like that game. This is what I wrote down:

Once upon a time, a baby was born and grows into a young adult. This is where the story begins.

1. You've arrived. You're just starting out as an adult.

2. Your world is still small but full of opportunities.

3. It's now expanding, you're going further and experiencing foreign things.

4. You begin to understand that you have an inner and an outer world and home is where you feel safe. Your world is still rather small and your focus is on your home and immediate family.

5. You're growing and starting to understand that you need to attend to your health.

6. Your first exposure to troubles. In everyone's life a little rain must fall.

7. You learn that there are hidden dangers and get your first taste of deceit.

8. You experience your first ending and now understand what death is. Maybe you lose a grandparent.

9. Everyone brings flowers and offers sympathy. There's still happiness to be found.

10. You begin to see life as a little more fleeting with sudden dangers. You learn that life is full of sorting – some things stay and some things go – and you're often faced with having to make rash decisions.

11. Ouch! Your first big fight. You learn to stick up for yourself but also the danger of pushing others too hard. You may experience discord in the home for the first time.

12. Life is so full of passing troubles, scattered thoughts, so much chatter in your ears and ideas flitting through your mind. You want to get it all done! This is my "crazy brain" card and it's here that you may get your first taste of gossip as others share their own crazy thoughts!

13. And, once again, as soon as life gets a little too crazy, you remember what play and fun are and realize that you still have that childlike wonder in it all! You're full of youthful energy, are excited about the future, and seek novelty. But, you are still a bit naive.

14. As is true in life, when your guard is down some may take advantage of you. You now see that not everything is as it seems and not everyone has your best interest at heart. In the Middle Ages, the Fox was often used to portray the devil. Don't trust the fox, but there's a little devil in all of us! You now realize that you have to watch out for yourself. Survival of the fittest!

15. So, you see that you need courage and strength in life and must protect what's yours. There's a division between the haves and the have-nots. The have-nots want what the haves have. You now get your first taste of envy. The Bear tells you to be on guard.

16. It's starting to appear that your life has meaning and you're meant to walk a certain path. You begin to seek out spiritual guidance and a

higher purpose. You have a vision and know what direction to go in. You are focused on following your guiding star.

17. Things are changing in big ways now. You move out of your family home.

18. You're now getting closer to friends and deciding who and what you'll be loyal to and are loyal to you. You realize that you can form close relationships outside of your immediate family.

19. Here comes authority! Now that you're an adult, you see that there are things in life that are much bigger than you, your family, and your community. Institutions and laws that have withstood the test of time. They are sturdy, sometimes rigid, but they endure. There are different levels in the world – some people are above you and some below. There's a separation. You may get your first taste of ambition and strive to reach the top for the best view.

20. You decide to expand your world beyond your personal friends. You see the benefit of networking and are introduced to the concept of respect – giving and earning it. You learn how to act in public, when to speak out and when to be silent. You can learn much from others and they can learn much from you.

21. But social life brings enemies too and you want to distance yourself from them. You see that you need to put forth effort and have endurance to overcome obstacles. The Mountain stops you temporarily and some effort is required to continue on.

22. You reach your first crossroad and realize the importance of the choices you make. The Game of Hope (GOH) tells us that not noticing the need for choice sends you back around the Mountain to the Garden to go through it until you figure it out.

23. You experience your first real sense of loss and squandering (waste in a reckless manner). If you didn't make the right decision at the Ways, you are back with enemies who may steal what's yours – literally or figura-

tively. Sometimes you can retrieve what was lost, other times it's gone forever. Wrong decisions can lead to big messes.

24. And just when life gets complicated again, you discover what real passion is! You may get your first taste of love for another or a passion for committing to something. Either way, your passion and joy lead to a union. If you land here in the GOH, you immediately move to or .

25. You now commit fully to something or someone outside of yourself. You take oaths, sign contracts, and make agreements.

26. You're studying and learning new things. You're also learning important life lessons. You want to know all the secrets of the Universe, though some you may wish you hadn't discovered. Innocence is disappearing. The more you learn the more you realize you don't know. (This sends you back to the Garden to figure it out in GOH.)

27. You begin to make things official, put them in writing, and realize the importance of clear communication. You learn that you shouldn't always communicate everything you feel. You may feel inclined to start keeping a journal or diary to record life's events.

28. Here it comes! You find a partner! Paternal, masculine, analytical, dominant.

29. At this time, you also get a stronger sense of yourself and what role you are to play as an adult. Maternal, intuitive, feminine, passive.

30. You get a taste of bliss and realize the strong bond of families. You are maturing and may gain a new appreciation of your extended family, possibly have children and want them to spend time with their elders. You now give more consideration to your values and principles and what you judge to be important in life.

31. You begin to appreciate the energy you have to live and realize that you need to use it while you have it. You seek warmth and joy and begin to see many things clearly.

32. Being recognized by others is now important to you and you may dream of fame. You want respect from others and carefully consider who you give your respect to. You also begin to recognize people for who they really are, not just on the surface. While the Sun clearly shows what's real on the surface, the Moon requires digging deeper to see what's below the surface. With the Sun followed by the Moon, you see that your days are limited – the Sun will rise and set only so many times. Enjoy every one!

33. You've found solutions, have opened some doors and have closed others. You now know that you hold the key to how you'll live your own life and it's up to you to pick it up and use it wisely.

34. Abundance flows. You have freedom, independence, and begin to amass your own fortune.

35. You've reached many goals. Life is good and you finally feel safe and secure.

36. But, as is the Universal law, life still has some hardships and burdens. You may have some regrets or some crosses to bear, though some crosses are carried for a very long time – until we realize that we can put them down when we decide to. As the law of thermodynamics states, energy cannot die but only changes from one form to another. As your energy finishes one form, it arrives new in another. The game will begin again at the Rider. The end.

Gilded Reverie by Ciro Marchetti

THEME GROUPS

K eep in mind that every one of the 36 cards can answer any question in some way. This makes every card applicable to every theme group. What I'm listing here are the cards that relate strongly to certain themes, making them more likely to show up for certain questions. These lists are not all-inclusive and don't fall into the trap of thinking that any card in a particular group relates only to that theme. All cards in the Lenormand system depend on the other cards that fall and the question for their meanings. For example, this is how you'll know whether Fish relates to deep feelings or many other people involved. I've only included this listing for general reference.

Topic/Object/Life-area:

We can look for these to find the themes in our spreads.

Ship – Travel/Where's your journey heading?

House – Home/Property/Private life

Tree – Well-being/Health

Dog – Friendship

Garden – Public life/Your environment and those in it

Heart – Love/Desires

Ring – Relationships/Commitments

Book – Study/Education

Lily – Family

Fish – Finances

Cards that explain or describe:

While all the cards can be used in this manner, I'm listing the primary cards that further describe the theme cards here. Some are also theme cards.

Clover – Makes something smaller, short-lived, or sudden

Ship – Distant

House – Foundation/Stability/Security/Traditional

Tree – Stagnant, slow-growth, boring

Clouds – Adds ambiguity

Snake – Complicates

Coffin – Dismal

Scythe – Sudden and dangerous

Whip – Repeating, requires effort

Birds – Frenzied

Child – Young, small, just beginning, growing

Fox – Sneaky

Stars – Spreading/Expanding

Stork – Changing

Dog – Staying-put

Ways – Alteration

Mice – Eroding

Heart – Passionate

Ring – Committed

Book – Unknown

Letter – Information

Lily – Relationship satisfaction/Sexuality

Sun – Success/Energy

Moon – Recognition and social success

Anchor – Security/perseverance

Cross – Painful/sorrow

Movement/Change:

Rider, Ship, Clouds, Scythe, Stars, Stork, Ways, Mice (a slow eroding change), sometimes Fish (because of its reference to being flexible, adaptable, going with the flow, or independence – going your own way).

Fixed/Resistant to Change:

House, Tree, Coffin, Whip (struggle, effort, repetition – not giving up!), Dog, Tower, Ring, Anchor, Cross.

Descriptive Groups:

Fast: Rider, Scythe, Birds, Fish

Slow: Tree, Mountain, Mice, Lily, Cross

Long-lasting: House, Tree, Dog, Tower, Ring, Lily, Anchor, Cross

Short-term: Clover, Clouds, Birds, Child

High: Birds, Stork, Tower, Mountain, Sun, Moon

Low: Clover, Coffin, Child, Mice, Fish, Anchor

Big: Bear, Mountain, Tower, Sun, Moon, Anchor

Small: Clover, Child, Mice (being made smaller)

Warning Cards: Snake, Scythe, Fox

Work:

Ship – commerce/money coming in,

Bouquet – offers/bonus,

Scythe – fired/cutting out/editing,

Whip – disagreements/hard repetitive work,

Birds – daily stresses/trying to do too much/too much on your mind,

Fox – something's wrong/sneakiness,

Bear – boss/manage/control/protecting what's yours,

Dog – colleagues/friends/loyalty,

Tower – corporate/organization/institution/ambition/levels,

Garden – public/advertising,

Ways – decisions/alternatives,

Mice – losses,

Ring – contracts/agreements,

Book – unknown information/learning/teaching/in-depth knowledge,

Letter – contracts/paperwork/communications,

Moon – being recognized/reputation/prestige/publicity,

Fish – cash flow/income/abundance of resources,

Anchor – stability/goals/achievement/security/perseverance.

Relationships:

Rider – someone's coming/someone new,

Clover – fun,

House – personal,

Tree – needs help/requires patience,

Bouquet – date/beauty/admiration,

Scythe – danger/break-up,

Whip – fighting/discord/sex as in a one night stand,

Birds – a couple,

Child – new/growing/innocent/fun,

Fox – something's wrong/trust your instincts,

Stars – new direction/meant to be,

Dog – loyal/friends/trustworthy,

Tower – rigid/boundaries/long-term,

Garden – going out/other people involved,

Mountain – a rival/enemy/challenging,

Ways – going another way,

Heart – passion/love/desire/joy,

Ring – committed/serious/proposal,

Lily – mature/harmonious/slow-moving/satisfaction/sex through love,

Moon – being recognized by someone/romance/night,

Key – certain, important, a "key" relationship, Karmic,

Fish – deep and abundant feelings/independence or many other people,

Anchor – secure/stable/consistent/long-lasting.

Communication:

Rider – incoming communication,

Whip – generally verbal and heated,

Birds – mental chatter or verbal communication that is often in the form of gossip or senseless talk that tends to upset but it can also indicate small talk or mindless chatter.

Book – secrets or the lack of communication/a closed book.

Letter – communication in general that will be explained by the accompanying cards, written, recorded, or formal/official but not necessarily.

Well-being:

Tree – shows the current state or what's needed. All cards have a well-being section in the card meaning chapter, though some cards are more relevant:

Clover, Clouds, Coffin, Bouquet, Scythe, Whip, Tower, Ways, Book, Letter, Sun, Key, Cross.

People:

The following is a list of all the cards that can represent people in your readings.

Keep in mind that you can set your intention before the reading to use the following cards to represent the people your client is asking about. In this case, you're charging these cards and want to see where they fall in a GT or if they fall in a small spread. You can also preselect one of them in a small spread. This is often done with a box spread where you place this charged card in the center or you can lay the card down and randomly select descriptor cards to describe personality and/or physical traits. At other times, these cards will show up randomly and according to the context of your question and their placement within your spread, you'll simply know that they refer to another person.

Man and Woman are the only cards that represent people and have no other meanings.

All cards containing court card insets can be used to represent people and their details are found in the card description chapter.

Rider – a young man, a lover, a visitor

House – your immediate family, those you live with. This can be used to represent father, brother, or uncle.

Clouds – ex-husband/boyfriend

Snake – another female/the "other" woman

Bouquet – a friendly woman. Can be used for mother.

Child – a child

Bear – an authority figure. Can be used for grandmother.

Stork – sister, daughter, or aunt

Dog – a good friend, partner, colleague, brother

Ways – a business woman, an assertive woman

Heart – a young man, male lover, male child

Man – male client, partner card, can be used for the most significant male in relation to the female client.

Woman – female client, partner card, can be used for the most significant female in relation to the male client.

Lily – father, grandfather, mentor, advisor

Fish – businessman

THE NUMBERS GAME

Many cards naturally reference a number or amount. I'm not talking about the numbers on the cards themselves, though you can see how to use those in the timing chapter, but a reference based on the card's meaning, emblem, or symbol.

Rider – a quickly improving number or receiving the right number.

Clover – lucky number. Or, it's small, sudden and temporary.

Ship – a long or distant number.

House – can refer to one consistent or manageable number. Your house number.

Tree – a slow-growing number. A boring number.

Clouds – an unpredictable or ever-changing number.

Snake – a difficult and complicated number.

Coffin – zilch

Bouquet – being offered just the right number.

Scythe – a reducing card. Slicing something in half or smaller. Fractions.

Whip – more than once as in repetitive actions rather than things, but in a specific number question, 2 or more.

Birds – a couple, two united.

Child – a small but growing number.

Fox – a false number.

Bear – large but more about managing or protecting a number of things.

Stork – a change in number.

Dog – a comfortable non-changing number.

Stars – a vast or infinite number or a growing number of things.

Garden – the opposite of house – it's the "many" card.

Tower – aiming for a higher number, a number that hasn't changed in a very long time.

Mountain – a very large and hard to manage number.

Ways – a split, fork, options – all reference more than one and at least two.

Mice – loss and reduction in number, though you might get it back. If the question warrants, it may refer to many more than you can see.

Heart – a heart-warming number, two.

Ring – circling around and no change in number.

Book – an unknown number.

Letter – recording numbers.

Man – one or a male's favorite number.

Woman – one or a female's favorite number.

Lily – a perfect and complete number.

Sun – a powerful number.

Moon – a recognizable, distinctive number. A number that stands out.

Key – accessing numbers

Fish – a multitude of independent number of things.

Anchor – reaching the right number.

Cross – a number that is difficult to deal with or reach.

PLAYING CARD INSETS

While many modern decks forgo the inclusion of the playing cards on their decks, most still include a small symbol of the playing card number and suit somewhere on each card. There's some debate over why the playing cards are there and whether or not they should be considered in our interpretations. Here is my view on this.

What we know is that this deck was originally called Das Spiel der Hoff-nung (The Game of Hope) and was designed by German Johann Kaspar Hechtel and first published in 1799, or thereabout. The cards contained both a Bavarian and Alsatian playing card inset. Hechtel's instructions stated that other than the board game, the cards could also be used to play all the popular card games of the period as well as being used to tell fortunes.

So, what, if anything, do those insets have to do with the Petit Lenormand system? Despite the belief by some that there's no correlation at all, I beg to differ. The cards clearly correlate with the Bavarian playing card insets in that the most inauspicious cards contain insets of the Clubs suit, with the only exceptions being the Bear (Positive/Neutral) and the Ring (Neutral). The Spades suit is connected almost entirely to auspicious cards, with only two exceptions, the Tower and the Letter, and they are both neutral. The Hearts are a warm and fuzzy suit with the only exception being the Tree and the Diamonds that correlate with the cards of excitement, tension, and twists of fate, which can be either positive or negative in a reading. Clearly, we can scan a small spread or any cluster in a GT and determine at a glance the general vibe of what we're dealing with based only on the playing card insets.

As for the pips, there are no 2-5 cards as these weren't used in the early Bavarian or Alsatian decks.

How can we use the insets?

1. We can use the suits to give an indication of the energy of the reading as I describe above. This is something that I always do.

2. We can use the court insets to represent people in our readings. This is also a technique I often employ.

3. Some choose to answer yes/no questions based on the color of the insets, generally red is positive and black is negative. This is a technique I tried but quickly discarded as I couldn't refrain from reading the cards themselves, which never correlated with the answer from the red or black insets. This is entirely up to you as I know many readers use this method.

4. Some readers choose to add up the numbers of the insets and relate that number to a card. Jacks = 11, Queens = 12, and Kings = 13. For example, if you drew three cards and got the Letter (7), Stork (13), and Sun (1), you'd add up the inset numbers and get 21 giving you the Mountain. They then use the Mountain as an underlying theme of the reading. I've never found this method to work as Lenormand, unlike Tarot, isn't based in numerology and the pips don't correlate fully with the card meanings. I'd like to mention a blog post by my friend, Serge Pirotte, titled, "Numbers". He explains very clearly why this method doesn't work. You can read it here: https://cartomancier.com/en/2018/03/18/numbers/

PLAYING CARD INSETS
QUICK REFERENCE

1.	Rider	9 of Hearts
2.	Clover	6 of Diamonds
3.	Ship	10 of Spades
4.	House	King of Hearts
5.	Tree	7 of Hearts
6.	Clouds	King of Clubs
7.	Snake	Queen of Clubs
8.	Coffin	9 of Diamonds
9.	Bouquet	Queen of Spades
10.	Scythe	Jack of Diamonds
11.	Whip	Jack of Clubs
12.	Birds	7 of Diamonds
13.	Child	Jack of Spades
14.	Fox	9 of Clubs
15.	Bear	10 of Clubs
16.	Stars	6 of Hearts
17.	Stork	Queen of Hearts
18.	Dog	10 of Hearts
19.	Tower	6 of Spades
20.	Garden	8 of Spades
21.	Mountain	8 of Clubs
22.	Ways	Queen of Diamonds
23.	Mice	7 of Clubs
24.	Heart	Jack of Hearts
25.	Ring	Ace of Clubs
26.	Book	10 of Diamonds
27.	Letter	7 of Spades
28.	Man	Ace of Hearts
29.	Lady	Ace of Spades
30.	Lily	King of Spades

31.	Sun	Ace of Diamonds
32.	Moon	8 of Hearts
33.	Key	8 of Diamonds
34.	Fish	King of Diamonds
35.	Anchor	9 of Spades
36.	Cross	6 of Clubs

THE COURT INSET GROUP:

HEARTS: Jack of Hearts-Heart, Queen of Hearts-Stork, King of Hearts-House

SPADES: Jack of Spades-Child, Queen of Spades-Bouquet, King of Spades-Lily

DIAMONDS: Jack of Diamonds-Scythe, Queen of Diamonds-Ways, King of Diamonds-Fish

CLUBS: Jack of Clubs-Whip, Queen of Clubs-Snake, King of Clubs-Clouds

THE HEARTS GROUP:

Ace-Man, 6-Stars, 7-Tree, 8-Moon, 9-Rider, 10-Dog, Jack-Heart, Queen-Stork, King-House

THE SPADES GROUP:

Ace-Lady, 6-Tower, 7-Letter, 8-Garden, 9-Anchor, 10-Ship, Jack-Child, Queen-Bouquet, King-Lily

THE DIAMONDS GROUP:

Ace-Sun, 6-Clover, 7-Birds, 8-Key, 9-Coffin, 10-Book, Jack-Scythe, Queen-Ways, King-Fish

THE CLUBS GROUP:

Ace-Ring, 6-Cross, 7-Mice, 8-Mountain, 9-Fox, 10-Bear, Jack-Whip, Queen-Snake, King-Clouds

THE FISH ALWAYS MEANS MONEY... UNTIL IT DOESN'T WHY WE DON'T WANT TO PIGEONHOLE CARDS IN LENORMAND

W hat are the most asked questions from new readers? "Which card means X?" I can remember asking those same questions like it was yesterday! But, the quickest way to learn Lenormand is by getting out of that mindset from day one! Let's dive into this.

While it's true that we see the Fish card as our money card, the Heart as our love card, and the Ship as our travel card, if that's all we see them as, we won't get very far in our readings. With the Lenormand deck containing only 36 cards, we need them to fit any context that we'll be asking about. What this means is that all the cards will have more than one meaning, which is why we don't read Lenormand cards singularly. They were designed for tableau-style reading and this is also why you won't find too many Lenormand spreads online or in books. Those that you find are all basically the same – a straight line of cards or a tableau of varying sizes, mostly square or rectangular with the exception of the Pyramid and Cross.

What I want you to take away from that fact is that the cards rely on horizontal and vertical interactions with other cards and their meanings will vary depending on the cards flanking them, above them, below them, their proximity to any significator cards, the cluster of cards they show up with, and any groupings of cards from the same theme group.

Let me get back to the Fish. In this book, I explain each card based on its primary vibe and the theme group it belongs to. So, what is the primary vibe of the Fish card? Abundance. A large quantity of something, a plentiful state, freedom of movement, independence, flow, and deepness. All these words relate to the Fish emblem, which is why it was chosen. This makes it very easy to remember! It's also the card of prosperity as it relates to success in your endeavors and flourishing financially. This makes perfect sense when you consider that fishing was one of the original commercial enterprises and the bartering of fish made it one of the original forms of currency.

So even if you're asking a question about money, rather than seeing the Fish card simply as "money", look at it as the "flow" of money, or better, the flow of abundance. Now, the other cards will explain the how, what, and where of the flow of the money. It's not just showing up because you asked about money. It didn't need to because the theme is included in your question and is understood. It has something more to say.

So now, we understand its primary vibe and we can relate this to any question we may ask, whether it's about business, a relationship, how you'll like your dinner, or what's your dog's favorite pastime. Now let's look at its theme group. This is something you need to understand to easily read Grand Tableaus but it's equally important in small spreads. The Fish belongs to the commerce/financial group. Other cards in this group are the Bear and the Ship. This group is related to the work/business group, which includes the three cards above as well as the Anchor, Moon, Ring, and Fox. What's important to notice is that every one of the cards I just mentioned fit into other groups as well. The Ring, for example, is in the business group as it relates to contracts, agreements, and deals, but it also fits into the personal relationship group as it relates to commitments among couples. On the flip side, we can say that every card in the deck can answer a business or financial question – not just the cards in the theme group.

For example, if I ask how well I'll do financially with my book during the first six months, and I lay a small spread of three cards, I don't need the Fish to show up at all because the entire question relates to money and all cards will relate to that context. If I draw Clover-Child-Moon, I know that I'll be recognized and see some small success and a small amount of money. I know that the Clover, and actually the Child too, relate to a small amount of money because money is what I'm asking about. If I ask what the outcome will be after six months of my book being published, I really want to see the Fish card in there! If I draw Bouquet-Lily-Stars, then I know it will be well-received by those who read it, and it may be the beginning of a satisfying path for me, but I won't make much of a profit in the time period I asked about.

Fish Card Examples:

Question: What are his feelings for me? Sun-Fish-Lily. Answer: They are warm (we can also say strong as this is the card of energy), deep, and pure. Nice!

Question: How will the subway commute go today? Rider-Fish-Child Answer: It will go quickly, you'll be able to move about freely and easily as it won't be too crowded. The Fish refers to a lot of something, but followed by the Child, it's made smaller.

There seems to be a lot of confusion about the Fish and the Garden in relationship questions. Both cards can refer to other people as well as a loose and casual relationship. But, as usual, that depends entirely on the question and context. The Garden for example, can also refer to opening-up and sharing. Here are a few examples:

Here's a great example from a reading I did over a year ago. This is a regular client, so I always get feedback.

Context: Querent (female) has been seeing a divorced man with a young child. They've been getting serious yet he didn't want to tell anyone about their relationship to protect his child.

Question: How will our relationship progress over the next six months? I laid a box, and the first card was Dog, the center card was Anchor, and the exit card was Garden. He'll remain loyal to her and will finally bring their relationship out into the open. They are now openly engaged.

Question: What can I do to improve our relationship?

Ring-Letter-Garden. Commit to opening-up communication.

Don't forget that Garden also refers to the environment, outdoors, or any location where social events take place. Garden + Ring + Bouquet is a common grouping for a wedding.

Another Fish example: How will I know that he's the one? Fish-Moon-Key. If you dig deep, you'll just recognize that he's the one among all the choices.

What will the outcome be of our dating? Rider-Fish-Garden. This won't be a committed relationship. You'll date casually and see other people.

What are his feelings for me right now? Heart-Fish-Dog. Passionate, deep, adoring, and faithful.

Do you see how the question changes the way we interpret the cards?

CAN THE MICE EAT THE MOUNTAIN? CAN THE SCYTHE KILL THE MICE? WILL THE COFFIN BURY THE SCYTHE?

As you know, the Lenormand cards can be grouped as positive, negative, and neutral with some falling somewhere in between. If you understand what each card means to you and whether it is favorable, unfavorable, or neither of these, then you're off to a great start in interpreting your spreads. But, there's so much more to consider.

When you use the cards for a descriptive reading, I think they're a little more straight-forward. For example, you ask about the personality of the new girlfriend that your son is bringing home. You lay a 3-card line to describe her personality and you draw Scythe, with its blade facing right, Mountain, and Mice. These are all negative cards. One could say that she'll be blunt – maybe even aggressive, cold and defensive as well as anxious. That's pretty clear. If you ask how you'll feel about her, that again, is a descriptive question. You may be shocked by her and feel a bit panicky, seeing her as a danger. You may see her as an enemy – large and looming – stealing your son away and leaving you feeling anxious and at a loss. Again, pretty clear.

But when you start laying narrative spreads, you're asking the cards to tell you a story. How will the evening go when you meet the new girlfriend? Now, using the same three cards you're confused because you've been taught that the Scythe cuts the card to the right and the Mice erodes the card to the left. If you follow this line of thinking, then everything will be great! The Scythe cuts through the Mountain and the Mice erode whatever's left of it. Think about that a moment. How did those cards make you feel as soon as you saw them? (Sorry, but I'm a Pisces and we feel the world before we see it.) If everything was going to be great, don't you think the deck would've given you more favorable cards?

So, if you read that line as a narrative, you might start by considering your meanings:

warning/sudden danger + obstacle/challenge + loss/anxiety. If you consider your directional cues, Scythe cuts or threatens the card it's facing OR the card it's facing describes the threat. The Mice erodes the card to its left and destroys the card to its right, but you still lose out in some way – you're still dealing with a loss in an anxious and unsettling way. At best, you could say that the danger will be to the obstacle, which will result in anxiety. So, if you saw the Mountain as the protective barrier between you and the girlfriend, that the Scythe cuts through and the Mice erodes, you're still left with a loss. There's no way that those three cards can describe a warm and fuzzy feeling.

Always remember that if negative cards fall near a significator in a Grand Tableau or show up in a small spread, they did so for a reason, and the Mice, Scythe, Coffin, and Mountain aren't going to make other negative cards disappear. Yes, the Coffin ends something but if it's the last card in a string, what are you left with? How are you feeling? A little down? Exhausted? Depressed? Sick? Stuck? You'd need to see a favorable card after it to make it better and if you have none, then that's where the story ends. Yes, the Scythe will cut through or bring danger to whatever it's facing, but it's what I call "hasty and hostile". The danger hasn't disappeared completely without favorable cards following. Yes, the Mice makes things smaller but in an anxious, uncomfortable way. Think of the word, "decay" when you see the Mice and you'll have a better idea of its core meaning. It's not the kind of easier or more pleasant smallness you see in the Child or the Clover.

SEX: THE LILY OR
THE WHIP?

First, let me point out that there is no mention of sex in any of the original Lenormand instructions. In eighteenth century Catholic/Christian Europe, sex wouldn't have been publicly discussed – those discussions took place in private and generally among groups of men or groups of women – never the twain shall meet! The act may have taken place in mixed company, but the discussions didn't.

The earliest reading traditions chose the Lily to represent sex for a simple reason, and that is due to how sex was viewed – or at least taught – during the period.

Traditional Catholic/Christian teachings strictly forbade sex outside of marriage including adultery, incest, and general promiscuity. They didn't acknowledge homosexual relationships at all.

What I find interesting about adultery is that it traditionally only applied to women. The primary reason supposedly was due to the issue of the children's parentage. A woman with multiple partners couldn't prove who the father of her children was before paternity tests existed.

There was no "universal law" prohibiting married men from taking a concubine, as long as he came home to his wife and children every night! But, the early church didn't acknowledge this either.

So, what does all of this have to do with the Lenormand cards? It means that traditional religious teachings about sex have always considered it to be a divine gift from God – pure and blissful – beautiful and holy. This is what the Lily card describes – not the Whip. And in studying the early reading systems for this deck, we have to remind ourselves that the pictures on these cards were intended as emblems, not symbols. When the Lily card shows up in a small spread where you're asking a general question about a personal relationship, or between the partner cards in a tableau, you can be quite certain that sex is part of it. It's difficult, though not impossible, to create bliss and complete harmony within a relationship without it. The Whip, on the other hand, is the card of discord and unless you're specifically setting your intention to use it to answer a question about the type of sex that you already know is taking place, it won't show sex at all, but instead, disharmony. Isn't this the issue that new readers have? I can't tell you how many times I've heard, "The Whip is my sex card but when it shows up, I can't be sure if they're having sex or fighting!"

But, we can certainly use the Whip card to describe a type of sex. So, in describing sex, the Whip represents everything outside of that pure and blissful form, from casual sex outside of love or commitment to adultery, rape, incest, or sexual deviance. The context and other cards drawn will tell you which you're dealing with. For example, if you simply ask about someone's relationship, neither card can definitively tell you that sex is involved, but the Lily is a much safer choice. If the Whip showed up, my first reaction would be that the couple isn't getting along. I certainly wouldn't say that they have a healthy sex life! This is a perfect example of why we need specific questions in Lenormand and multiple cards to answer them. If sex is what you're really wondering about, you need to specify that with the cards.

Consider the questions that you might ask and how these two cards might answer them.

1.   Has she been faithful while I was away? Lily – yes, Whip – no.

2. You want to date J. However, you know that J and S are currently intimate but in an open relationship. So, you ask, "What type of sexual relationship do they have?" Lily – you'd better move on – he's taken, Whip – they're having sex but there's no love or commitment, so if that doesn't bother you – go for it.

3. How does K view our sex life? Lily – you're safe, Whip – you're in trouble.

4. What did last night's copulation mean to C? Whip – you were just a notch in his belt – it was nothing more than you just got screwed! Lily – he'll be calling you soon – it's the real thing!

What might the cards look like for a cheating male? Here's a possibility: Man + Rider + Whip + Snake + Clover.

What might the cards look like for a virtuous and trustworthy female partner? They might look like this: Heart + Lily + Woman + House + Ring.

So, when we consider the reference to sex through these two cards, they may be polar opposites, and yet we can use both to give us clear and specific answers to some of today's questions. The Lily will show that someone's intentions are pure and their motives are virtuous. Consider the primary vibe of the card. Peaceful, satisfying, harmonious, and mature. The Whip will show the opposite. It's the card of the whore, the sexual pervert, the nymphomaniac, or the sexual deviant. Think about the core meaning of the card! Tension, struggle, repetition, discord. In order to stay clear on how we interpret the cards in this system, we need to stay in alignment with the primary vibes or core energies of the cards. For the same reason that it makes no sense to me to choose a negative card (Fox) to represent one's beloved career, it equally makes no sense to me to choose a negative card (Whip) to represent the beautiful consummation of true love. By always adhering to the primary vibes of your cards, you will always know what they're trying to tell you.

LENORMAND POSITIVE-
NEUTRAL-NEGATIVE

W hen we consider which cards are positive and which are negative, we're talking about their overall energies. This is an important aspect of the Lenormand cards because it's what gives us the feeling of which way the reading is going. Having a solid understanding of the energies of the cards will make the work of answering yes/no questions quick. For example, if you're laying a small spread for a specific question, you'll first notice the positive or negative values of the cards. Are they all positive? All negative? All neutral? Or, as in most cases, a mix? Does the line start out positive and then deteriorate into negative cards or vice versa?

Let's look at exactly what we mean by positive and negative. These words were originally used to describe electrical charges, which are the physical properties of matter that cause them to experience a certain force when placed in an electromagnetic field. Charges are either positive (carried by protons) or negative (carried by electrons). An object with the absence of a net charge is referred to as neutral (carried by neutrons).

The terms positive and negative have also been used to describe numbers as far back in recorded history as the seventh century, where the concept of negative numbers was first used to describe debts.

In today's vernacular, we use these words to describe something good or an addition of something for positive, and something bad or a reduction for negative.

The reason I wanted to mention exactly what the words positive and negative mean is that in Lenormand reading, we need to understand that certain cards will be auspicious or favorable to our questions, while others will be inauspicious or unfavorable. Some will add something while others will subtract or detract. Some will increase something while others will decrease. Some will give us a yes, others a no answer, while still others will lend no influence.

In making my positive/negative list, I followed the original translations of the cards but I noticed that most neutral cards were leaning one way or the other, so I chose five categories: Positive, positive-neutral, neutral, neutral-negative and negative.

What's important to understand about these groupings is that while all Lenormand cards have a core energy, most of these energies will be affected by the surrounding cards. For example, while the positive cards will share their positive effect with the surrounding cards, those in the positive-neutral category will still share their positive energy but also can be brought down by negative surrounding cards. In other words, their positive energy is weaker.

By grouping the cards in this manner, I have a nicely balanced deck with ten positive cards, nine positive/neutral cards, five neutral, three neutral/ negative, and nine negatives. From this, we can see that ten cards are positive beyond a doubt, while nine others are somewhat positive, but possibly not positive enough to give you a yes answer. I only have five cards that are so completely neutral that they won't help me lean one way or the other, three are somewhat negative, but still not negative enough for a no answer, and nine are beyond a doubt a no. To look at these another way, we can group the positive and positive/neutral cards to give a total of nineteen predominantly positive cards, only five neutrals, and twelve predominantly negative cards. This gives us a nicely balanced reading system.

My list is as follows:

Positive: Clover, Bouquet, Star, Heart, Sun, Moon, Key, Fish, Anchor. 10

Positive/Neutral: Rider, Ship, House, Child, Bear, Stork, Dog, Garden, Ring, Lily 9

Neutral: Tower, Ways/Crossroads, Letter, Man, Woman. 5

Neutral/Negative: Tree, Birds, Book. 3

Negative: Clouds, Snake, Coffin, Scythe, Whip, Fox, Mountain, Mice, Cross. 9

How did I arrive at these values? I simply based them on my interpretation of the Philippe Lenormand original translations (PLOT), which you can find under the individual card description pages.

THE 36 CARDS

1 RIDER/CAVALIER/KNIGHT

"Her Legacy Lenormand" by Teri Smith.

Number and Name: 1 RIDER

Playing Card Inset: 9 of Hearts.

Primary Vibe: Arriving/Incoming news, people, ideas. If you've been waiting for something to happen, it's about to!

Energy: Positive/Neutral.

Influence: Fast, energetic, exciting, new.

Theme Group: Movement, communication, fast

Base Keywords: News, messages or the messenger, feedback, updates, replies, visit/visitor, thoughts, ideas, deliveries, conversations, mobility.

Basic Concept: People, news, or ideas that are coming to you. Something is arriving, moving, or changing, and quickly. You're making plans and taking action. A fast and energetic card. An action card. A card of plans, thoughts, ideas, as well as people coming into your life. This is one of the communication cards in the deck and when you read it as such, it always refers to incoming communication. On its own, it's a positive and exciting card.

As this is the first card, I'd like to start off by sparking your creativity. When you read about these 36 cards, consider all the ways that you'll use them to answer any question that could possibly be asked. For example, say you're wanting to start a new project and you lay some cards to guide you. What would the Rider indicate? It would be the new and exciting idea that has to come to you before you can start a project. The House would represent giving it structure. The Bouquet could indicate adding your creative touch or making it attractive. The Stars would tell you that you're focused and heading in the right direction. The Letter might indicate making it tangible by putting it in writing. The Moon could say that it'll be successful and you'll be recognized for it. These are simply one of the many interpretations that could be gleaned from these cards. My point is that rather than trying to memorize someone else's list of card combinations, start to see the cards as words, ideas, bits of information, that when combined will tell you a story.

Broader Concept: It can represent a horse or bike and may show inland travel of short distance (in contrast to the Ship). When representing another person, while traditionally male, it can refer to any new person coming into one's life. If this represents a new love interest, you'll have other cards around such as the Heart, Ring, or Lily.

As a card of activity and mobility, it can indicate general exercise or dancing.

In a spiritual reading, it may refer to incoming messages from Spirit.

In relationship readings, it's generally a positive and active card and may indicate someone new coming into your life.

Descriptive Words: Athletic, well-dressed, sporty, attractive, lean, fit. A person that may come in and out of your life quickly. They're charismatic and like to hold the reins. Communicative, active, outgoing, ambitious. A courier, athlete, equestrian/jockey, messenger, newscaster, witness.

Advice: As a con: Too much information, too fast, don't be too hasty, you're letting too much in too soon, get off your high-horse, stay home, don't meddle in others' affairs. As a pro: Go for it! Pay attention to the new ideas, information, feedback that's coming to you now. Take action. Do it! Deliver.

Directional Cues: The directional cue for this card relates to what the news will be about or what the person may be bringing to us rather than whether the energy is moving toward or away from us. This is always an energy coming to you.

Philippe Lenormand Original Translation (PLOT): THE CAVALIER is a messenger of good fortune—if not surrounded by unlucky cards, this brings good news that the Person may expect, either from his own house or from abroad; this will, however, not take place immediately, but some time later.

Game of Hope (GOH): N/A Because the game was originally played with a pair of dice. It was impossible to land here, so there's no mention of this house in the game rules.

Method of Distance (MOD): The traditional view says that when it's close to us the news or visitor is coming from our local environment or someone within our own home, while being far it will show that the energy is coming from a distance. What we can say from this OT is that the cards touching it will tell us what will be coming and whether the news or visit will be favorable or not.

Compare To: What cards can show energy moving away from us? Stork = Change, Crossroads = A split or different path. Ship can also show going out to seek opportunities or adventures. Also compare to cards that show no energy movement such as Tree, Coffin, Mountain, or Cross. As a communication card, compare to the Letter, which is communication that we create as opposed to the Rider, which is communication that we receive.

Emblem Meaning: Horses were the primary mode of land transportation of the period. While trains and horse-drawn carriages were used for transporting goods and larger numbers of people, horseback was the fastest method and they could go anywhere regardless of roads or tracks. Visitors and mail arrived primarily by horseback.

House Meaning: Thoughts, messages/news, or people coming to you.

Timing: Soon, next, one day, week, month, first of the month, January, on a visit, it's on the way.

Well-being: Shows general improvement, news coming to you about healing, a visit from or to a healthcare professional, or your overall mobility and horsepower. Anatomically, it represents the legs, knees, feet, paws, hooves. For example, Rider + Scythe = Broken leg;

Scythe + Rider = Knee surgery.

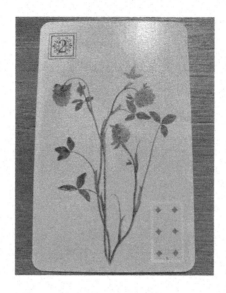

2 CLOVER

Number and Name: 2 CLOVER

Playing Card Inset: 6 of Diamonds

Primary Vibe: You just stumbled upon an unexpected opportunity. Grab it before it's gone!

Energy: Positive

Influence: Happy, carefree, fast/short-term, small, fun.

Theme Group: Fast, short-term, low, small.

Base Keywords: Fun, easy, fortunate, unexpected, sudden opportunity, spontaneous, pleasant coincidence, ease, carefree, brief, small. Taking chances. Small amounts of money or luck. Enjoying the simple things in life! Carpe diem! When it shows up with unfavorable cards, it may be interpreted as irresponsible, a gambler, a dabbler.

Basic Concept: Clovers are small, fragile, and short-lived. They grow quickly and easily and require no help to survive their short lives. Therefore, they represent being carefree and happy-go-lucky. They show luck when they're close enough to find and not hidden by Clouds. Their association with luck can give them the meaning of a gamble, but not in the risky way of the Scythe.

It's more like catching a break. I generally see it as a "throw caution to the wind and seize the day" card. They are something that you find or stumble upon, not given to you like the Bouquet. The happiness and luck they represent is rather small and simple – that which you find in your own home or daily life. Be spontaneous. Be in good humor.

Broader Concept: Because of the association with luck, the Clover can represent extra money coming in but it will be a small amount. Something sudden and unexpected but good as long as favorable cards are around. It can represent grass, herbs, finding something, a gambler/risk-taker, synchronicity, nature, funny/comical, fun, short-term, green, short, small, easy-going, sociable.

In a spiritual reading, it can ask you to pay attention to small signs that you'd normally miss. Are you open to the unexpected? Should I be more carefree?

In a relationship reading, it may refer to a casual, carefree, and short-term relationship such as a fleeting encounter, a fling, an unexpected meeting, or a new (or renewed), lucky or happy relationship.

Descriptive Words: Short, great smile, fun, a great sense of humor, a prankster, carefree and happy go lucky, green or hazel eyes, of Irish descent, easy-going, cheerful. A comedian, gambler, gamer, stunt person, opportunist, herbalist, cannabis grower.

Advice: As a con: Short-lived, a gamble, risky, too small, someone isn't taking it seriously. Stop shirking your responsibilities. As a pro: Don't worry, be happy! Grab the opportunity before it's gone. Stay positive. Take a chance. Don't overlook the small things. Throw caution to the wind.

Directional Cues: N/A

Philippe Lenormand Original Translation (PLOT): A CLOVER LEAF is also a harbinger of good news; but if surrounded by clouds it indicates great pain; but if # 2 lies near # 29 or 28, the pain will be of short duration, and soon change to a happy issue.

Game of Hope (GOH): If you land on the house of Clouds, you're sent back 4 spaces to the house of Clover. What we can derive from this is that while the Clouds card and the card that falls in its house will tell what troubles you'll encounter, you then look to the house and card of the Clover to see what luck/opportunities you'll have to deal with those troubles.

Method of Distance (MOD): From the PLOT, we can say that this is a lucky and favorable card though if near Clouds or other unfavorable cards, it can show bad luck or a twist of fate. It's a card you want near, because if it's far from you in a GT and surrounded by unfavorable cards, then you're out of luck! If this little Clover is far, you won't see it and can't pick it!

Compare To: Compare to Tree for slow-growing and requiring much care whereas Clover is short-term and easy. Clover is temporary and Tower and Anchor are more permanent. House and Anchor is for stable or a sure-thing. Bouquet is for something that's given to you because you earned it as opposed to something you find.

Emblem Meaning: The oldest reference to the clover's connection to good luck comes from the Irish Druids. In 1620, Sir John Melton wrote: "If a man walking in the fields finds any four-leaved grass, he shall in a small while after find some good thing." The Druids believed that they could thwart evil spirits and danger by carrying a shamrock. A three-leaf shamrock would enable them to see the evil spirits and escape in time. A four-leaf clover was said to ward off bad luck and offer magical protection. The Druids helped establish the clover as a Celtic charm, and other folklore indicates clovers helped people see fairies and chase the little sprites. Around 400AD, when Christianity began to overturn Pagan beliefs, the clover came along for the ride and was likened to the Holy Trinity. Some stories suggest that St. Patrick used a shamrock to teach principles of the Trinity to the masses. A three-leaf clover represents the Father, Son and Holy Spirit. Should a four-leaf clover be found, it is considered the Trinity plus God's grace. The four-leaf clover looks like a cross, which gives the four-leaf clovers special meaning to some people. Of course, the rarity of four-leaf clovers makes some people who find them feel as if luck is on their side. Among naturally occurring clovers, the odds of finding a four-leaf clover instead of the more common three-leaf clover is 10,000 to 1.

I began to search my decks for the Clover cards to see if they contained four leaves and only found it on a few decks. Whether three- or four-leaves, the clover was a common symbol of luck and still is today.

House Meaning: Sudden and short-term luck or opportunities.

Timing: Unexpectedly/when you least expect it/ by chance, fast, February, two weeks, days, months, second of the month.

Well-being: Shows progress and improvement, a pick-up of mood or energy. It refers to greens and vegetables. Temporary illnesses. Holistic herbal or homeopathic remedies. Cannabis. May describe a vegan or vegetarian. For example, Tree + Clover + Clouds = Medical marijuana.

3 SHIP

Number and Name: 3 SHIP

Playing Card Inset: 10 of Spades

Primary Vibe: Journey – either literal (travel and physical movement of a person or thing) or metaphorical (striving, yearning, longing). Represents distance, something foreign, a venture or an adventure. Will your ship come in? Look at the surrounding cards and especially the card it's heading toward!

Energy: Positive

Influence: You're going somewhere – you're on the move and things are changing. You may be going the distance to get what you want. A journey of seeking adventure or something better – physically, mentally, emotionally, or spiritually. The Ship represents slower movement and over a greater distance than Rider, and while the Rider represents something coming to you, the Ship is more about outward expansion, moving forward, a venture (business or any undertaking with an uncertain outcome) or an adventure! It may simply indicate taking a trip or remuneration coming in from business or inheritance.

Theme Group: Movement/Change, slow, work.

Base Keywords: Travel, vacations/going on holiday, business/commerce, long-distance or a distant location, slow, voyage, passage, transportation, seeking/going for opportunities, a long-distance between things, trying to or getting from one place to a distant one, foreign, longing, new adventure, opportunity for betterment, making progress, exotic things/people/locations, departure, farewell. Extra money coming in, inheritance.

Basic Concept: The original translations give us travel, commerce, and wealth. This wealth is related to distance, that is, the wealth is coming from a distance as in an inheritance, or you have to go the distance to achieve this wealth. This card involves a journey or adventure of some sort. It's connection to longing stems from its relation to great distance and slow movement. As it relates to opportunities, the cards surrounding it will describe what those opportunities are. Whether you're on the Ship or not will be known via the context and the other cards that fall. If you're not on the Ship, you may be longing or searching. It's a card of big opportunities for betterment and enrichment. It's the passage whereby one transitions with the intention of reaching a better state. It may bring in adventure, money, interaction with foreign places, people, or ideas. It's also the card of long distances and foreign or exotic places so this may show itself as a physical trip or a distance between the client and what they want, which is where the concept of longing comes into play.

Broader Concept: The Ship may reference navigating, vacations, holidays, being adventurous, exploring, searching far and wide, or a big change in location or environment. As Albert Einstein said, "Ships are always safe at shore but that's not what they were built for." So, unlike Anchor, which shows that you've arrived, it's a card of movement, of going out and seeking your fortune, of longing for adventure. It tells you that your chances are good now. It can also simply refer to your mode of transportation and can represent a car, ship, or plane.

In a spiritual reading, it may refer to your soul's journey, transcendental meditation, lucid dreaming, or astral travel. It can also suggest that we search longer and further for an answer. "We wander for distraction, but we travel for fulfillment." – Hilaire Belloc

In a relationship reading, the Ship may indicate a long-distance relationship that you're traveling to or longing for, an exotic or foreign love interest, the "love boat", going the distance, playing away from home, that ship has sailed or your ship is coming in – it will all depend on how you phrase the question and the Ship's position as well as the other cards in the spread. With unfavorable cards, it can indicate someone leaving, but that would depend on the question asked. Always remember to let the cards give you the complete story and don't jump to conclusions by taking one or two cards out of context.

Descriptive Words: Foreign-looking, exotic, olive skin, adventurous, someone who loves to travel, a big dreamer, unpredictable – doesn't like to stay in one place, a free spirit, immigrants, emigrants. A successful business person, shipping/transport, import/export, the travel industry, with Stork = Airlines, translator, sailor, someone who travels for business.

Advice: As a con: Too far away, too slow, too foreign, it's time to put down roots, are you traveling toward something or escaping something? As a pro: Be adventurous! Go the distance. Make the trip. Seek your fortune!

Directional Cues: The direction the Ship is heading shows the next step on your journey or the direction in which you should go.

Philippe Lenormand Original Translation (PLOT): THE SHIP, the Symbol of Commerce, signifies great wealth, which will be acquired by trade or inheritance; if near to the Person, it means an early journey.

Game of Hope (GOH): If you land on the house of the Ship, you sail ahead 9 spaces to the house of Birds. The Ship represents your journey and where it's heading. By looking at the card that falls in the house of Birds and the house that the Birds card falls in, we'll see what minor stresses and annoyances, if any, we'll have to deal with at the next step of our journey. Because the way to win the game is to be the first to reach the end, moving ahead 9 spaces makes the Ship a very positive card.

Method of Distance (MOD): We can say that finding the Ship near the PSC in a GT may signify a journey, which can be literal or metaphorical depending on the type of reading.

Compare To: Rider for movement over shorter distances or travel by horse, motorcycle, or bike. Anchor, which also refers to success in business but infers that you've arrived whereas the Ship says that you're starting the journey or still have a distance to go. Anchor shows hope and faith that everything will work out as planned, whereas the Ship simply shows a yearning or longing for something that may never materialize as it's too far out of reach. Fish is for the flow of cash or assets while Ship refers to the opportunities to receive it, or more traditionally, to receive extra. The House for a homebody, while the Ship shows wanderlust.

Emblem Meaning: During the period these cards were created, foreign trade took place via shipping whereas domestic business could be handled via trains. Foreign trade represented the big money, so the Ship was placed on the card to represent wealth gained through commerce or inheritance. In a reading regarding finances, you could see this card as, "your ship has come in!" Ships represented foreign travel, moving great distances, and opportunities for great wealth and adventure. Planes had yet to be invented, so the Ship represented exotic travel, big business, and possibly inheritance from your family abroad. We can also consider a connection to Fortuna, the Roman Goddess of Luck, Fate, and Fortune, who is generally depicted as holding a ship's rudder or steering wheel to indicate that She is the one who controls how lives and fates are steered. She's considered to be the bearer of prosperity and increase and her association with ships indicates that ships are associated with these ideas as well.

House Meaning: Movement toward goals, travel, change. Where are you heading? What is distant?

Timing: When things start to move in a certain direction. On a Trip, march, three weeks, days, months, third of the month.

Well-being: The Ship may refer to illness or disease from foreign travel, motion sickness or vertigo, or a fear of travel. In its relation to money, it may refer to extra money that comes in from insurance or possibly a lawsuit related to an illness. Anatomically, it refers to the liver/spleen/ pancreas/gall-bladder. As it relates to motor vehicles, it may represent an ambulance. For example, Ship + Stork + Tree = Medevac.

4 HOUSE

Number and Name: 4 HOUSE

Playing Card Inset: King of Hearts. He's also known as the man of hearts as he's one who your heart goes out to. He's typically the same age or older, family-oriented and traditional, financially stable, and friendly. Can be a father, brother or uncle.

Primary Vibe: Personal, domestic, inner world, private, home, personal property, immediate family or those you live with. What grounds you and provides basic security.

Energy: Positive/Neutral

Influence: It's the personal card. Safe. Comfortable. Familiar. It represents your sanctuary. Where you live and who you live with. It also references internal, private, keeping something to yourself as well as how you're prospering in your personal life.

Theme Group: Fixed/Resistant to change, long-lasting, relationships, people

Base Keywords: Home, immediate family or those you live with, personal endeavors or affairs, real estate, your safe place, the general quality of your life, your traditions, home or family businesses, small companies or satellite offices. Intimacy, familiarity, certainty, security, domestic.

Basic Concept: Your shelter, home, family, and neighborhood. Where you feel safe and secure. What goes on behind closed doors. How you live your daily life and what you bring into your personal life. This card represents things that are familiar and close to home. This card has traditionally described personal enterprise as in an undertaking to bring prosperity or at least improvement into your personal circumstances. If you're asking about relocating, the cards around the House will describe your new home. In a business reading, the House can represent a small business, family-run business, home office, or the surrounding cards will describe what a business venture will improve your personal circumstance. In describing a person, we can say that they are stable, traditional, a home-body, seeking homey comforts – not the adventurous type.

Broader Concept: This card speaks of contentment and safety and a place that we can retreat to and find security and protection. It falls into the private sphere of life as opposed to the public sphere of the Garden card. One of the two "building" cards designating the smaller building. Tower is the larger building. For companies, House is smaller, family-owned, the one you're comfortable with. Tower would be a large company, an official company, an institution. It can refer to traditional views, solid structure, or a website homepage.

In a relationship reading, it connects to your home and family life. It may indicate a traditional relationship, aka marriage.

In a spiritual reading, it may refer to an altar or area of your home where you practice meditation or divination.

Chakra: Root/Muladhara. The Root Chakra is connected to our sense of safety and security. It's what keeps us grounded, practical, and of the earth as it relates to our basic needs while on the physical plane. It's the lowest Chakra, which connects us to Mother Earth and gives us our practical sense of self as human beings. When it is healthy and open, it allows us to function comfortably in the world, feeling safe and secure while receiving and offering practical and useful advice for daily living.

Descriptive Words: Stocky/square build, conservative, traditional, family-oriented, reliable, patriotic. A realtor, landlord, homemaker, homeowner, home-business, interior designer, furniture-maker.

Advice: As a con: Too conservative, someone is a home-body and you're not, agoraphobia. As a pro: "It starts at home," keep things private, remember where you come from, preserve traditions. Focus on your home. Success begins inside yourself. Build a solid foundation. Protect your home life/private affairs.

Directional Cues: N/A

Philippe Lenormand Original Translation (PLOT): THE HOUSE is a certain sign of success and prosperity in all undertakings, and though the present position of the Person may be disagreeable, yet the future will be bright and happy. If this card lies in the center of the cards, under the Person, this is a hint to beware of those who surround him or her.

Game of Hope (GOH): Landing here didn't send you back or forward but you did have to pay two tokens, inferring that there's a price to pay for shelter and security. Rent or mortgage!

Method of Distance (MOD): The House is a card that was seen as very favorable when landing close to the PSC as long as it wasn't in the center of the GT, or worse in the center directly above the PSC. The center being the heart of the story would give you concern that there's something amiss in your personal life in the same way that the Tree falling close tells us that we need to pay attention to our health. Therefore, landing nearby in any other position brought the message of prosperity or improvement in circumstances.

Compare To: Garden for public, exterior, or out in the open whereas House is private and internal. House is domestic and Ship is foreign.

Emblem Meaning: I was curious as to why the original translations for this card referenced success as opposed to simply your home or family. During the eighteenth century, your immediate family had an even greater impact on your financial and social standing than it does today. Where you lived depended on the family you were born into and that rarely changed. The image on this card was always a beautiful home, not a hovel. This was an image of success and high social standing. This is why the House in the early Lenormand and Gypsy cards referred to material well-being and the economic health of you and your family.

House Meaning: Personal and inner life, home, family, and security.

Timing: Evening. Not soon, you're too comfortable, when at home, April, four days, weeks, months.

Well-being: In a health reading, the House may refer to small health-related businesses such as a doctor's office, clinic, or treatment center. Anatomically, it stands for the bones of the skeleton and when near speaks of a strong and solid constitution. Because it was originally one of the "Tree" cards (*See Well-being for #5 Tree), it could somewhat offset the negativity of the Tree card when landing near the PSC as it's a card of security and a strong foundation. For example, Tree + House + Dog = Veterinary office.

5 TREE

Number and Name: 5 TREE

Playing Card Inset: 7 of Hearts

Primary Vibe: Well-being, life, nature. Something requires time, care, healing.

Energy: Neutral/Negative

Influence: References the health of the client or situation being asked about and falling near or in a small spread infers slow-growth or something is needed to create an optimal situation. The Tree is slow-growing, rooted, patient, organic, and natural.

Theme Group: Fixed/Resistant to change, slow, long-lasting, well-being.

Base Keywords: Well-being, life force, health, healing, holistic, slow but steady growth, a slow pace, inertia, rooted, long-lasting, immobile, patient, quiet, enduring, natural.

Basic Concept: Our life force, striving to thrive, well-being, time for recuperation or bringing something to a healthier state. This is a slow-paced card whose effects are long-lasting.

I think this is the card that confused me the most when I was learning. There are so many differing opinions on what this card is referring to, especially in small spreads. In keeping with my quest to understand the original meanings, I reminded myself that the emblems for this deck were chosen based on the commonly understood Christian symbolism of the period as well as everyday symbols such as a Rider, Ship, and House, and well-known stories such as Reynard the Fox. This enabled me to grasp the meanings that were intended for each card. Because this is a balanced divination system, changing the meaning of any card will change the balance of the system. I'll point this out with every card that it applies to.

For the Tree, most if not all readers agree that it's connected to health. I did a little research on what exactly the word "health" means. Health is defined as the absence of disease. Well-being is defined as the state of being comfortable, healthy, and happy. Life is defined as the condition that distinguishes animals and plants from inorganic matter, including the capacity for growth, reproduction, functional activity, and continual change preceding death. I think that sums up the meaning of this card best. You can look at the Tree as a, "how's your life going?" card. When I see this card, I don't think only of illness, but rather how the card is trying to answer the question asked by suggesting that something is needed to make a situation optimal. When it shows up in a small spread we know that something is needed in order to bring the person or situation asked about to a healthier or more stable state. It references development, duration, patience, and possibly deeply rooted issues. To be in balance and achieve true health in a situation, we need to respect all aspects of what's needed. This is where the word, "organic" comes into play as it references the integral elements of a whole system.

The Tree represents life, not disease, but it makes little sense for the life card to show up in a small spread just to tell you that everything is fine. Depending on the question, if it shows up and is accompanied by favorable cards then it will still refer to something that will require time and care in order to thrive. The surrounding cards will give you more information or may show you how to go about bringing the situation to a healthier state.

In researching similar card systems to see what card is used for health, I found this: Whitman's Old Gypsy Fortune Cards. Card #5 isn't a tree, but rather a "sick person". It describes the card as a clarion call that yes, something is actually wrong, and it's time for you to make it right. The key indication listed for this card is that when near the subject's card, there will be great misfortune. When it lands in a small spread, your challenge is, "What will make me well?" This correlates with the Near meaning of the Tree card.

In summary, the Tree, when near, tells us that energy/care/ attention is needed to bring something to a healthier state. Always look at the surrounding cards because unfavorable cards will give us an indication of a problem and favorable cards may indicate the remedies. My grandmother used to say, "Don't ignore your health because good health doesn't grow on trees, you know!" Thanks, Grandma!

Broader Concept: Trees are stationary and stay where they're planted. They grow, of course, but at a very slow rate. Tree is unlike a clover, which sprouts up overnight but also dies quickly. This is why they are connected to the idea of patience or boredom. Watching a tree grow is like watching paint dry. Not very exciting. In a GT, the cards next to or under the tree are being shaded, which slows their growth. Quite the opposite of the Sun card.

This card tells me that there's a need for patience and care to bring something to its full potential or to enable growth or branching-out. In a relationship reading, it can tell you that something is needed or that a relationship is stagnant and unexciting.

In a relationship reading, the Tree indicates a bond that has roots but is stagnating, boring, convenient, or at best, will require time and effort to bring to a healthier state.

In spiritual readings, it can represent our connection to different planes of existence. It's associated with ancestors due to a tree's reference to one's roots and the family tree. I'd like to mention that the Celtic Lenormand deck has two distinctly different Tree cards, one is covered in snow and the other is thriving. You can then use one for general well-being and the other for ancestors or one for thriving health and the other for health issues. (*See Stars for spirituality.)

I also use it to stand for the Earth, the Fish is the seas, and the Stars is the heavens.

"When the roots are deep, there's no reason to fear the wind" – Chinese Proverb

Descriptive Words: Unfit or with health issues, green eyes, someone who's grounded, slow-moving, boring. A natural and holistic-minded person, hippie (tree-hugger), healer, doctors, patients, shaman, all healthcare workers, environmentalists, arborists, gardeners, ancestors.

Advice: As a pro: This will grow big and strong if you give it the time and care it needs. Put more time and energy into the roots/foundation. Take a holistic view of the situation to see what will bring it to an optimal state. As a con: You're stuck, too boring. It will take too much effort/time/energy.

Directional Cues: N/A

Philippe Lenormand Original Translation (PLOT): A TREE, if distant from the Person, signifies good health; more trees of different cards together leave no doubt about the realization of all reasonable wishes.

Game of Hope (GOH): Landing on the house of the Fox will send you back to the house of Tree. In the GOH, the Fox shows what drives you crazy. What can we say about it sending you back to the house of Tree? That you are hiding in the forest until you recuperate. Hence, there is a relationship between the Tree and a need for healing, care, or patience.

Method of Distance (MOD): So, we don't want to see this card near as it brings concern regarding health issues. The mention of other tree cards refers to the fact that several favorable cards originally had trees on them. These cards are House, Child, Bear, Garden, and Ways (while the Ways is by its nature a neutral card, in relation to the Tree it will show options and alternatives). There are a few other cards that had trees on them, but their inauspicious nature has kept them out of this list. They are the Snake, Birds,

Fox, and Mountain. It is from the MOD instructions that we arrive at the idea of the Tree falling in a small spread receiving its near meaning. The fact that you drew only three to nine cards out of a deck of 36 gives us the idea that all those cards are near, while the rest of the deck is far.

Compare To: Rider for legs – moving whereas Tree is rooted and immobile, Coffin for serious illness, Mice for diseases, Bear for strength. Tower for longevity or long-lasting whereas the Tree represents slow (a long period of time) growth. (*See Well-being for #19 Tower for more information.)

Emblem Meaning: The most obvious reference to a tree's connection to health is the Tree of Life. The Christian Bible contains many references to trees as they relate to humans and our well-being, growth, and health. The Tree of Life is mentioned in the Bible in the Book of Genesis. It is the tree that grows within the Garden of Eden and is the source of eternal life. The tree is believed to have healing properties and its fruit grants immortality.

"That person is like a tree planted by streams of water, which yields its fruit in season and whose leaf does not wither—whatever they do prospers." (Psalm 1:3)

"He is like a tree planted by water,

that sends out its roots by the stream,

and does not fear when heat comes,

for its leaves remain green,

and is not anxious in the year of drought,

for it does not cease to bear fruit." (Jeremiah 17:8)

Trees also have a long history of representing humans. Their size, rate of growth, strength and resilience, and even the fact that they are rooted to the earth yet reach for the heavens. They are natural and organic, as are we. They require the right conditions to thrive – nutrients, water, sunlight, fresh air, and space. Trees also breathe and the fact that they inhale CO_2 and exhale O_2 correlates with our own inhaling of O_2 and exhaling CO_2!

House Meaning: Health and well-being. What is needed to thrive? How is the environment affecting the health of you or the situation? How is your health impacting the situation or how is the situation impacting your well-being? What needs help/time to grow?

Timing: Slow growth that takes years or only if its needs are met, May, five days, weeks, months, the fifth of the month.

Well-being: It is the card of well-being and represents overall health as well as oxygen and genetic disorders (family tree). Appearing near the PSC, it will indicate that some element of physical, mental, or spiritual health isn't at its full potential. In a general reading, falling with the House card, it refers to physical well-being; with the Stars, it will refer to spirituality; with the Clouds, it will relate to mental health. In a reading specifically about health, these cards have their own health references. Tree with the Snake = Allopathic/conventional medicine; with the Ways = Alternative approaches; with the Clover = Herbal medicine; the Bouquet = Homeopathic or Bach Flower Remedies. Keep in mind that as with any specific small-spread question, the primary theme card does not have to show up as it is built into the question, so if we're asking about someone's health, the Tree card, in a small spread, doesn't always appear. If it does, it's needed to explain the flanking cards or it may reference one of its more specific meanings of oxygen or a genetic disorder that the other cards and context will explain. For example, Tree + Tower = Hospital.

6 CLOUDS

Number and Name: 6 CLOUDS

Playing Card Inset: King of Clubs. As a person, this is someone the client typically has a bad relationship with. He will be complex, unhappy, or even passive-aggressive. The card the King is looking at will tell you what troubles this man will bring. Can be used for an ex-husband or boyfriend or a hustler.

Primary Vibe: Unstable, confusing, and turbulent. Blocks the light. Stormy weather.

Energy: Negative

Influence: Murky, misfortunate, changeable, elusive.

Theme Group: Movement/Change, short-term, Well-being.

Base Keywords: Confusion, passing troubles, unfocused, uncertainty, fear, doubt, unsteady, ambiguous, obscured, unpredictable outcomes, deceptive or elusive, something's brewing, cloudy, hazy. Weather, clouded perception, smoke, a smokescreen.

Basic Concept: Buckle your seatbelt – turbulence ahead! In everyone's life, a little rain must fall. This is the card of confusion and troubles that, just like the weather, are out of our control. A dark cloud can dampen any sunny day

– but clouds are unstable and eventually float away! Think about clouds on earth, better known as fog. Suddenly, the world as we knew it is obscured and our imaginations may run wild. We may think we know what's beyond the foggy patches, but suddenly appearances become elusive. Something's brewing and things may get dramatic.

I think the most important thing to understand about the Clouds is that it is unique among the negative cards in that it's the only one that actually "clouds" or has the ability to change the meanings of other cards. This is why you'll see it mentioned throughout the PLOT. Think of it this way, when it's above a card or the dark side is touching another card, it's clouding it so that you won't see that card in exactly the same way that you normally would. The card on the dark side is made darker, while the card on the light or clearing side is made a little clearer or more positive, so a negative card falling on the light side of the Clouds will be clearing-up.

When it appears with communication cards, the news or messages will be difficult and troublesome at worst or confusing and creating uncertainty at best. Early decks and many modern decks show an obvious light and dark side of the clouds, while some decks show an obvious thicker side to the cloud formation. This makes the dark/thick side the side you want facing away from the PSC or any important cards. It indicates the storm is coming. The other side is the clearing side, indicating that the storm is passing.

In describing a person, it can represent anything from mental illness to having one's head in a fog where they simply can't see clearly which way to go. The surrounding cards will tell you if the fog originates internally or externally as well as how problematic it is. In a GT, you can look to the Stars for guidance through the fog and the Sun to see how to burn through it.

Broader Concept: It can literally stand for bad weather, clouds, fog, smoke, incense, air pollution. Avoidance, something's brewing, clearing the air, thunderstorm phobia, can't find their way home, it's there but you can't see it, a humid place, gray or multi-colored, something hidden.

In a spiritual reading, the Clouds has already appeared to me as a nimbus or aura. Keeping in mind that it's an unfavorable card, it suggested auric problems (I saw it as Pig-Pen from the Peanuts with a dirty cloud around the client) and I then looked to the surrounding cards for more details regarding the Chakras. It can indicate a need to practice focused breathing.

In a relationship reading, it references ambiguity, hidden motives, an unclear agenda, or a lack of understanding. It may describe a person who is always changing their mind, so the risk of being hurt is great.

Descriptive Words: Gray eyes, gray or different shades of hair color, smoker. They may be vague, moody, confused, unpredictable, insecure, pessimistic, widower, someone who's very hard to read, an eccentric. A meteorologist, illusionist, mental health worker. The tobacco industry, incense producer, smoke-damage technician.

Advice: As a pro: Don't be afraid to ask for directions! You may be too fixated on a particular path or are being inflexible. Practice nephelomancy. Loosen-up and let things form as they will. You don't need to see the road ahead, trust that it will lead you where you need to go. Look at solutions that at first appear troublesome. A good rain will clean the air. You'd better bring your umbrella. As a con: You're heading into stormy weather, you're not seeing things clearly. Don't move forward until you can see the path clearly.

Directional Cues: The card to the dark side receives the trouble/issues. The card to the light side is lightning and becoming positive.

Philippe Lenormand Original Translation (PLOT): CLOUDS, if their clear side is turned towards the Person, are a lucky sign; with the dark side turned to the Person, something disagreeable will soon happen. While you never want to see Clouds close by, having the light side facing the PSC was a "lucky sign" in that it showed a clearing of the troubles.

Game of Hope (GOH): Landing on the house of Clouds sends you back 4 spaces to the house of Clover. So, your troubles set you back and you wind up in the house of Clover, looking for luck and an opportunity to overcome them.

Method of Distance (MOD): This is a card that you always want far, but if it's close, you at least want the light side facing the PSG or any SG's. Also, it's better to find it below than above. Clouds above block the sun and obscure visibility. This is the only unfavorable card that is mentioned many times in relation to the other cards in the PLOT as it's the only unfavorable card that literally clouds or rains on the other cards, changing their meanings. Other unfavorable cards add their energy to the spread and overall message, but don't actually change any other cards' meanings. It changes the meanings of Clover, Stars, Tower, Ways, Letter, and Lily when close.

Compare To: Snake for problems and difficulties that are directed at you and coming from outside of you; Mountain for problems that slow you down but it's up to you to overcome them (you have no control over Clouds); Book for things that are hidden or yet unknown as opposed to the Clouds for things you aren't seeing clearly.

Emblem Meaning: Dark clouds symbolize gloom and disaster as well as hampering our optimism and obscuring our vision. They are also symbols of change as they quickly come and go.

House Meaning: Troubles. What aren't you seeing clearly? Where are your fears and insecurities? What is creating confusion or uncertainty?

Timing: It's currently unclear/uncertain, when it's raining or overcast, June, six months, weeks, days, sixth of the month.

Well-being: As always, the Clouds refers to confusion or uncertainty in a health reading. Anatomically, it refers to the respiratory tract including the lungs, trachea, chest, and bronchial tubes. It references breathing, airborne diseases, smoking, air pollution, bronchitis, asthma, pneumonia, respiratory viruses and colds. With the Snake and Bear it can refer to intestinal gas. With the Birds, it may indicate vision problems. If the other cards indicate, it may refer to hidden addictions or mental illnesses. Any inhalation intoxications or respiratory diseases. For example, Tree + Garden + Clouds + Mice = Rhinoviruses, influenza viruses.

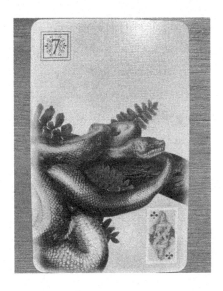

7 SNAKE

Number and Name: 7 SNAKE

Playing Card Inset: Queen of Clubs. As a person, she is unpleasant and possibly dangerous. She can be cunning as she knows what she wants and will do whatever it takes to get it. At best she will be intelligent but not easy to get along with. It is often seen as "the other woman" in a relationship spread and with the Fox, she is definitely a rival.

Primary Vibe: Treacherous, twisted, complicated, a detour, a roundabout way.

Energy: Negative

Influence: Problematic, dangerous, convoluted. It's not what you expected. It often is or feels personal. It's the card of the rival - human or not.

Theme Group: Relationships, people, warning.

Base Keywords: Complexities, difficulties, complications, twists and turns, entanglement, detours, lies, betrayal, jealousy, poisonous, seduction, a competitor or rival, infidelity (be careful not to jump right to this one!), deceit, desire, unpredictable, untrustworthy, jealous, hurtful sarcasm, venomous as in malice or spite.

Basic Concept: This is a card of a twisted path. A card of complexities. Think of a kink in a chain or receiving a bent envelope in the mail that has one of those large, "Do Not Bend" stickers on it. When you see the Snake card, something isn't right. It brings troubles, upsets, and complications. Most of us fear snakes because we usually don't see them and their bites can be poisonous. In an interpersonal relationship reading, the Snake can represent both deceit (to trick or mislead) and betrayal (to stab someone in the back/deliver into the hands of the enemy by treachery) and this is often a personal attack. It represents anything that's complicated and indirect. It can show side-stepping, procrastinating, or taking a detour. It's my Judas Kiss card and it's not a nice card no matter how you look at it!

Broader Concept: Physically, it can represent tubes, pipes, wires, chains, catheters – anything that can twist and tangle. Rivers or streams, a winding path. Things or situations that aren't straight and with many twists and turns; blackmail; things or situations which are slick, slippery, or which 'snake' around, poison. In an addition to the playing card inset, the snake itself has a historic symbolic reference to women. Michelangelo's "Fall and Expulsion of Adam and Eve" hanging in the Sistine Chapel depicts the serpent as being half woman is but one example. You can charge this card to represent another woman in a reading, but if you don't want to take any cards out of play, you can simply add enough people cards to any reading to represent all the players. (*See the section on adding extra cards to a reading.)

In a spiritual reading, it may reference Kundalini yoga, which is a yoga practice that attempts to release the Kundalini energy which lies coiled like a serpent at the base of the spine and includes breathing, physical positions, meditation, and chanting.

In a relationship reading, it will refer to anything from complications to jealousy of a rival to adultery and will rely heavily on the question and the surrounding cards.

Descriptive Words: Attractive in a dangerous and provocative way, smooth/slick, dry skin, piercing eyes, tattooed, complex, unpredictable, disloyal, manipulative, calculating, a female rival, widow, a stalker, "snake-oil sales-man", poison-control, snake charmer, herpetologist, electrician.

Advice: As a pro: Take a round-about approach but proceed at your own risk. It's complicated – you'd better charm your way out of it! Identify the issue. As a con: Don't get tangled in the lies. It's time to straighten things out. Be careful and proceed at your own risk.

Directional Cues: The card the snake is facing shows from where the betrayal comes. The other cards touching the snake will reveal the source of the betrayal.

Philippe Lenormand Original Translation (PLOT): A SERPENT is a sign of misfortune, the extent of which depends upon the greater or smaller distance from the Person; it is followed invariably by deceit, infidelity, and sorrow.

Game of Hope (GOH): If you land here, you must pay three tokens to stay safe from the snake's bite.

Method of Distance (MOD): Whenever it's near it brings adversity and tension. The cards touching the Snake may show what it's hiding. You never want it within reach to be struck with its venom or strangled, so it warns one to be on guard. When far, it indicates that the problems it brings to the surrounding cards are lessened or will soon be solved.

Compare To: Comparing it to the Fox, the Snake's goal is to hurt you and doesn't take a straight path. The Fox just wants what it wants – self-interest – so if it hurts you it's just because you were in its way. So, the Fox simply lies and cheats to get what it wants. It's not directed at you. The Snake is the back-stabber. Compare to the Ring for inclusive (included within a circle) while the Snake is exclusive (limited and/or private).

Emblem Meaning: Based on eighteenth-century Christian Europe, the emblem of the Snake isn't related to healing or transformation, but rather lies, vengefulness, and vindictiveness. This is based on the fact that venom-ous snakes often deliver deadly bites without giving prior warning to their victims. While they may simply be defending themselves or their territories, it's their unannounced attacks that give them their reputation of being vengeful.

House Meaning: Complications, betrayal. Where are the complications? Who or what is betraying you? Where are the difficulties that may require a detour?

Timing: Whenever the enemy decides to make their move, during a negative event, July, seven days, weeks, months, seventh of the month.

Well-being: The standard meaning of the Snake may apply to treatments or diagnoses in a health reading. Being the card of deception, it may indicate false disease as in a false pregnancy (more common in animals) or imaginary disorders as with hypochondriacs. Anatomically, it represents the lower gastrointestinal tract of the intestines, bowels, the rectum; the umbilical cord, and veins. It may represent poison, worms/tapeworms, or dry skin. In the right context and with favorable cards, it may point to seeking an alternative approach. For example, Snake + Mountain = Constipation, Snake + Fish + Mice = Diarrhea, Bear + Snake + Ways (going a different way) + Scythe = Projectile vomiting.

8 COFFIN

Number and Name: 8 COFFIN

Playing Card Inset: 9 of Diamonds.

Primary Vibe: End, loss, illness.

Energy: Negative

Influence: Halting, dark, heavy.

Theme Group: Slow, low, fixed, well-being.

Base Keywords: Painful endings, injurious loss, sickness, crisis, mourning, depression, closed, finished, empty, boxed-up or feeling boxed-in, reclusive, restricted or restrictions.

Basic Concept: It's a card that represents something dark, depressed, or gloomy. While it can simply indicate an end, it always decreases the positivity of any favorable nearby cards. By its very nature, it's a card that expresses an inability to do anything – move, proceed, let go, live, grow. You're stuck, buried, in the dark, so deep you can't get out. It's dark and still in the cold ground – alone. It's a card of finality. This can relate to health, finances, relationships, or work and the loss is a major one with lasting effects. It's a card that doesn't leave you with a good feeling. It confuses many people when it follows another negative card because they think the ending will make everything better. The problem here is that it's still a negative card and even if it ends something negative, it still leaves you feeling disempowered, depressed, ill, helpless, or with some sort of loss or lasting negative effect. Only a positive card following a negative card will truly improve things. As one of the three "stop cards" of the deck (along with Mountain and Cross), it indicates no forward movement.

Broader Concept: In a broader sense, this card can show up to represent a box, something buried, something underground, in the basement, at the funeral home or graveyard. While it's the card that is supposed to represent death, I've found that it is more likely to represent a serious illness that will keep you in bed rather than death. How death appears in a reading seems to differ from reader to reader as well as from client to client, so please be aware that it is very difficult to predict death. You have to consider who you're reading for and how they view death. If you're reading for someone who's asking about a loved one's health, you may get grimmer cards than if you're reading directly for that person, who may be ready to go! It may depend on how you, the reader, views death also. I see death as something that is painful for those who are left behind, but a gateway to another world for those who are leaving here.

In a spiritual reading, endings are often powerful indicators that something new is about to open-up in one's life. Sometimes, people need something that knocks them off their feet to force them to change their ways or views. While the Coffin isn't a card of rebirth as in Tarot, in a spiritual reading, it can certainly indicate the need for a spiritual rebirth or awakening.

In a relationship reading, it may indicate a dead-end union, a painful ending, or the death of feelings. With favorable cards, it points to buried feelings or something stopping one from feeling or from expressing their feelings.

Descriptive Words: Dark features, sickly-looking with dark circles under the eyes, exhausted, depressed, pessimist, fatalistic, wears black, gloomy, stuck in the past. Ghost, archaeologist, grave-digger, coroner, funeral director, someone from your past.

Advice: As a pro: This is the right time to end things. Finish what you start. Box it up and put it in the basement. Take a long rest. Lay low until the sun comes out. Take time to grieve, it ain't over till the fat lady sings! As a con: It's over and it hurts, but you have to accept it. As painful as they are, endings are a natural part of life. You're suppressing your feelings and it will only make it worse, claustrophobia.

Directional Cues: This is a stop card that ends whatever comes before it. The card following it in a horizontal line is also diminished a bit so you want the most favorable cards in this position.

Philippe Lenormand Original Translation (PLOT): A COFFIN, very near to the Person, means, without any doubt, dangerous diseases, death, or a total loss of fortune. More distant from the Person, the card is less dangerous.

Game of Hope (GOH): The one who lands here is deemed to be dead until another player lands here or until he throws a double.

Method of Distance (MOD): As the card of endings and loss, you will always want it far. When it refers to loss, it's a loss that leaves one with bad feelings and a sense of powerlessness. If close in a health reading, it indicates an illness severe enough to send you to bed. In comparing it to the Tree, the Coffin sucks the life out of other cards while the Tree sucks the energy out of the other cards. This certainly makes the Coffin a worse card. When the Coffin follows any life-area card, always look to see what follows the Coffin to see what will come after the ending.

Compare To: Compare to the Cross for suffering and pain that we endure in life; to the Mountain for obstacles rather than a dead-end; Mice for diseases and/or slowly eroded losses that may be recouped; Stork for change whereas Coffin is no change. When near the PSC in a health reading, compare to the Tree, which drains your energy, whereas the Coffin drains the life out of you.

Emblem Meaning: The Coffin is a universal symbol for a final ending or death.

House Meaning: Endings. This house often shows the greatest problem the seeker faces. What needs to die or is dying? What have you been suppressing/burying?

Timing: Winter. It's done, over, not meant to happen, never, after a death or ending, August, eight days, weeks, months, eighth of the month.

Well-being: In a health reading, it can refer to a loss of money or courage as well as health. It can indicate chronic illness, depression, severe headache, pain, fatigue, exhaustion, terminal disorders, or claustrophobia. Things that make you bedridden. Don't jump to a conclusion of death when you see this card in a health reading. It rarely indicates that. In my readings, the Ship, Stork, Stars, and Lily are generally involved when death is imminent. To claim that you see death is to play God and even with many cards pointing to death, I NEVER use that word as it will take away all hope and I've seen miraculous reversals happen. Instead, I may state that things look grim, recovery will be extremely difficult, things have taken a turn for the worse, etc. It ain't over till it's over! An MRI. For example, Tree + Mice + Coffin = Cancer.

9 BOUQUET/FLOWERS

Number and Name: 9 Bouquet

Playing Card Inset: Queen of Spades. As a person, she'll be pleasant and helpful. She can stand for a mother, godmother, aunt, older sister, teacher or mentor. In any event, she'll be someone you have a pleasant relationship with.

Primary Vibe: Surprise, invitation/offer, gift. Something offered that brings delight. Beauty, grace, generosity, pleasantries, creativity, aesthetics.

Energy: Positive

Influence: It adds a happy and uplifting mood to the reading. It's a warm fuzzy feeling to be given flowers and often shows that someone cares or appreciates you. It adds a delightful, beautiful, surprising, and giving element to the reading.

Theme Group: Relationships, people, work, well-being.

Base Keywords: Reward, gift, invitation, something offered – especially assistance, pleasure, something offered in appreciation, pleasant surprise, achievements that bring joy and happiness, compliments, gratitude, pretty, creative, charming, enjoying life's simple pleasures such as taking the time to smell the roses! Flowers, compliments, flattery, manners.

Basic Concept: This is one of the most positive cards in the deck. The original instructions give us nothing more than "happiness" – no matter what. Of course, we have several cards that imply happiness so we need to consider what a bouquet of flowers represents and in what situations we give or receive it. What we know from the PLOT is that the Bouquet will always bring an improvement in mood to the reading. You could say that it flowers things up. It represents something pleasant that's offered to us. A pleasant surprise, reward coming to you for appreciation of something you've done, or just because you're being recognized or appreciated in some way. It's something that's given to you, not something you find like the Clover or being honored for something you've worked hard to achieve like the Moon. It can be a gift, an invitation, or a compliment, and in all of these cases, it represents receiving something a little extra in life. Whatever form it takes, it's quite lovely and pleasant and will always make you happy!

Broader Concept: This is the card of aesthetics. It relates to art, beauty, colors, and creativity as well as representing flowers and insects. It may also show-up to describe our own gifts and talents.

In a spiritual reading, it may recommend using art to connect to your spiritual side. It can also indicate being inspired and even enlightened by the beauty that's all around us and even the offer of Divine grace.

In a relationship reading, it may indicate general joy and pleasure, receiving an invitation, flowers, or a gift; or a blossoming relationship.

Descriptive Words: Attractive, blonde or red hair, smells great, wears colorful clothing, beautiful smile, gracious, giving, a "Martha Stewart" type, artistic, creative. Someone with style, flair, and good taste. It's a card of pigments and colors. A florist, artist, beautician, make-up artist, fashion or interior designer, model.

Direction – East.

Advice: As a con: Your allergies will flare-up. It may look pretty on the surface but appearances can be deceiving. False flattery. Don't be so vain. Stop flowering things up. As a pro: Accept compliments with grace. Make it pretty. Be creative. Accept the offer. Count your blessings. Bring a gift.

Directional Cues: N/A

Philippe Lenormand Original Translation (PLOT): THE BOUQUET means much happiness in every respect.

Game of Hope (GOH): N/A

Method of Distance (MOD): Nearby it adds its beauty and fragrance to any situation. Because it references receiving something extra, it has no negative meaning when far, but will bring pleasantness to whatever cards it surrounds. In the far position, it simply won't bring any extra pleasantness to the client.

Compare To: It's happiness that comes to us. We don't go and get it (Key). We don't unexpectedly find it (Clover). When it refers to our gifts/talents, compare to the Moon for being recognized or known for them.

Emblem Meaning: This is a topic of great interest to me as I LOVE flowers! Growing up as the undertaker's daughter, I naturally associated flowers with funerals. When anyone in my family received flowers, the first thing we'd ask is, "Who's died?" But that didn't stop me from adoring flowers, although my preference to this day is wildflowers – I even wore them in my hair and carried them at my wedding!

In considering what this emblem was intended to mean, we simply need to consider the fact that this deck was designed during the Victorian era. The Victorian era was a period when certain topics weren't discussed openly, instead, personal feelings were conveyed through the giving of certain flowers. Each flower was assigned a particular meaning. Giving someone flowers conveyed a literal message during this period but today, we still offer flowers to relay general sentiments. They're offered to others to convey admiration or ardor, appreciation, sympathy, congratulations, and apology. Most people would agree that flowers lift our moods – unless you suffer from severe allergies – and studies have actually proven this fact.

Based on all that I just shared, it's easy to understand the meaning of this card.

House Meaning: Happiness, beauty, surprises. What's blossoming or being offered?

Timing: Once you deserve it, September, nine days, weeks, months, ninth of the month.

Season: Spring.

Well-being: Always a great card to draw in a health reading, it represents the gift of recovery or healing. It may indicate flower essences or allergies. Anatomically, it represents the face, general appearance and coloring/pigmentation. It may recommend bringing flowers or any display of care and concern for another who's ill. For example, Tree + Bouquet + Fox = Cat allergy.

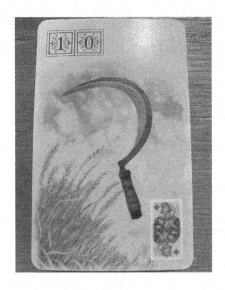

10 SCYTHE

Number and Name: 10 Scythe

Playing Card Inset: Jack of Diamonds. A young person who isn't easy to understand. He'll be disruptive, unpredictable, impatient, impulsive, and often manipulative.

Primary Vibe: Warning! Blade side or at worst: dangerous, hasty, and hostile, cut away. Handle side or at best: sort out, make the final cut or decision, a need to take immediate action.

Energy: Negative

Influence: Sudden, shocking, risky, radical, aggressive, threatening. Anything sharp, be it an object, words, or a happening. Whatever the Scythe cuts away will be lost permanently. It sometimes appears as the "final straw" card that forces you to take radical action.

Theme Group: Fast, movement/change, work, well-being, relationships, warning.

Base Keywords: Danger, risk, accident, cut, edit, separate, dissect, slice, injury, threat, aggression, sharp, swift, breakup, separation, urgent, sudden interruption, divorce, a final good-bye, sharp pain, fear, insecurity, panic, risk, settle the score, a radical act out of a sense of urgency.

Basic Concept: This is a card of cold, quick and sudden endings or severing ties. Whoever is holding the Scythe will determine whether it's a tool or a weapon. It often shows up when you're at the end of your rope and must let go of something. Cutting things out of our lives can be very painful, whether the choice is ours or not. At its best, the Scythe can represent sudden and shocking events that happen unexpectedly. It's even shown-up at the end of a line as a sort of exclamation mark, as if to say, "I told you so!". In my daily draws, it sometimes appears to indicate a sudden break in my daily routine, a papercut, or a broken dish. It also appears when I finally sort through something that had been troubling me - but it won't be easy or pleasant!<$n>

Broader Concept: This is one of the primary warning cards in the deck and often indicates a threat to your safety or well-being. I've seen quite a few new readers using this exclusively as their "decision" card, but that belongs to card #22 Ways. First and foremost, the Scythe refers to something being cut out. This card may show up as a hasty decision or a need to deal with something immediately and in an extreme way. It can also appear to represent a surgeon's scalpel, making it a tool for healing, though dangerous in the wrong hands. Because I own a dog grooming salon, the Scythe often appears to represent scissors. If all the other cards in the draw are favorable, my new shears might be arriving. Unfavorable surrounding cards may indicate an accident or dropped/damaged shears (very common in a grooming salon!). It also represents knives or any sharp tools. The Scythe can represent military, police, sudden aggression, or a stabbing.

In a spiritual reading, it indicates a need to cut ties, cut ethereal cords, clean and align your Chakras, or cutting out anything that poses a danger to your spiritual well-being.

In a relationship reading, it often indicates danger, aggression, splitting-up, divorce, being harshly rejected, or a sudden crisis.

Descriptive Words: Dangerous looking, sharp features, short hair, eyes that appear to look right through you, aggressive, intimidating, dangerous, with physical scars. Personality descriptors include being sharp-tongued, analytical, blunt, and rudely to the point! Anyone who uses sharp objects such as a surgeon, dentist, farmer, barber, groomer, tailor, grass-cutter. A risk-taker, risk assessment officer, soldier.

Direction – West.

Advice: As a pro: Slice through the BS. Cut it down to size with speed and precision. Prioritizing what goes and what stays. Dangerous or not, you must make that decision – now! Get moving now before it's too late! As a con: Danger, danger, Will Robinson! Haste makes waste. You reap what you sow. Watch out! Be careful you don't get cut!

Directional Cues: Like the Clouds, this is a card with an obvious worse side. The blade side does the cutting, so it stands to reason that the cards on that side are being threatened. The cards on the handle side, however, are still too close for comfort. You can view these cards as being drawn into the danger or they will represent an action that is required to avoid the danger of the blade side. Positive cards surrounding the Scythe may indicate how to avoid the threat.

Philippe Lenormand Original Translation (PLOT): THE SCYTHE indicates great danger, which will only be avoided if lucky cards surround it. From this we can see that the card was intended to infer danger, but favorable surrounding cards will show us how to avoid it, or at least give us hope that we can. The CC verse: "Wait quietly for the harvest, proportionate to your labor; for everyone is the maker of his own fortune," indicates only that we not rush into things which certainly acts as a warning.

Game of Hope (GOH): N/A

Method of Distance (MOD): As a card that threatens the safety and security of the client, you want to see it far from the PSC. It brings risk into the story and the direction can show where it's directed. The danger of the Scythe can be eliminated or lessened when surrounded by favorable cards as well as favorable cards surrounding the PSC, which offer protection. It can be lessened to fear, uncertainty, or a narrow escape when favorably positioned. In the far position, the swinging blade can't reach you but it will have a negative impact on any cards it touches. Consider that the handle side will still deliver a blow, though not as severe as the cut of the blade side.

Compare To: The Coffin for endings – period – with no indication of danger or a possibility of avoiding it. Compare to the Fox for something wrong, while the Scythe is a sudden danger. Compare with the Ways for having alternatives, while the Scythe is eliminating alternatives.

Emblem Meaning: The Scythe is an agricultural tool that dates back to 5000 BC, and was still in use in Europe during the early nineteenth century as the gas-powered mower wasn't invented until a century later in 1902. Scythes were very sharp, required a fast action in order to cut, and were quite dangerous. This gives us a clear meaning for this card – cutting via a fast, sharp, and dangerous action.

House Meaning: Danger and separation. Where is the danger? What is or needs to be cut out?

Timing: Suddenly and often before you're ready! Very fast, strikes when you least expect it, October, ten days, months, weeks, the tenth of the month.

Season: Fall/Autumn/harvest time.

Well-being: Always a card that indicates danger. It's not one you want to see in a health reading. It can refer to surgery, injections, fractures, accidents, stabbing pains, cuts, trauma, and surgical tools. For example, Garden + Clouds + Scythe = Flu vaccine.

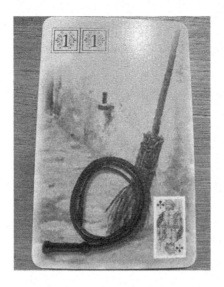

11 WHIP/ROD/BIRCH

Number and Name: 11 WHIP

Playing Card Inset: Jack of Clubs. The Jacks are the children or young people of the deck and being a Club card, this will represent a difficult child. They can be complex, controlling, self-centered, unhappy, or aggressive. Jacks can be of either gender.

Primary Vibe: Discord, drama, effort, and struggle.

Energy: Negative

Influence: Tense, repeating, disharmonious, and conflictual.

Theme Group: Fixed/resistant to change (as in struggle/effort/repetition), work, relationships, well-being, communication.

Base Keywords: Discord, conflict, dispute or intense discussion, heated negotiations, to irritate, to inflame, angry, repetitive, recurring, addictive, punishing, harsh discipline (cracking the whip) or tongue-lashing, fighting, hard work. Agitation, friction, aggression, accusation.

Basic Concept: The Whip depicts a back and forth effort but one lacking in harmony as you might see in a repeating cycle of the Ring. Everything is a struggle and it makes me think of the saying, "One step forward and two steps back." It can show up as criticism, correction, arguments. Whenever this card is in a position of describing another card, it will show something being repeated.

Broader Concept: It's intensity and repetitive nature can infer addictive behavior depending on the context and surrounding cards. It often shows difficult negotiations (unless surrounded by favorable cards) or interference. Throughout the final stages of putting this book together, the Whip showed up for me regularly in my daily cards to show the repetitive struggle of editing and proofreading.

In a spiritual reading, it may indicate a need to eliminate addictions or bad habits. With favorable cards, it may recommend chanting or interpretive dancing. It may also tell the client that it's time to bury the hatchet and make amends.

In a relationship reading, it will indicate general disharmony, arguments and disagreements, not seeing eye-to-eye, and anything from hot and heavy sex to make-up sex to sexual perversion.

Descriptive Words: Verbally assertive, loud, combative, agitated, quick-tempered, overly disciplined, obsessive exerciser or body-builder, a sexual deviant, argumentative, echolalia, combative, judgemental, OCD. A lawyer, debater, critic, sex therapist, defendant, complainant.

Advice: As a pro: Don't stop – extra effort will bring results. Train/work hard. Competition can be a good thing. Take the challenge! Defend yourself! Make an effort. As a con: You're whipping a dead horse – Give it up. Stop beating yourself up needlessly. Sharp tongues hurt others and hurtful words can never be taken back. You're stuck in a negative pattern.

Directional Cues: The card next to the whipping end of the emblem will show the cause of the discord or what needs to be admonished.

Philippe Lenormand Original Translation (PLOT): THE ROD means quarrels in the family, domestic afflictions, want of peace among married persons; also fever and protracted sickness.

Game of Hope (GOH): So as not to be castigated by this Rod, one pays two marks. For this, one gets to move forward 2 spaces to the house of Child. So, you pay to avoid the whipping and are then placed in the Child's house. It's like being sent to your room to think about what you've done!

Method of Distance (MOD): As the card of battle, if it's near, you can expect disagreements or a need to defend yourself. You don't want it near any life-area cards and if it's near the PSC, it indicates disruption of harmony in their personal life.

Compare To: Rider for activity and general exercise, while Whip is strenuous and repetitive exercise. Birds for nervous chatter, while Whip refers to heated discussions or arguments; or Birds for a couple and Whip for multiples of something. The Ways for more than one option while the Whip refers to repeating something more than once. The Scythe for sudden aggression while the Whip refers to repetitive, back and forth discord, or Whip for persistent pain while Scythe is sudden and stabbing pain.

Emblem Meaning: A whip is a device for hitting or threatening and is a universal symbol for punishment, coercion, or discipline. Think of "spare the rod/whip and spoil the child."

House Meaning: Discord, conflict, repetition, and intensity. Where are you struggling? Who's stirring up trouble?

Timing: After something repeats, it may happen more than once, during a difficult time, November, eleven days, weeks, months, eleventh of the month.

Well-being: The Whip generally refers to recurring health conditions that you're fighting, relapses, fever, and back-and-forth pain. It can signify inflammation, which is the body's localized reaction to tissue irritation, fever, infections, muscle aches (especially from overuse), stiffness, or stretch marks; rheumatic disorders such as Osteoarthritis, Fibromyalgia, or Lupus; hoarseness or stuttering, OCD. Male fertility (female is Moon). It may refer to a medical dispute that the client will have to fight. It's more serious if found with the Tree near the PSC. Anatomically, it relates to the muscles as well as the vocal cords and throat. With Clouds, it can indicate addictions that will

be further explained by the other cards such as Fish for alcoholism or bulimia, or Snake for drug addiction. For example, Mountain + Whip = Arthritis,
and Man + Whip + Mountain = Male infertility.

12 BIRDS/OWLS

Number and Name: 12 BIRDS

Playing Card Inset: 7 of Diamonds

Primary Vibe: Aflutter – as in mental agitation or nervous excitement.

Energy: Neutral/Negative

Influence: Nervous, exciting, or uneasy state of short duration. Noise. Mental clutter.

Theme Group: Communication, relationships, short-term, fast, high.

Base Keywords: Temporary upsets, fuss, busyness, stress, hectic, distraction, startling, excitable, flighty, scatterbrained, mental clutter.\mental clutter, chatter, gossip, idle talk, chitchat, superficial conversations, noise, exciting announcements, informal meetings, daily comings and goings, a couple or pair.

Basic Concept: The Birds card adds a sense of arousal to the reading. It can show itself as unease, nervousness, or excitement stemming from expectation, speculation, or conjecture. It brings in a hectic, flighty, or possibly frustrating or disappointing feeling, which is short-lived. This can manifest itself internally or via verbal expression. Its connection to verbal communication relates to the noise that birds make as they anxiously chatter, so it is connected to anxious talk and gossip.

When I began to study this system seriously, there were a few cards whose meanings were inconsistent and the Birds was one of them. Some see this strictly as a verbal conversation card while others argue that it has no connection to communication at all and is a card of anxieties and troubles. I imagine the latter is based solely on the PLOT. Interestingly, the GOH instructions consider this a very positive place to be – the Canary Islands where the beautiful birds live – which you're lucky enough to visit if you land on the Ship space. Looking at the original Coffee Cards, we have #26 Bird/Turtledove. The phrase on the card says, "You are very happy, but love entirely swayed by passion will leave you very unhappy." From this we get the idea of happiness in love, passion, and stress, as well as being swayed, which is defined as being influenced by others. We can also start to understand the idea of the meaning of "a couple". So, here we have a connection to talk, gossip, and chatter. From all of this, I can see the Birds as a card of a break in homeostasis. This means that it is indeed a card of stress, but stress can be positive or negative, which is something that we animal trainers understand all too well. Positive stress, also known as eustress, is the excitement we feel when our best friend brings us some juicy gossip, or when we compete in a favorite sport, ride on a roller coaster (if we love them), or possibly going on a blind date. What we're really talking about here are aroused emotions, which can be good or bad. It's all relative, my friends. So, does the Birds card represent stress? Yes. Does it represent talk? Yes. On its own, it leans more toward the negative, but the surrounding cards will make the meaning clear.

This often shows up as my TMI (too much information) card – too many external forces hitting you such as too many opinions, too much to do, too much information in general. It's also my card for mass media, of which I'm not a fan as I see it as nothing more than a barrage of funded opinions and professionally-written propaganda intended to paint a picture of what those in power want us to see as reality. I share this not to sway anyone in their opinions, but to drive home the point that the cards will show up for us according to how we view the world. Sometimes, this card indicates one of those days where you have way too much to do, too much on your mind, and everything bothers you! It often shows up in my advice readings to say that there's too much talk, chatter, conflicting opinions or ideas coming from others that are clouding your judgement. It's also my "crazy-brain" card where it can indicate that all the chatter is in your own head and not coming from an external source.

"Silence is the language of God, all else is a poor translation." – Rumi

Broader Concept: Some of the early decks call #12 Owls rather than birds and picture owls on the card. For the purposes of this book, the meaning will be the same. The Celtic Lenormand deck includes a separate Owls card to include the meaning of wisdom if you should choose to use it.

The Birds may simply refer to verbal communication or phone calls with the Letter or Rider, or with favorable cards such as the Bouquet, it can indicate singing. With the Stars it may refer to Twitter, Skype, or Web chat. It can also refer to short trips (think of the short distances birds fly on a daily basis) such as running errands. It may refer to actual birds and bats.

In a spiritual reading, it may recommend talking something out or not letting the little things in life get to you. Don't sweat the small stuff!

In a relationship reading, it traditionally refers to a couple, but in keeping with the card's meaning, it will refer to a lot of little stresses and misunderstandings. This meaning then moves into the realm of a need to talk things out and clear the air.

Descriptive Words: Sharp/beady eyes, long nose (beak), tense/irritable/nervous, quick movements, flighty, scattered, light-build/frail, chatty, gossipy, a snitch or tattletale. Someone who constantly changes their minds, changes directions, and is easily distracted. Singer, gossip columnist, speech therapist, talk-show host, twins.

Advice: As a pro: Couple-up. Hurry-up and get it all done. Talk it out. As a con: Take your time and you won't be so frenzied. It's time to slow-down and clear your mind – there's too much fluttering around in there. You've got too much on your plate. Too stressful. Too noisy. Shut up!

Directional Cues: N/A

Philippe Lenormand Original Translation (PLOT): THE BIRD means hardships to overcome, but of short duration; distant from the Person, it means the accomplishment of a pleasant journey.

Game of Hope (GOH): The only mention of this card is in relation to the Ship card. Landing on the Ship sends you ahead 9 spaces to land in the house of Birds but there's no discussion in the game of the meaning of this card.

Method of Distance (MOD): When near, the Birds bring stress, annoyance, and chaotic situations. This will cause a lot of chatter about the annoying state, which will be described by the surrounding cards. In the earliest traditional near/far instructions for a grand tableau, the Birds falling very far from the PSC suggested a short trip was to take place (as opposed to the Ship, which needed to be near and referred to a distant journey).

Compare To: Letter or Book for written information whereas the Birds refers to oral communication. Mice for gnawing worries (which implies a length of time) whereas the Birds indicates fleeting and temporary stresses.

Emblem Meaning: The nature of bird behavior gives the emblem its meaning. Watching and listening to birds is all you need to do to understand this, as they nervously and noisily flit around. A book entitled, All Birds Have Anxiety by Kathy Hoopmann relates dealing with daily stresses to a bird's life and fits the meaning of this card perfectly.

House Meaning: Restlessness, chatter, gossip. What's upsetting you?

Timing: Morning. A time of year when the birds migrate (Spring or Fall), during a stressful time or stressful conversation, fast. December, twelve days, months, a year, annual, twelfth of the month.

Well-being: The Birds brings transitory stresses, tension, and agitation to a health reading. It may indicate hyperactivity, impulsivity, or ADHD. Anatomically, it represents the nervous system and the eyes (think of bird's eye or hawk-eye). With the Sun it may indicate hot flashes, with the Heart it may indicate high-blood pressure (low blood pressure is Heart + Stars). For example, Tree + Birds = Vision problems such as myopia. Add Book and you need reading glasses.

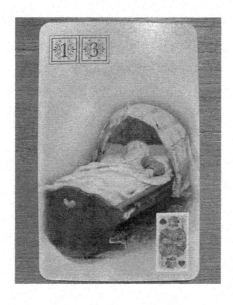

13 CHILD

Number and Name: 13 CHILD

Playing Card Inset: Jack of Spades. A child or young person who is well-behaved, kind, and dependable. The Spades courts tend to be practical and are often familiar to the PSC.

Primary Vibe: Childlike innocence and ease – new and wondrous, small and just beginning. The significator card for a child.

Energy: Positive/Neutral

Influence: Think of all the attributes of a child and you'll get the right feeling for this card. Its influence is young, novel, trusting, kind, naive, or something that's just starting out.

Theme Group: Short-term, low, small, relationships, people.

Base Keywords: Small, new, innocent, amicable, playful, young, children, simple, trusting, immature, inexperienced, naive, unsuspecting, youth, good company, kindness, a fresh start, new beginning, innocence, goodness, new developments, littleness, naiveté, childlike trust. Negatively, it can show pettiness (uncaring in a small-minded or spiteful way).

Basic Concept: This card can represent an actual child or children, which would be determined by the question and surrounding cards. If you're reading for someone with children, you can set your intention for this card to be the SC for their child or children. It's a card that shows good associations with others, kindness, naiveté, as well as innocence, curiosity and wonder. It can ask you to look at things from a new perspective. It may refer to childhood or younger days. It also references things that are small, new, and just beginning; taking baby steps or easing into something, a desire to learn, being spontaneous or just having fun. With unfavorable cards, it may indicate immaturity, childish behavior, being overly trusting or incapable of caring for oneself.

Broader Concept: Games, play, make-believe, playfulness; new opportunities, a new project, initiating, starting something new, little things, small steps, a tiny amount, the early stages of development; loving-kindness. In animal readings, other than referring to puppies, kittens, and the like, it refers to play and toys.

In a spiritual reading, it may indicate a need to look about the world with a new sense of wonder, allowing yourself to succumb to child-like curiosity and question all that you think is "real". It also refers to lightening-up and being more playful in your spiritual and divination practices.

In a relationship reading, it can indicate a new romance, spontaneity and playfulness, or easing into a relationship by taking things slow and keeping it light.

Descriptive Words: Short, youthful appearance, energetic, spontaneous, frivolous, simple-minded, irresponsible, naive, playful, a novice. A student, debutante, kindergarten teacher, paediatrician, child-care worker, toy maker.

Advice: As a con: Don't be so naive. You're too immature. Grow up! Curiosity killed the cat. Don't belittle it. You're thinking too small. As a pro: Lighten-up and don't be so serious. Take that first step. Take a playful approach. View it from a childlike perspective. Try something new. Innocence is very attractive.

Directional Cues: When it refers to an actual child, the card the Child is facing will describe their relationship with the parents.

Philippe Lenormand Original Translation (PLOT): THE CHILD is a sign that the Person moves in good society, and is full of kindness towards everybody.

Game of Hope (GOH): No mention of this card other than the fact that you move to this space after landing on the Whip.

Method of Distance (MOD): The Child, along with the Dog and the Garden cards relate to how you interact with others and on their own, they are all rather positive cards. When near, the Child indicates that the PSC is in good company and is interacting with others in a positive way. In the near position when describing the PSC, they will be seen as good-natured and amiable as well as retaining a sense of child-like wonder. This can describe a fun and spontaneous person. In the far position, you'd see the opposite of all or any of the aforementioned.

Compare To: Whip is tension and Child is ease. Tower is tall and formal, whereas the Child is small and informal. Child is impatient and the Dog (and Lily) is patient. Child is the beginning of life (of a person, project, or thing), whereas the Rider can represent the beginning of adult life (as the first card/house – see "LENORMAND: THE GAME OF LIFE"). Compare to the Clover, which is also new, small, and carefree but also unexpected and temporary and primarily references luck or opportunities that you stumble upon. The Child is also carefree but due more to immaturity or lack of knowledge or experience. Clover says, "I'm going to do it no matter what. I'm going to take my shot. It's now or never." Whereas Child says, "I'm going to do it because I don't know any better, or maybe I should say, any different as in blind trust."

Emblem's Meaning: When you see a picture of a child, what do you think of? Children, of course, but also the future – something that is just starting out. Something small, sweet, playful and simplistic. It represents ease and being carefree making it the opposite of work or anything that's rigid and structured.

House Meaning: What's fresh, new, or wondrous. What's small and just starting? Where do you need to trust/lighten-up? What's new? Children.

Timing: Dawn. A small amount of time, on a new day, when something is new and just starting, related to your child's birthday, during childhood, thirteen days, weeks, months. thirteenth of the month.

Well-being: Generally, it will indicate a disease or ailment that is in the early stages as well as just starting a new treatment or medication. It may refer to childhood diseases such as measles or chickenpox, things that decrease in size such as rashes or tumors, congenital disorders, dwarfism or growth issues, or diseases that manifest as a return to childlike behavior such as dementia. For example, Tree + Book + Child = Dementia; Tree + Child+ Stars = Diaper rash.

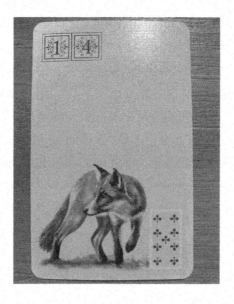

14 FOX

Number and Name: 14 FOX

Playing Card Inset: 9 of Clubs

Primary Vibe: Wrongness. Pay attention. Sly and strategic. Survival and self-interest.

Energy: Negative

Influence: Something's wrong, someone's up to something, being or a need to be sly.

Theme Group: Work, relationships, warning

Base Keywords: Wrong, sneaky, a trick, covert, masked, manipulation, cunning, stealthy, shrewd, mischievous, caution, distrust, self-interest, fraud, strategic, vigilant, street-wise, behind the scenes, spying, use your instincts, taking advantage or being taken advantage of.

Basic Concept: If you think about the phrase, "to outfox someone", you'll understand the meaning of this card perfectly! To "outfox" is to beat someone using your wits rather than physical strength. Don't let the concept of "wrongness" throw you. While that's the first thing you should think of when you see this card, there are so many levels of wrongness. The fact that not all is right in your world can lead to a need for cunning, shrewdness, and the devising of a strategy or plan. Something being wrong may simply indicate a need to keep your wits about you or think outside the box. If you're asking whether your thinking or reasoning is correct and it shows up, then the answer is no, you're wrong. The same would be true of the Clouds or Snake. But if you're asking how you should handle yourself at an upcoming meeting or interview, it won't tell you to be wrong, of course, but will infer a need to be strategic, clever, and not so forth-coming with personal information that isn't related to the position you're applying for. When it refers to someone else, it will describe someone who will do whatever necessary to get what they want, and if that includes throwing you under the bus, that's exactly what they'll do – and they may smile to your face while doing it! It's not personal like the Snake, but you'd better keep an eye on them nonetheless. They're not to be trusted.

Broader Concept: In keeping with the theme of wrongness, let's consider that the Fox's association with a struggle for survival, being crafty, clever and strategic are all the result of something being a bit wrong to begin with. Why else would one need to be cunning or crafty if everything was fine and dandy, life was running smoothly and all was above board? If the world was made up only of rainbows and unicorns, we'd have no need for foxes. So, yes, there are foxes in the world, and yes, sometimes we are the foxes. This card shows up a great deal in work-related readings, and that should be of no surprise. When it comes to money, surviving, or gaining power and control, even the sweetest of colleagues may become a little foxey!

This card can describe something that is masked or disguised, someone with ulterior motives, a lurker, or avoidance. It may refer to a detective, a spy, a stalker or a criminal.

In a spiritual reading, it may indicate that we aren't being honest with ourselves or we're not trusting or paying attention to our basic, mundane or secular survival instincts. Because of its connection to the sense of smell, it may suggest the use of incense or aromatherapy.

In a relationship reading, remember the mask the fox wears. The other person is not completely forthcoming. They're up to something, being sneaky, dishonest or deceitful in some way. They may have a secret life.

Descriptive Words: Red hair, freckles, prominent or pointy nose, slight build, light on their feet, wears dark glasses, masked (in animals – a natural mask). A loner, liar, criminal, false friend, opportunist. A teenager. A detective, spy, con artist, imposter, criminal, survivalist, swindler. Someone with a hidden agenda.

Advice: As a pro: Be sly to get what you want, sneak in the back door, be clever and do what you have to do. It's time to think of yourself first. Something's wrong and you need to trust your instincts. Be cautious! Think outside the box. Be silent but stealthy. As a con: You're wrong! Stop pretending. Don't deceive – you'll get what you want if you're up-front and honest.

Directional Cues: The Fox's nose points to the wrongness.

Philippe Lenormand Original Translation (PLOT): THE FOX, if near, is a sign to mistrust persons with whom you are connected, because some of them try to deceive you; if distant, no danger is to be apprehended.

Game of Hope (GOH): The cunning Fox leads the player astray and he has to find refuge in the Woods (Tree). The Tree, being the card of health, is the perfect place to recuperate after being negatively exposed to the Fox.

Method of Distance (MOD): You don't want this shady character nearby as it's better to avoid his attention. When near, it recommends that you be on guard and protect yourself from those who may be out to trick you or manipulate a situation to their benefit. When far, you are not on his immediate radar but should check the cards that are touching to see what he's trying to manipulate.

Compare To: The Snake is the hidden enemy intending to manipulate, whereas the Fox is interested only in self-preservation and most likely is present in plain sight. Fox=covert and Snake=overt.

Emblem's Meaning: The Fox was chosen for this card because of the many fabled foxes and most likely the popular Reynard the Fox tale in particular, which was made into a classic story by Johann Wolfgang von Goethe in Germany in 1860. What all these foxes had in common was their use of cunningness and trickery to get what they wanted. The Lenormand deck was designed using emblems that every one of the period could easily relate to and this was a widely-known fable of the time. In the story, Reynard meets the bear and it relates to the classic story of the have-nots trying to get what the haves have! The Bears have it and the Foxes want it! The fox works indirectly by manipulation and control to achieve its own end.

House Meaning: Falsehood and caution. What lands here is wrong or a call for action due to something being wrong.

Timing: At the wrong time, fourteen days, weeks, months, fourteenth of the month.

Well-being: As with any reading, the Fox indicates that people or situations are misleading or intending to manipulate you in some way. Proceed with caution and get a second opinion if possible. The Fox may indicate a misdiagnosis or an ailment that is masked by another. This card may infer issues with medical deontology. Anatomically, it stands for the nose and sense of smell. Because it's the card for the Cat, it may refer to toxoplasmosis or with the Bouquet, a cat allergy. For example, Fox + Scythe = A broken nose.

15 BEAR

Number and Name: 15 BEAR

Playing Card Inset: 10 of Clubs.

Primary Vibe: Large and in charge.

Energy: Positive/Neutral.

Influence: Strength, possession, controlling, powerful, and protective.

Theme Group: Big, work, people.

Base Keywords: Prosperous, strength, supporting, courageous, powerful, influencing, attracting envy, assertiveness, dominance, leadership, taking charge, protection, management, economy, success that brings a need to protect your resources, weight.

Basic Concept: This card shows power and control, the good fortune of obtaining resources along with a need to protect them. This, of course, can attract envy or jealousy in others. The Bear separates the haves from the have-nots. It shows that someone has something to protect. The PLOT clearly gives us the positive and negative aspects of this card, the GOH makes no mention of it, and the CC (the Bear emblem was clearly taken from the CC Lion) states,

"Be always on your guard; he who easily believes is easily deceived." The Coffee Grounds interpretation is: "At the top in the clear it signifies all kinds of prosperity with people of quality. At the bottom it warns the consulter to shun all such intercourse as he will at all events find persons who will envy him and his fortune, and not see it with indifference." This meaning is in keeping with the PLOT and the MOD in that if favorably placed, the Bear references prosperity, but when unfavorably placed, we'd better watch our backs.

Broader Concept: This card can refer to management or being in charge, hence the common reference to a boss. It may show up to describe resourcefulness or support when flanked by favorable cards. At its worst, it can relate to jealousy, being overbearing, unbearable, intimidating, and controlling. This would require the addition of unfavorable cards. On its own, the Bear references greatness and the fortitude to protect it. It's a "take charge" card and often points to doing things in a big way. Maybe it's time to start throwing your weight around! While the Mice may be the eaters in the deck, the Bear is the card of overweight, stocky, or muscular as well as hairy. In my animal readings, it often indicates resource-guarding and may show up to signify any large wild animal.

In a spiritual reading, it can ask you to look for your personal strengths and sources of power or may reference a need for more protection. Because of its connection to support, it may also ask you to seek a mentor.

In a relationship reading, it indicates a prosperous relationship. One of strength, support and protection. If flanked by unfavorable cards, it may refer to a partner who is jealous and domineering.

This is one of the other traditional "people" cards, though it doesn't have a court card inset. Interestingly, some see it strictly as male, while others (myself included) see it as female. I often use this card as a mother or grandmother card in a reading.

Descriptive Words: Large, strong, burly, heavy, motherly, protective, hairy, assertive and commanding, supporting but easily offended, "a big softy". Courageous, powerful and authoritative. A strong personality. Bear people often don't know their own strength. A leader, manager, someone in charge, a guardian, an official.

Advice: As a con: You're overbearing. Don't force it. Your jealousy will get you into trouble. You don't always have to be in charge. Control-freak. Time to lose weight. Your hair is a mess. Don't be so bossy. Hoarding. As a pro: Protect what you have. Take charge. Provide for your family. Be more assertive.

Directional Cues: When far, the direction the Bear looks points to who is jealous.

Philippe Lenormand Original Translation (PLOT): THE BEAR is either a messenger of good fortune, or admonishes us to keep away from company, particularly from that of the envious.

Game of Hope (GOH): N/A

Method of Distance (MOD): The good fortune that the Bear represents comes with a price. The more one has, the more one attracts attention from those who don't have. When near, it tells you that the PSC has resources and a need to protect them rather than flaunt them. It may also show that you are being protected and supported, depending on the surrounding cards. When far, there's no good fortune coming your way, no power or control over matters, and no assistance in protecting yourself.

Compare To: The Snake for jealousy while the Bear indicates a need to protect ourselves from those who are envious of our success. Child for small and innocent while the Bear is large and in charge. Fish for abundance and cash flow while the Bear references luck and success and the strength and courage to protect it. Compare to Mice for eating and metabolism with the Bear for overweight or overindulgence.

Emblem's Meaning: The Bear, along with the Fox, was chosen because of the well-known fable of the time, Reynard the Fox. In the story, the fox represents self-interest while the bear represents established power. This gives us the meaning for the Bear card as the one who has the power or resources that need to be protected and attract jealousy in others who want to infiltrate that power.

House Meaning: Power, protection, strength. Who's in control or what are you in control of? How are you protecting what you have? Where is your power/strength?

Timing: When you take charge and make it happen, fifteen days, weeks, months. fifteenth of the month.

Well-being: In a health reading, the Bear will offer its usual strength, support, and courage. As a person, it may signify a strong and helpful woman who will play an important role in the reading, be it a doctor, nurse, mother, or grandmother. It can reference obesity issues, sleep patterns, or your own strength to fight a disease or illness. Anatomically, it stands for the stomach and hair. For example, Heart + Birds + Bear = High blood pressure due to obesity.

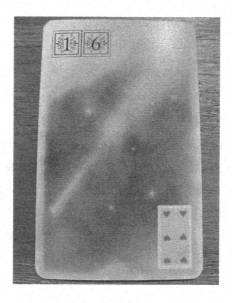

16 STARS

Number and Name: 16 STARS

Playing Card Inset: 6 of Hearts

Primary Vibe: Guidance, crystallization – making or becoming definite or clear.

Energy: Positive.

Influence: It can show up like a big arrow saying, "Look here, this is the direction in which you want to go! This is where you should focus your efforts." It's guiding, aspiring, encouraging, and gives us hope. The stars are aligning. Things are starting to shape-up. This is where we're meant to be!

Theme Group: Movement/change, relationships.

Base Keywords: Progress, aspirations or designs (what are you conceiving in your mind?), successful new path, guidance, healing, recovery, encouragement, direction, clarity, wishes, ideals, possibilities, intuition, spirituality, esotericism, connection to the Divine, the Internet, science, technology, night, dreams, visions, success, a positive influence.

Basic Concept: The Stars has a dreamy and ethereal quality. It shows what we are attracted to (the shiny things) and where we're meant to go. It is my GPS card so I take note of the cards touching it to find my way. It sometimes shows up as an "aha" moment where I suddenly gain clarity on a matter. In a spread with vertical interactions, I always check to see what card falls under it. When describing a person, they have a dreamy, idealistic, visionary quality. A "head in the stars" type. Being a double Pisces, this card often shows up in descriptions of myself! Being the card of prophecy and destiny, you could call this the "fate card".

This is the card that shows up when we're ready to move toward our goals. In a GT, when your card is facing the Stars, your plans are moving in the right direction. If it's near the Ship (showing where your current journey is heading) then you know your path is clear and correct! (Compare this to the Anchor, which shows the end result.)

What exactly is the difference between goals, ambitions, and aspirations? I see goals as the desired result coming from effort and ambition. Aspirations (Stars) are still in the planning phase born of hopes and ambitions to achieve those goals (Anchor).

The Stars is also a "going within" card – especially with Lily (meditation, prayer), as opposed to cards such as Book (learning from outside yourself), Garden (including others), Bear (taking control physically), or Dog (support from someone you trust).

The Star is all about the realization of potential. With this card, the hidden becomes clear. Inspiration (what comes to you mentally – the mental stimulation) becomes aspiration (a plan to make it happen – the ambition to achieve it).

As one of the three luminaries in the deck, it is a very positive card that you want near in a GT or to show-up in a small spread. The other two are the Moon and the Sun. What they all have in common is the light they shine on the surrounding cards, which adds something beneficial and advantageous. We can say that the Sun adds energy and optimism – you're on fire, baby! the

Moon shows that we are or will be looked upon favorably and acknowledged for this, and the Stars shows a positive outlook, being inspired to follow this path, and a confidence that we're going in the right direction.

Broader Concept: Because of its relation to a spread of many similar connected things as well as its ethereal nature, the Stars has become the card of the Internet. Consider all the ways this may show itself. With Book = Facebook; with House = Personal home pages, domains; with Garden = Social media; with Whip = Internet porn, etc. It's also the card of science and technology and can refer to electricity, GPS, computers, or a map.

More symbolically, it can refer to myriads of things, a spreading or scattering of items, vastness, a connection among many similar things, or many small items of a similar nature. It references something clear, clean, and vast.

It's the only card that the original translation relates to the Divine, so it is my spirituality card. Ancient writings refer to stars as, "The canopy of the Heavens". As Jiminy Cricket sang in Pinocchio, "When you wish upon a star, makes no difference who you are." We are all equal under the stars! I LOVE this card!

It can refer to psychic ability, prayer, divination, astrology, fortune-telling, a medium, psychic, diviner, or mystic, dreams, visions, Heaven, the Universe. Magic (w/Book). Shaman (w/Tree). Famous people (stardom).

In a spiritual reading, the Stars card may suggest a need to gain clarity through seeking divine guidance. Ask and thou shalt receive!

In a relationship reading, this is a very positive card as it relates to moving in the right direction. It's also a card that gives hope for success.

Chakra: Crown/Sahasrara. This is the Chakra that connects us to the Divine. It gives us access to higher states of consciousness, allowing us to leave behind all secular concerns and personal preoccupations. It is where we get in touch with the Universe. I guess you could call it our long-distance telecommunications carrier! When it is open and healthy, we gain an awareness of the higher wisdom of the sacred. It's a connection to all that is, ever was, and ever will be. It's formless, faceless, and limitless. It is here that we are free from all human limitations and gain full realization of Universal immutable realities.

Descriptive Words: Charismatic, talented, someone who stands-out, bright twinkling eyes, famous-looking, interesting birthmark. Intuitive, a dreamer (starry-eyed), inspiring, a thinker, a planner. An astrologer, psychic, mystic, IT, Web developers, map maker, astronomer, scientist, inventor. With Lily = Introvert. As opposed to Sun + Garden for an Extrovert (when describing people).

Direction: North.

Advice: As a con: You're spreading yourself too thin. You're following the wrong path. Get your head out of the stars and face reality. As a pro: Keep the faith. Reach for the stars. Thank your lucky stars.

Directional Cues: N/A

Philippe Lenormand Original Translation (PLOT): THE STAR confirms good luck in all enterprises; but if near clouds, it means a long series of unhappy accidents.

Game of Hope (GOH): Arriving at the Star of good prospects, the player receives six marks. Obviously, a very favorable card!

Method of Distance (MOD): As one of the three luminaries in the deck (Sun and Moon are the others), you want this card near to bask in its light, and having it above you is best. When the Stars card is near, you have hope for success in your endeavors. You know that you're heading in the right direction. If it's near and the other near cards are all favorable, success is guaranteed! When far, your goals may currently be out of reach. Look at the surrounding cards to see where the light is shining.

Compare To: The Stars card is extraordinary while the House is ordinary. Stars infers divine inspiration, which contrasts with the Tower's earthly ambitions. Compare to the Key, which says that you have the solution to the problem and it's in your hands. The Key is more physical, as in, do it now! The Star shows that you are on the right path, you're now seeing it clearly, and you know which way to go.

Emblem's Meaning: Stars have been watched and admired since the beginning of recorded history. Our ancestors looked at the stars and prayed. People used stars in navigation, which is even mentioned in the Bible. To dream of a starry night suggests that a dream or wish will come true and is said to bring good luck in which you will enjoy wealth and fame. From this we get the intended meaning of this emblem, that of aspiration, inspiration, imagination, wonder, dreams, pursuits, creative brilliance, and Divine guidance.

House Meaning: Spirituality/divine guidance. What is taking shape/forming/spreading? What potential are you realizing? Where are you meant to go? Where will you find inspiration?

Timing: Night. When it's destined to happen, on a clear night, sixteen days, sixteenth of the month.

Well-being: It's an overall healing card as it's a card of hope and success. Anatomically, it refers to the cells, the skin/pores, pills or tablets (w/Snake = Allopathic or

Bouquet = Homeopathic), low blood pressure (w/Heart). As it relates to the skin, it can indicate anything from rashes, rosacea, acne, moles, psoriasis, eczema, candidiasis, herpes, shingles to measles or dermatitis herpetiformis (a sign of Celiac disease). For example, Tree + Rider + Stars = Athlete's foot; Stars + Mountain = Clogged pores.

17 STORK

Number and Name: 17 STORK

Playing Card Inset: Queen of Hearts. An adult woman with any of the "Heart" qualities of empathy, romance, sympathy, intuition, openness, and a love of family. Can be a sister, daughter or aunt.

Primary Vibe: Change/evolve

Energy: Positive/Neutral

Influence: An evolving of a situation, an addition, a movement, with favorable cards it will show an improvement.

Theme Group: Movement/change, high, people.

Base Keywords: Change, evolving, advancing, progressing, relocating, improving, alteration, shift, reorientation, improvements, transitions, migration, birth.

Basic Concept: "Turn the tide," "Out with the old, in with the new," "Breathe new life into something."

You won't be staying where you are when this card appears. This card brings significant changes into your life, and unless this card is surrounded by unfavorable cards, they're generally for the better. The Stork stirs things up and breaks inactive or stagnant situations. The surrounding cards will show what will change and how. Is it next to the PSC and the House or Tower (apartment building)? Then they may be relocating their home. With the Child card, a baby may be coming! With the Ship, it may refer to an airplane. Near the Ring, it can indicate a change in a relationship. Near the Moon (or whatever your primary work card is), it may indicate a job change or a change within your job such as a promotion. Always examine the surrounding cards when you see the Stork.

Broader Concept: Because this card can refer to moving on as well as returning, there are a few things to consider. Is the card referring to a change to something new or a return to something familiar? Keep in mind that the Stork generally brings improvements and something new in your life. Returning is going back to what was, which can be a positive change such as when the kids return from college for a family holiday. As always, take all the cards into account. What cards surround the Stork? Stork + Dog may indicate a return to something or someone you're already familiar with and faithful to, or it could say that the client is moving in with a friend. It all depends on the context and surrounding cards.

The Stork may refer to air travel, especially when it's with the Ship. It may refer to babies, pregnancy and delivery in the right context. It may also refer to restlessness (a need for change) or flexibility (the ability to change).

It can signify home renovations, job promotions, new additions to your life, moving on to new projects, and general movement.

It may show up to represent waterfowl/game birds.

In a spiritual reading, we'll consider the three main themes of this card, which are change, birth, and the legs. It may indicate a need to change your spiritual practice and allow something new to be born. The legs may tell you to get moving, whether that is through dancing or walking in nature (my favorite way to meditate!).

In a relationship reading, the Stork implies some sort of change that will require other cards to explain. It may refer to a positive change within a relationship or a need to change to another. Consider your exact question and examine the other cards carefully.

Descriptive Words: Long legs, slender, graceful, bad hearing (birds actually hear differently than humans). Adaptable, flexible, restless, loves change and variety. A pilot, flight attendant, mover, midwife, natal nurse, orphanage/adoption agency.

Advice: As a con: It's not time to change. Not the right time to move. As a pro: Make a fresh start, change can be hard but it's necessary.

Directional Cues: N/A

Philippe Lenormand Original Translation (PLOT): THE STORK indicates a change of abode, which will take place the sooner the nearer the card lies to the Person.

Game of Hope (GOH): N/A

Method of Distance (MOD): When near, this card always represents a significant change in the PSC's life. The flanking cards will determine whether this is a favorable change or not or will relay what the change is about. When far, any changes won't be significant but check the cards it touches to see what changes it may bring to those areas.

Compare To: Compare to Dog and Anchor for staying. Ways for having options, whereas Stork is simply a change that occurs.

Emblem's Meaning: The European white stork is what you'll see on all early decks as well as most modern decks. My research showed that its association with babies actually originated in Northern Germany centuries ago. One theory as to the correlation is that storks return to central and northern Europe in late March to early April, just about nine months after Midsummer's Day, June 21, the summer solstice and longest day of the year. This day was celebrated with a major festival in pagan Europe and was a time for weddings and general merrymaking which of course, included a lot of drinking of fermented beverages. My guess is that many babies were born nine months later! Being highly migratory, Storks change residences annually, giving us the meaning of change, especially a change of residence.

House Meaning: Change. Pregnancy, if applicable. What is or needs to be changed, relocated or improved?

Timing: When the seasons are changing or when you make a change. In some cases it can refer to nine months. Seventeen days, weeks, seventeenth of the month.

Well-being: In a health reading, the Stork refers to change which will require other cards to elaborate on. If it's with all neutral cards, you can expect some improvement in the condition asked about. It may refer to pregnancy and all that's related to it. Anatomically, it stands for weak limbs – both the legs and knees as well as the elbows. In determining pregnancy in a reading, my general rule is that I need to see the Child card nearby. Add the Birds and there's nervous talk about it or possibly a premature announcement. With the Letter, there is a confirmed birth announcement. For example, Tree + Stork + Whip = Tennis elbow;

Child + Stork + Scythe = Cesarean section.

18 DOG

Number and Name: 18 DOG

Playing Card Inset: 10 of Hearts

Primary Vibe: Loyalty, devotion. Who or what are you friendly or loyal to or what or who is friendly and devoted to you? Supporting and helpful.

Energy: Positive/Neutral

Influence: As a card of loyalty and devotion, on its own, it's rather positive. The important thing is to see it primarily as loyalty rather than a physical friend. While it will often show up as a friend, if that becomes your primary vibe, you'll miss out on all of the other ways to view devotion. Is the card describing you, as in what or who you're devoted to? Is it describing a situation or career position that's loyal to you rather than a person? Is your best friend a dog – or an animal other than a dog? For example, while the traditional card for cats is the Fox, if your cat is your best friend, then the Dog card can represent it. Don't limit this card by seeing it first and foremost as a human friend.

Theme Group: Fixed/resistant to change, long-lasting, relationships, people, work.

Base Keywords: loyalty, fidelity, support, faithfulness, steadfastness, friendly, reliable, dependable, supporting, helpful, trustworthy, a companion, an ally, a friendly colleague, close friend, pet.

Basic Concept: A friend is defined as one who is attached to another by affection or esteem or one that favors or promotes something (showing loyalty). These are two very different things but this card can represent either. Look at your question. Is the seeker the dog or is the dog someone else who is impacting them? This can also be determined by the positions in a larger spread and by the context and question in a small spread. What is the seeker loyal or devoted to? Who is supporting or helping the seeker?

Broader Concept: This is the card that represents actual dogs or domestic pets in general. It can also refer to other people, such as a close friend, a partner, or friends in general. It can also refer to a close sibling of either sex, though traditionally, it's been used for a brother.

The Coffee ground meaning: At the top, in the clear, it signifies true and faithful friends, but if his image be surrounded with clouds and dashes, it shows that those whom you take for your friends are not to be depended upon; but if the dog be at the bottom of the cup, you have to dread the effects of extreme envy or jealousy. This is the same as the PLOT definition.

Coffee Card Verse: You will easily find better friends among strangers than among your own relations. Anyone with a dysfunctional family will certainly relate to that!

In a spiritual reading, the Dog brings up the idea of what or who we trust or look to for support. It may speak to us about how we're treating our friends or are we depending on them too much? The Dog may represent an animal guide or totem or simply a Spirit guide who wants to help us.

In a relationship reading, the Dog refers to unwavering loyalty and staying-put, but without cards such as the Heart, Ring, or Anchor, it may simply indicate someone who'll stick by you without love or commitment.

Descriptive Words: Large or distinctive ears, loud, a big mouth of teeth, brown eyes and hair, touchable-looking hair, friendly and welcoming appearance. Familiar-looking. Someone loyal, dependable, waits patiently, warm and loving. Maybe too dependent. A trusted colleague, close friend, a fan, club member, chaperone, police, those who help and support you, a pet, pet care workers, anyone who works with dogs.

Advice: As a con: You're too needy. Stop whining and be more independent. Those whom you think are your friends, aren't. Don't be so trusting. You're too submissive. What you've been loyal to needs to change. Doggedness (stubborn tenacity). As a pro: Blood may make you related but loyalty makes you a family. "Be loyal and trustworthy. Do not befriend anyone who is lower than yourself in this regard." – Confucius "Loyalty is what makes us trust. Trust is what makes us stay. Staying is what makes us love, and love is what gives us hope." –

Glenn van Dekken

Directional Cues: The card the Dog faces shows the loyalty when near and disloyalty when far.

Philippe Lenormand Original Translation (PLOT): THE DOG, if near the Person, you can consider your friends faithful and sincere; but if very distant and surrounded by clouds, be cautious not to trust those who call themselves your friends.

Game of Hope (GOH): N/A

Method of Distance (MOD): When the Dog falls near the PSC, it shows support from friends, colleagues, or alliances. An alliance isn't necessarily a person, but may reference anything you've aligned yourself with and are loyal to. When far, the PSC won't be able to count on those he trusts or may experience disappointment with regards to his or her alliances. When the Clouds falls near the Dog it's a warning not to trust those you're unsure of and even your closest friendships may be at risk.

Compare To: Garden for social groups/other people, the Dog as a person is singular. Compare to Anchor for faithfulness, while Dog represents loyalty. The difference is subtle but important. Loyalty represents allegiance based on a long-term affiliation, whereas faithfulness goes much deeper. It infers a sincere and strong commitment to someone or something which involves vows or promises. Loyalties include benefits, but faithfulness is unconditional. The Dog shows things going your way or the same way as opposed to Mountain, which shows things going against you. Mountain = Enemy and Dog = Ally. Dog is patient and Child is impatient. The Tower is judgemental but Dogs never judge.

Emblem's Meaning: The dog is widely accepted as a symbol of steadfastness, loyalty, trust, devotion, protection, and someone who supports and assists you.

House Meaning: Loyalty and devotion. Friends/supporters. What are you devoted to or who's devoted to you?

Timing: You'll have to wait so be patient. On your friend's birthday or when you're with your friends, eighteen days, eighteenth day of the month.

Well-being: As a card of someone who's helpful and supporting, the Dog can refer to anyone who provides assistance and care during an illness. Anatomically, the Dog refers to the ears and the immune system. Some choose this card for the voice and vocal chords, but I gave that to the Letter as it's my primary card of communication. Still others choose the Birds. Whichever makes sense to you is the one you should choose as you don't want to have to stop and think about what any cards mean during your readings! For example, Tree + Dog + Mice = Ear infection, while Dog + Mice = Hearing loss.

19 TOWER

Number and Name: 19 Tower

Playing Card Inset: 6 of Spades

Primary Vibe: Authority, institutions, restrictions, regulations, hierarchy, solitude (by personal choice).

Energy: Neutral

Influence: Long-standing and unchanging, high/tall, official, established, organized, solitary. Structured, organized and firmly-established.

Theme Group: Long-term, high, big, work, relationships, well-being.

Base Keywords: Authority, institutions and organizations, large public buildings such as school, hospitals, or courthouses; government, bureaucracy, officialdom, hierarchy, ambition, solitude, isolation, confinement, rising above, a need to isolate or protect privacy, long-term, rising up to gain a higher perspective, striving to advance, placing oneself above others, egotistical, judgemental, superior, boundaries, an uneven relationship, power struggles. Conformity, confinement, limits, rules, laws, red-tape, formality, formal, legal, rigid, corporate, executive, politics, high-status, lofty self-image, high

155

expectations. It's also the card of ego and life-span – think tall, high, solid, and rigid and you'll get the right idea.

Basic Concept: A tower is tall, high, rigid, structured, and has many levels. It has an upper level, middle, and lower, which separate those at the bottom from those at the top. It can reference ambition and solitude, which is chosen or intentionally inflicted upon you rather than the natural isolation of the Mountain. It's something that withstands the test of time and refers to longevity of life of a person or thing. The Tower represents the duration of something that's existed or has been developing for a long time. It can also indicate moving up in increments. An interesting note is that when I ask about an expected delivery, the Rider + Tower tells me that it will take longer because it is being shipped using more than one carrier or it has to go through customs. Either way, there's nothing wrong, it simply has to go through channels. This differs from the Rider + Mountain, which tells me that it's held-up or stuck somewhere or my mail carrier is "fertummelt"! The Tower tells me to be patient but the Mountain suggests I may need to make a phone call.

Towers are organized, structured, and bigger than one person. Towers are structured, organized, governing, and separating. It can represent establishments, administration, arrangement and order and is rigid and resistant to change as well as cold and isolating. When accompanied by favorable cards, it can reference rising above, staying on top of things, or seeing things from a higher perspective. It may reference a need to raise your standards or create healthy boundaries. Think big, high, or long-term when you see the Tower in an advice reading. In a descriptive reading, it can indicate a big ego, big ambitions, high standards, big buildings, big power and control. This is a card of rules, regulations, bureaucracy, and red-tape, which is the opposite of the philanthropic and benevolent Lily card.

Broader Concept: There's another aspect of this card that sometimes comes up, and that's the idea of secluding yourself and moving to higher ground to gain a new perspective on something. I liken this to the Hermit card in the Tarot. Borders, any large buildings or institutions such as universities, hospitals, corporations, prisons, apartment buildings, banks, airports, courthouses, the military. Hard-to-reach goals. It references all large buildings, while the House references small buildings. Things with many steps. Tall pieces of furniture with many drawers.

In a spiritual reading, with favorable cards it tells me that I need to be more organized and structured in my spiritual practice. With unfavorable cards, I'm being too cold and rigid. It may indicate a need to rise above, take the higher ground, or strive to reach new spiritual heights. While the Mountain tells me to spend more time alone the Tower tells me that I'm too isolated or placing myself above others.

In a relationship reading, the Tower indicates a formal, official and long-term relationship, though there's nothing warm and fuzzy about it. With unfavorable cards, it indicates an unevenness (in age, culture, values, ideals, etc.), power-struggles, isolation, or a formal and business-like relationship.

Descriptive Words: Tall, thin, older appearance, a big ego, arrogant. A loner, introvert, rigid, selfish, ambitious, an entrepreneur, an authority figure, someone who's made it to the top, CEO, an official, someone with status. Top dog, the big cheese, the el jefe, an executive, politician, legislator, architect.

Advice: As a pro: Rise above. Become more ambitious. Aim high and work hard. Work toward something bigger than yourself. Isolation is your friend now. Take the higher-ground. Gain a higher perspective. Distance yourself from the situation. Take that corporate/government job. As a con: You're too rigid. Stop being so cold. Don't be such a snob! Stop working so much. Leave your ivory tower.

Directional Cues: The card sitting above the Tower explains what the client needs to gain clarity in a situation.

Philippe Lenormand Original Translation (PLOT): THE TOWER gives the hope of a happy old age; but if surrounded by clouds, it forebodes sickness, and, according to circumstances, even death. As a tower is long-lasting, solid, and sturdy with a strong structure and solid foundation, it stands to reason that it would reference a long and healthy life in a health reading when favorably placed. Towers are long-lived buildings so this card will refer to longevity in general such as a job, project, or relationship. There's no CC for the Tower and the GOH simply references a better view from the top.

Game of Hope (GOH): To enjoy the pleasant view, you must pay two tokens. You don't move forward or backward but there's a price to pay to enter the tower and gain a higher perspective by reaching the top, or possibly to reach the top level of your career.

Method of Distance (MOD): The instructions only mention health, and what we get from this is that the card relates to something long-standing and sturdy when near and surrounded by favorable cards, but there's a complete 180 if unfavorable cards such as the clouds are near, changing the interpretation to illness – even death. This isn't the card of a long life, but a card of life expectancy. Therefore, it is completely dependent on the surrounding cards and distance from the PSC when asking about health. It's a card you want close to the PSC and surrounded by favorable cards in a GT or small spread for health.

Compare To: With regard to the solitary aspect of this card, we can compare it to the Mountain. In this sense, the Mountain represents being isolated by external forces or location, whereas the Tower is self-imposed solitude through personal choice. If the Mountain is borders, the Tower is border control. Tower is the introvert, whereas Garden is the extrovert. Tower is reserved, whereas Mountain is defensive and stubborn and Child is shy and insecure. Tower is formal and rigid, while Dog is friendly and casual.

Emblem's Meaning: The symbolism of a tower really depends on whether you're inside the tower by choice or not, whether you're on the top or the bottom, or whether you're inside or outside. It's long been a symbol of protection and fortitude as well as confinement, hierarchy, restriction, and guarding. You only have to consider who builds towers to fully comprehend this card's meaning.

House Meaning: Anything related to government, associations, organizations, laws, all things official. What separates you from what you want?

Timing: It could take a long time, in increments, on a government/bank holiday, when in a large building, nineteen days, weeks, nineteenth of the month.

Well-being: Because the Tower refers to longevity, where it lands will have great impact. If it lands next to the Tree, it indicates a long-term health condition. Landing near the PSC in a health reading and far from the Tree, it indicates long life expectancy. It may indicate health related buildings such as hospitals and medical universities. It's my quarantine card. Anatomically, it references the spine and neck. For example, Tree + Tower + Dog = Veterinary hospital.

20 GARDEN/PARK

Number and Name: 20 Garden

Playing Card Inset: 8 of Spades.

Primary Vibe: Public, outside, environment, events.

Energy: Positive/Neutral

Influence: This card focuses on the outer world, where things are out in the open. The public, community, or society in general. The environment outside of your four walls.

Theme Group: Work, relationships.

Base Keywords: The environment, outside, atmosphere, your surroundings, exposed (Book is hidden), on display, society, public, the community, large gatherings or the places where they take place, external world (House is internal), groups, crowds, socializing, friends, social events, entertaining, guests, audience, networking, contacts, alliances, interacting with others, parties, festivals, sharing, coming out, expansion, an extrovert (Tower is an introvert).

Basic Concept: This is the social card as well as the card of the outdoors and your community. It may represent all those in your social group, the people that you work with, people who support you, or going out in public, any group of people. This card can indicate parties, social events or public celebrations as well as the locations where they're held. It may reference entertainment, networking, any outdoor activity or simply the park, your yard or garden. It may indicate large meetings, conventions, consumers, public opinion or refer to publishing or advertising in business readings.

Broader Concept: It can represent something being shared, something out in the open, disclosure, coming out, announcements, expansion, outward view, what's outside of the inner situation (House), involving others, the environment. Garden + Bouquet = Hospitality.

Garden + Rider = The media. Garden + Stars = Online social media.

In a spiritual reading, it may ask you to seek or form a group of like-minded people, join a Tai Chi group, meditate or perform yoga outdoors, or simply commune with nature. It can also reference a need to evaluate how you're interacting with others.

In a relationship reading, it can refer to a public meeting, especially with regard to first dates. It can also refer to the involvement of others in a relationship based on accompanying unfavorable cards. It can indicate a wedding with the Ring nearby or a public exclusion with the Coffin. It may reveal a loose or shallow relationship that lacks depth and is based on going out together or being seen together.

Descriptive Words: People who are active, open and easy to read. They care for their appearance and are articulate. Sociable, popular, influential and outgoing, they love interacting with others and want to make a good impression as reputation is important to them. Their emotional fulfilment comes from outside of themselves. They tend to be open-minded. They love to entertain. These are the team-players. Entertainers/actors, party or event planners, gardeners, partiers, socialites.

Advice: As a pro: Get out there and meet new people. Share. Be a team-player. Open-up and go public. As a con: Keep it to yourself. Don't follow the crowd –

do your own thing. Don't include others. Stay in the house. Looking to others for your own happiness is always a temporary fix.

Directional Cues: N/A

Philippe Lenormand Original Translation (PLOT): THE PARK prognosticates that you will visit a very respectable company; if very near, that you are to form a very intimate friendship, but if distant, it hints to false friends.

Game of Hope (GOH): Landing on the house of the Book will send you back to Garden space. From this we can surmise that the secrets held within the Book stem from your social environment. You must go back there to sort it out.

Method of Distance (MOD): The original deck referred to this card as the Park and it was a well-manicured park where people went to see and be seen by others. Hence, the near/far reference is linked to your social standing. When near, it promises respect and alliances with others that will help you get ahead. Being socially active is equated with success. When far, you could see this as people shunning you or turning their backs to you. You're not being seen, noticed, assisted, or appreciated by others.

Compare To: Tower for isolation and unsociability. House for inner/private life as compared to Garden for outer/public life. Book for keeping secrets as compared to Garden for openly disclosing information. Coffin or House (introversion isn't necessarily a bad thing!) for introvert and Garden for extrovert. Garden can refer to friends in general while Dog is your best friend or one friend.

Emblem's Meaning: Parks and formal gardens were very important to those who lived in the cities and larger towns of the period. The seventeenth century developed the formal Renaissance gardens, while the eighteenth century gave us the more natural Baroque gardens. What they all had in common was that they were built to impress and were a sign of prosperity. For the city's inhabitants, they were the place to go to mingle, schmooze, and network. They functioned as centers for most outdoor social activities from open-air dining to musical and theatrical performances as well as sports and games.

We can truly understand the card's social meaning when we consider the importance of parks during the time this deck was developed.

House Meaning: Publicness and outer life. What's going on in your social life? How are others around you or your environment affecting the situation? In what way should you be connecting with others or opening up?

Timing: Afternoon. At the time of an event – Wedding, birthday, a large gathering, outdoors, twenty days, weeks, twentieth of the month.

Well-being: Being the card of people, it may refer to any group of people who play a role in a health reading. It's one of the traditional "tree" cards, so you want it close to the Tree as it shows there will be support. It's the card of contagion, public diseases and infections, and pandemics. It's connection to fruit (Garden of Eden) says that it may refer to a need for more fruit, vitamin C, or an allergy. It may indicate recovery through fresh air, rest, relaxation. A spa or retreat. For example, Tree + Garden = Patients; Tree + Tower + Garden = Hospital staff.

21 MOUNTAIN

Number and Name: 21 Mountain

Playing Card Inset: 8 of Clubs.

Primary Vibe: Obstacles, challenges, enemies.

Energy: Negative

Influence: At best, a speedbump. At worst, a temporary road closure. Something or someone that stands in your way. You may be standing in your own way!

Theme Group: Big, high, slow, relationships.

Base Keywords: Enemies, cold, hard, distant, foreign, remote, delays, obstacles to overcome, resistance, struggles, challenges, uphill battles, detachment, defensive, isolated, inaccessible, refusal, rejection. The odds are against you. Something you need to face. Boundaries, borders, blockades.

Basic Concept: "Every mountain top is within reach if you just keep climbing." – Barry Finlay. "Over every mountain, there is a path, although it may not be seen from the valley." – Theodore Roethke. An enemy isn't always a person. Think of anything that prevents you from accomplishing something. A challenge. A struggle. Along with the Coffin and Cross, it's one of the three "stop" cards, so what is stopping you? Or, are the cards asking you to stop and get yourself together before proceeding? It may show that you're at an impasse or dealing with an obstruction. It may reference enemies when close and powerful friends when far. There's something you need to overcome, it's not all clear sailing as something is in your way. It can reference patience, tenacity, or persistence. With other unfavorable cards, it may indicate a rejection, detachment or having the odds stacked against you.

Broader Concept: The Mountain may represent borders, anything that is foreign or in the distance, isolated, or tough to maneuver. It is cold, and detached and can represent inhibitions, stubbornness or frustration. It may indicate an uphill battle, a wall, malice, stasis, or general inactivity. A test, a deadlock, the summit, the peak, silence. It may refer to the "elephant in the room".

In a spiritual reading, the Mountain may indicate that there's something blocking you from reaching your spiritual goals or that your path won't be an easy one. You're facing a challenge and shouldn't give up until you reach the peak. You may be too detached from your higher self or your own worst enemy! Are you too inhibited? Seek warmth, release blockages, perform a colon cleanse or fast.

In a relationship reading, it warns of a challenging situation, someone who's stubborn and defensive, cold and distant. The relationship may be at an impasse or require too much effort if flanked by unfavorable cards. It may also suggest a separation.

Descriptive Words: Large and imposing, stubborn, holds grudges, headstrong and persistent. White-haired or balding. Harsh appearance, cold, detached, and stone-faced (shows no emotion). Large head, busty. An enemy, bully. Guarded, defensive, and self-protective. Lonely, isolated. Frustrated and stagnated. A hermit, recluse, someone who lives off the grid. Customs or border patrol, mountain climber, geologist, seismologist, shepherd, skier, wilderness buff. May refer to someone with disabilities.

Advice: As a pro: Be an immovable obstacle and don't let anyone get by you! Accept the challenge! Stay silent. The greater the challenge, the greater the reward! As a con: There's an enemy in the midst, don't be so stubborn, you're too cold, too distant.

Directional Cues: N/A

Philippe Lenormand Original Translation (PLOT): THE MOUNTAINS, near the Person, warn you against a mighty enemy; if distant, you may rely on powerful friends. So, the card referred to enemies, but enemies aren't always people. What is an enemy? A challenger, an opponent, opposition, adversary. Apply those same words to situations and you have the full meaning.

Game of Hope (GOH): On these steep Alps, the player has to remain until another arrives to release him or he has to cast a double. This is considered one of the "stop" cards in the game where you are stuck for a period. The others are the Coffin and the Cross, so we get an idea of the negativity of these three cards, though the only card that's a true "stop" card is the Coffin. But it's valuable to consider this when any of these three cards show up in a reading. You want to pause and consider that there's a problem when you see any of these cards.

Method of Distance (MOD): When near, this card represents an enemy or some other sort of obstacle or challenge for the seeker. The severity of which will be explained by the surrounding cards. It may represent anything from a minor setback or delay to a need to defend yourself from a mighty opponent. When far, it won't create any issues directly but as always, look at the cards it's touching to see where it may pose a problem.

Compare To: With regard to the solitary aspect of this card, we can compare it to the Mountain. In this sense, the Mountain represents being isolated by external forces or location, whereas the Tower is self-imposed solitude through personal choice. If the Mountain is borders, the Tower is border control. Mountain = Enemies or things going against you, whereas

Dog = Friends/supporters or things going for you.

Emblem's Meaning: Mountains can symbolise many things, but the constant among the coffee card meanings, the Game of Hope instructions, and the PLOT is that of obstacles, large and looming challenges, and enemies from foreign lands (those who lived on the other side of the mountains).

House Meaning: Obstacles and challenges. What obstacles are in your way? What is being delayed? What enemies (literal or figurative) are causing adversity?

Timing: Something that will take years or once you tackle the obstacles, when alone, twenty-one. Three weeks, twenty-one days, twenty-first of the month.

Season: Winter.

Well-being: The Mountain is a card of blockages and obstacles, so this can pertain to the treatment of a disease as well as the disease itself. It refers to blockages in the body such as constipation, large swellings such as tumors, abscesses, hemorrhoids, are any abnormal growths. It can also indicate hardening, stiffening, or compression, so consider hardened or blocked arteries, arthritis or rheumatism. It may also refer to any type of resistance in the body. Anatomically, it stands for the head, skull, and breasts. For example, Whip + Mountain = Muscle stiffness; Snake + Mountain = Constipation; Snake + Stars + Mountain = Medication resistance.

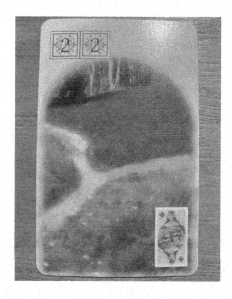

22 WAYS/CROSSROADS/PATH

Number and Name: 22 Ways/Crossroads

Playing Card Inset: Queen of Diamonds. As a person she represents an adult woman who likes to be in control though she may not actually be sure what she's doing. The diamonds people can be impatient, impulsive, assertive, independent, and unpredictable. Can be a business woman.

Primary Vibe: Decisions, alternatives, more than one.

Energy: Neutral

Influence: Another way, a split, duality, options, differences.

Theme Group: Movement/change, people, well-being, work, relationships.

Base Keywords: Decisions, choices, alternatives, split, diverge, diversify, deliberate, escape route, a new path, mediation, elections, duality, dichotomy, variety, more than one.

Basic Concept: This card is linked to the number two or higher in that we know there are at least two things to consider.

I chose not to call this card the "Path" (though it's a perfectly acceptable name if you choose it) as that infers a single path and there's a reason why the card shows a fork. At worst, it's the card of being at a crossroads and not knowing which way to go – being perplexed or in a quandary, having doubts, or feeling that you're being forced to make a choice. It can show apprehension and indecision. At best, it's a card of options, diversifying, finding alternatives or diverting from your current path to something better. With favorable cards, it's my "free-will" card.

In a health reading, it indicates options and alternatives.

The coffee card verse is: "Excesses will certainly make you unhappy, avoid them therefore while it is time." This indicates making a change while there's still time.

This card may also indicate being at a crossroads, literally, which can include hesitation, deferment, or procrastination. For me, this generally shows itself with cards such as the Cross, Snake, or Clouds.

Broader Concept: The surrounding/connecting cards may show your choices or will elaborate on the situation. For example, in small spreads of 3-7 cards, when it falls at the beginning of the spread it generally shows me that a choice has already been made and the following cards will elaborate on that. In the middle, the cards to the left show one choice and the cards to the right show another. Falling at the end gives me a storyline that's leading up to a need to make a choice. This card often shows up in my dailies to indicate taking a different route or a different path on my daily hikes. It may simply indicate a road, sidewalk, or trail.

In a spiritual reading, it may be telling you that now is the time to make some important decisions as to which way you want to go in life. It may indicate searching for alternative spiritual practices. Maybe it's time to try something different.

In a relationship reading, it may show that someone is being double-crossed or that the partner is making another choice, splitting-up, moving on, or looking for a way out. It can show separation or divorce.

Descriptive Words: Someone who's hard to figure-out. They may be indecisive or non-committal. Maybe of two minds, searching for alternatives.

Independent and likes to take the road less traveled. They may prefer to stay neutral and mediate for others. They love options and alternatives but you never know which way they'll go. At worst, can be reluctant, indecisive, back and forth, an escapist, two-faced, a hypocrite, or leading a double life. A mediator, life-coach, a drifter, a hiker, tourist or tour guide, prefers temporary or several part-time jobs, a dabbler.

Advice: As a pro: Go your own way. Give yourself options. Take another route. You can do more than one thing. If you don't see another option, create one! As a con: If you veer off your path, you'll be sorry. Stay on the straight and narrow. Stop procrastinating and make a decision already!

Directional Cues: When we have a card on either side, they can indicate our options.

Philippe Lenormand Original Translation (PLOT): THE ROADS, surrounded by clouds, are signs of disaster; but without this card, and if distant from Person, that you shall find ways and means to avoid the threatening danger. From this, we can say that the near meaning is one of tough decisions, near unfavorable cards can show difficult or bad decisions, and distant and with favorable cards, we have options and choices. For me, whether I want to see this card near or far is entirely based on context.

Game of Hope (GOH): Unnoticed, this path leads around the mountains right back to the Garden at number 20. The word, "unnoticed" infers that not making a decision, or making the wrong decision, sends you back in the game. At the same time, it infers that you have another choice! I see it as, go back to the park, think it over, and try again. If the Garden is our social card and it's followed by the Mountain, which represents enemies that attempt to block us, the Ways following this pair indicates that there's always a way out.

Method of Distance (MOD): This is a card that the two best known authorities on the MOD disagree on. Andy Boroveshengra sees it as a negative card when near and Bjorn Meuris sees it as the opposite. While Andy's view seems to be more in alignment with the PLOT, I'm in agreement with Bjorn on this as this is a card of at least two options so if I'm faced with a challenging situation, I'd rather have options available. I always want to know that there's a way out and that's exactly what this card indicates! My guess for the opposite view is that seeing it near indicates that an issue exists and there's a need to take a different route, make a split, or diversify. Because I see variety as the spice of life, this still isn't a bad option in my mind! Another way to see this is when this card falls close to the PSC in a GT or in a small spread, it can indicate that it's time to make a decision – you can no longer put it off. A choice needs to be made and it will lead to changes. Change can be difficult and many avoid it at all costs. Doing nothing is a choice and this card suggests that the seeker "fish or cut bait!" When this card shows up, the worst choice you can make is no choice.

The closer this card falls to the PSC, the more urgency there is in a need to make a choice, but also the clearer the choices will be and the more control they'll have over them. The fact that it's near indicates that at least two options exist, because you can't make a choice unless you have at least two things to choose from. Consider this scenario: There is a challenging cluster of cards surrounding an important life area such as health (Tree). Regardless of its distance from the PSC, this indicates that there will be some health issues to face within the time frame of the GT. Would you rather have the "way out" card close by or out of your reach? Personally, I want it close!

If the Clouds card is near the Ways, you can see that there will be stormy weather on your path – at least for one of the options. If the other cards are favorable, you may only experience confusion and/or doubts regarding your options, but if all the cards are unfavorable, you're in for problems. At worst, you may hit a brick wall regarding the choices you're considering. When far, your choices and options are out of reach. What I want to see in a GT is this card near the PSC if the seeker is indeed facing difficulties and surrounded by favorable cards. Otherwise, I'd like to see it further away, near no significant life-area cards, and not touching any unfavorable cards.

Compare To: Tower for restricted, whereas Ways represents free will. As it relates to more than one, compare to Birds for a couple or pair and Whip for repeating something more than once. Compare to Cross for being stuck at a crossroad with no way out, whereas the Ways says you have options.

Emblem's Meaning: Obviously, a path with more than one option as to which way to travel, gives us the meaning of this card. We have at least two options and a choice needs to be made. The GOH instructions give this emblem a clearer meaning as it states that if your choice goes unnoticed, you're going to circle back around the mountain. So, we can say that this is an important decision.

House Meanings: Ways/Crossroads – Decisions, choices, and altering your direction. The card that lands here will tell you about your decisions or describe your options.

Timing: It won't happen until you make a final decision, when a choice is presented, twenty-two days, weeks, twenty-second of the month.

Well-being: As the card of alternatives and choices, it may refer to a need to make an important choice regarding an illness. It's another "tree" card and with favorable surrounding cards, it can indicate having options or it may suggest alternative health care or getting a second opinion. Anatomically, it stands for the lymphatic system, whose primary function is to transport lymph throughout the body. It includes lymph vessels, nodes, and the spleen. The Ways can also represent the capillaries, veins, arteries and all transport pathways in the body in general. For example, Coffin + Ways + Clover + Sun = Choosing a holistic treatment leads to a brilliant recovery.

23 MICE/RATS

Number and Name: 23 MICE

Playing Card Inset: 7 of Clubs

Primary Vibe: Erosion, reduction

Energy: Negative

Influence: Slow and degrading, something is lost or taken away leaving a mess behind!

Theme Group: Movement/change, slow, low, small, work.

Base Keywords: Loss, damage, theft, pilfering, deprivation, reducing, eroding, corroding, decay, waste, wearing-out, spreading illness or disease, mess, filth, contaminate, infest, infect, damage, destruction, defective, depleted, disappearance, waste, gnawing worries or regrets, persistent annoyances, pests, restlessness, avoidance, energy vampires, undermining, nagging, nit-picking, depriving.

Basic Concept: This card always represents some sort of loss, whether this is literal or symbolic. Constant worries are a loss of your cool – your zen. Disease is a loss of good health. Filth is a loss of the cleanliness and order that is necessary for our existence. This card confuses many new readers when it's next to unfavorable cards due to the fact that it takes something away or reduces something. If you've already read about the Coffin, you'll be able to follow this line of thinking. While it's true that the flanking cards will be reduced in some way, this is still an unfavorable card that will leave the situation with some sort of loss, decay or damage. Think of how mice reduce things and what they leave behind! Always remember that the only way to improve upon or make a reading more positive is when positive cards follow negative cards. As always, if this card is surrounded by favorable cards, and depending on the question and context, we may be looking at the least offensive aspect of this card. For example, a minor aspect of this card is one of a group of laborers working diligently together. This is a valid meaning of the card but it doesn't refer to a pleasant working environment for those who are laboring or whomever they are laboring for. Now, think about another card that can refer to a number of people in a more positive light. We have the Garden. What is a more positive card that refers to effort? Sun. A positive card for work? Anchor. A positive card that shows you're all on the same page and united in your goal? Ring. A positive card for reliability? Dog. A positive card for assistance? Bouquet. This brings us back to the concept of tableau-style reading and the need for groupings of cards to give us a specific meaning. Stick to your primary vibes and card energies and you won't ever have to stop and wonder what the answer is!

Broader Concept: While I don't perform specific health readings and never attempt to diagnose, I will share what I see in the cards with the understanding that everything must be confirmed by a medical professional and I do this more in my animal readings than for humans. Ok, there's my little disclaimer! So, the Mice card is my general card for germs, bacteria, and viruses, especially those received from the environment. Inhalant would include the Clouds card. Contact with other humans would include the Garden card. The surrounding cards will help you differentiate between these. The word germ is a catch-all phrase that refers to all microscopic disease-causing particles. Bacteria are larger than viruses, so you'll look for large cards versus small cards. Bacteria can also be beneficial, so favorable cards might indicate this. Viruses can't survive without a host, so you'd need a host card nearby such as one of the animal or human cards, though there are plant viruses as well. You can get as specific as you want to!

This is also the card of debts, group consciousness, being deprived, missing something, and general lack. This card has already shown up to represent the company that just won't leave, stresses you out, eats all your food, and makes a big mess! I'm sure some of you can relate! It appeared in many readings during the pandemic to represent the group consciousness of the masses in a state of stress and fear from the constant barrage of media propaganda.

Because the biggest problems mice cause relate to places where humans reside (houses, barns, work-places, storage buildings), this card can represent issues with or damage to these structures in general.

It may represent infestations, mobs, and swarms.

There's an element of hidden activities, things that go on behind your back and remain unnoticed until the damage is done.

In using this card to show what items may be lost or stolen, consider these possibilities: Rider = Horses, bikes, motorcycles, cattle or any large animals. Ship = Cars, trucks, boats. Scythe = Tools. Book = Books, laptop computers. Letter = Documents. Bouquet = Artwork. Stars = Electronic devices, GPS. Birds = Cell phones.

The Mice can represent actual mice, rats, rodents, small domesticated animals such as hamsters, gerbils, or guinea pigs; or small wildlife such as chipmunks and squirrels.

In a spiritual reading, it may indicate an energy vampire or a need to release something that's been bothering you for a long time. As it relates to loss, it may suggest that you let something go, forgive someone for taking something from you, or it may recommend being more of a giver than a taker. It can also suggest a need to slow down, simplify your life, and stop scattering or draining your energies.

In a relationship reading, it may indicate a loss of love, instability, hidden unhealthy issues that are eroding the relationship. There may be restlessness and nervousness creating a decline of an otherwise solid bond.

Descriptive Words: Small, short, nervous/constant worrier, prominent teeth, a nail-biter. Irritable and with weak-nerves. Someone who lacks concentration and possesses hidden vices. Dirty and wasteful. One who takes, borrows without asking, or is careless with your things. Has experienced deprivation. Mice people need to stay busy to dispel all that nervous and misguided energy. Someone who always follows the crowd. A thief, beggar, garbage-picker, energy vampire, looter, trash collector, factory or pieceworker, loss-assessor, exterminator, dental hygienist, orthodontist.

Advice: As a pro: Rise above and don't be one of the crowd. Nibble away at the issue gradually. Discover what's eating you. Identify security breaches. Check your stock. Graze rather than eat big meals. As a con: Don't worry incessantly about every little thing. Stress can lead to alopecia. You're being ripped-off. Beware of energy vampires.

Directional Cues: Both sides show a loss but the card to the left is being slowly eroded or damaged while the card to the right will show what will be lost or what you will lose out on.

Philippe Lenormand Original Translation (PLOT): THE MOUSE is a sign of a theft, a loss; when near, it indicates the recovery of the thing lost or stolen; if at a distance, the loss will be irreparable.

Game of Hope (GOH): N/A

Method of Distance (MOD): Near, the mice will still bring anxiety but the loss may be recovered or recouped. In the far position, the damage is done and there's no chance of recovery. In order to understand this concept, consider that the Mice card when far and if surrounded by any cards of concern, will show a loss that is permanent, at least for the timeframe of the spread if you established one. You can view this as the Mice are already safely back in their holes and out of your reach. Always check the surrounding cards to see if they are favorable or not as this may bring some relief.

Compare To: With regards to worry, stress, anxiety and nervousness, the Mice card represents those small ongoing worries that gradually wear you down, whereas the Birds represents temporary everyday stresses or excitement. Compare to the Scythe for a sudden loss, whereas the Mice bring a gradual loss. Compare to the Sun for gain or increase, whereas the Mice represents loss.

Emblem's Meaning: Mice are universally understood to represent thievery and disease.

House Meaning: Loss, erosion, nagging worries. What is decaying/eroding? What is causing you underlying anxiety? What is lost/missing/stolen?

Timing: After a slow erosion, during an anxious period, after a loss or theft, twenty-three days, twenty-third day of the month.

Well-being: As the card of loss and damage, this isn't a card you want to see in many health readings. While it's true that the Mice can gnaw away at something such as a tumor or indicate needed weight-loss (after the Bear), there will still be a mess to clean-up such as side-effects or unhealthy end results. You'd need a card of success or healing following to show a truly positive result. The Mice card represents regrets, damage, and worries in general. It's the card of metabolism, deficiencies, nervous tics, decay, infections, parasites, bacteria, and viruses. Anatomically, it represents the teeth. For example, Mice + Scythe = Dental extraction;

Clouds + Whip + Mice = Anorexia/bulimia.

24 HEART

Number and Name: 24 Heart

Playing Card Inset: Jack of Hearts. A young person, often one whom the client is fond of. They are often attractive, charming, romantic, sympathetic, and family-oriented. Can be a male lover or a male child if you use the Child for a female child.

Primary Vibe: Passion, especially love. Emotions. Compassion, affection.

Energy: Positive

Influence: The Heart is the card of our feelings and emotions and brings an element of sensitivity, passion, joy, and warmth.

Theme Group: People, relationships.

Base Keywords: Love, romance, warmth, joy, sensitive, passionate, compassionate, desire, attraction.

Basic Concept: This is my card for feelings and emotions in general, though on its own, it's a very positive card. As the card of emotions, it references all matters of the heart including love, passion, caring, desire, adoration, and attraction. It can represent any type of love from platonic to romantic. You can love a job, your family, your hobby, your pets, your friends, money, etc.

Also, keep in mind that loving emotions have the greatest power when we act on them via affection. The Heart may represent fondness, altruism, benevolence, generosity, compassion, sensitivity, mercy, forgiveness or tenderness. It may imply doing something with all of your heart, reconciliation or infatuation.

Broader Concept: So much emphasis is placed on the power of our minds and our thoughts and yet science has proven that the heart is much more powerful! The heart is known as the "little brain" and contains 5,000 times more electromagnetic fields (Source: Heart Over Brain, available at thrive-global.com). Research suggests that the electromagnetic signals produced by the heart can change the brainwaves of those around us. Ancient traditions viewed the heart as the place where our true intelligence resides along with our emotions. It was also viewed as the house of our spirit – where the true essence of who we are resides. If you consider all of that, the Heart may very well be the most powerful card in the entire deck!

In a spiritual reading, it may suggest a need to work on your heart Chakra, open your heart to others, be more sensitive and compassionate, work on forgiveness, or allow your heart to swell with joy and gratitude for nothing more than the opportunity to experience life on the earth plane! It may ask you to examine more closely what truly makes your own heart sing!

In a relationship reading, it indicates pure feelings, harmony, support, affection and joy as well as romance and passion. It's probably the first card anyone looks for in a love reading, but don't forget that cards such as the Ring (commitment), Anchor (security/faithfulness) or Dog (trust/support) will portray important aspects in a love reading as well.

Chakra: Heart/Anahata. Ah, the Heart Chakra! The center of love, compassion, and appreciation of beauty. It governs our emotions, our compassion, our ability to forgive ourselves and others, and our ability to allow ourselves to grieve or feel empathy for others. When it is open and healthy, we're able to feel deeply connected to the Earth and all its inhabitants in a truly peaceful and harmonious way. It allows us to filter all truths, either sent or received, through a place of love. Without this Chakra in alignment, we cannot perform useful and accurate readings for others with any consistency. Opening this Chakra is the first step in communicating with animals and without it, we won't have their trust or cooperation.

Descriptive Words: Attractive, curvy, heart-shaped features, voluptuous, likes to wear red or pink. Romantic, flirty, caring, sensitive, emotional, kind, generous, helpful, sympathetic, enjoys physical contact, appreciates beauty. Vulnerable, idealistic, hates conflict, does everything whole-heartedly. Couples therapist, match-maker, romance novelist, cardiologist.

Advice: As a con: Protect your heart. Are you overly emotional? Time to take off the rose-colored glasses! Don't be a doormat. As a pro: Follow your heart. Have a heart. Follow your passions. Put your loved-ones first.

Directional Cues: N/A

Philippe Lenormand Original Translation (PLOT): THE HEART is a sign of joy leading to union and bliss. From this, we can say that on its own, the Heart is a very positive card.

Game of Hope (GOH): Whoever wins this Heart will immediately offer it to the Young Gentleman at #28 or to the Young Lady at #29. That is to say, if the player arriving at the card #24 is a woman, she will move up to #28, if it is a man to #29. For this we can see that the game relates the Heart only to romantic/personal relationships.

Method of Distance (MOD): When it refers to a romantic/personal relationship, this is one of the three cards in the MOD that need to be favorably placed. The other two are the Ring for commitment and the Anchor for stability and loyalty. When the Heart is near, it always shows passion and desire, but it requires the other cards in the right positions to show more than that. When near in a reading for a single person, it will show romantic feelings and/or desire. In a reading for a couple, it will show love and passion. When far, we can see this as a cold heart. For a single person, there's no love or it's not there yet. For a couple, it can show deterioration of love and passion. When the reading doesn't refer specifically to a relationship, the Heart near will show some sort of passion or strong feelings for something. The surrounding cards will indicate what it refers to. If far, you need to examine the surrounding cards to see what it refers to, but being far from the PSC, passion isn't at the forefront of the reading.

Compare To: The Heart represents the emotional (also see Moon), the Tree the physical, and the Clouds, Birds, Book and Sun all relate to the mental. The Tower is formal and unemotional, the Mountain is cold and distant, while Heart is warm and sensitive. The Heart represents love, affection, passion, and desire, compared to the Fish that can indicate an abundance of or deepness of those feelings.

Emblem's Meaning: In researching the symbol of the heart – you know, that red thing with two bumps on top and a point on the bottom – there are various theories as to its origin, none of which resonated with me except that Aristotle's writings on human anatomy described the heart as having three chambers with a dent in the middle. We could view the two upper humps as two chambers with the narrow, pointed section being a third. The dent in the middle is the crease running down the center. Scientists and artists of the Middle Ages began drawing images of the heart that closely resembled what Aristotle described. Because the human heart has long been associated with pleasure and emotions in general, the shape eventually became a symbol of love and romance. It became especially popular during the Renaissance when it was used to depict the Sacred Heart of Jesus in religious art. By the early fifteenth century, heart symbols were universally understood and were then used as one of the four suits of German and French playing cards.

House Meaning: Passions, desires, emotions, love. What brings your heart joy? Where is your desire? What or who do you love or desire?

Timing: Early Spring. When in love, around an anniversary or Valentine's Day, twenty-four days, twenty-fourth of the month.

Well-being: The heart is the hardest working muscle in the body. It never stops! It's like an engine that never runs out of gas. The Heart card may refer to compassion and care received or given during an illness. Anatomically, the Heart card can represent the heart itself as well as the blood. For questions about specific health issues, it may indicate any cardiovascular disorders such as abnormal heart rhythms, congenital heart disease, aorta disease, heart valve disease, cardiomyopathy, pulmonary embolism, heart attack, or stroke. For example, Heart + Scythe = Heart attack; Tree + Tower + Scythe + Heart = Heart surgery; Heart + Birds = High blood pressure; Heart + Cross = Low blood pressure.

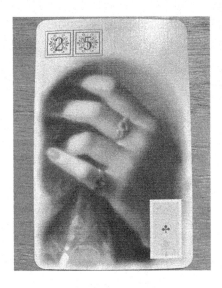

25 RING

Number and Name: 25 Ring

Playing Card Inset: Ace of Clubs.

Primary Vibe: Connections, agreements and continuous cycles.

Energy: Positive/Neutral

Influence: Constant, continuous, committed.

Theme Group: Fixed/resistant to change, long-lasting, work, relationships.

Base Keywords: Commitment, obligation, agreement, promise, proposal, bond, agreement, alliance, vow, a meeting, a joining together, a union, merger, a contract. Something cyclical, continuous, recurring, a routine. Engagement, marriage, partnership. Something binding.

Basic Concept: The Ring is a card of obligations, routines, cycles, patterns, and promises. It represents a union or an agreement. The Ring is a card that links or connects things together and shows cohesion or something shared. It infers reliability as well as indicating a continuous cycle.

Broader Concept: The Ring can represent jewelry, something circular, spinning, going in circles, something of value, contracts, valuable, coming full circle, binding objects such as handcuffs, a place where only members are allowed, progressive things. It often appears in animal readings to indicate separation anxiety when followed by the Mice. Because it's a card that connects, it can represent bridges and can bridge the cards on either side in a reading.

In a spiritual reading, it may ask you to commit to a spiritual practice or ritual, to honor your commitments, or to place more value on the relationships with those whom you're bonded to. Depending on the other cards, it may suggest the opposite, as in, what relationships or commitments no longer serve you and should be released.

In a relationship reading, it represents a solid bond or union, or with other cards such as Heart, Bouquet, and Anchor, it may indicate an engagement or marriage.

Descriptive Words: Round body shape, blonde, likes bling, stylish. Consistent, committed, agreeable, and reliable. Someone who values social connections. One who compromises, looks for a common ground and works well with others. Mediator, marriage counselor, contract administrator, contractor, bail bondsman, jeweler.

Advice: As a pro: Commit, keep your promise. Bridge the gap. As a con: You're going in circles – break out of the vicious cycle, it's too binding – get out of the deal while you can.

Directional Cues: The Ring located in front of the PSC (either where they're facing when reading directionally or to the right when reading left to right) indicates a solid connection or happy union, while behind or to the left indicates separation or little regard for the union.

Philippe Lenormand Original Translation (PLOT): THE RING, if on the right of the Person, prognosticates a rich and happy marriage; when on the left, and distant, a falling out with the object of your affection, and the breaking off of a marriage.

Game of Hope (GOH): Whoever finds the Ring gets three marks. This makes the Ring a favorable card, which increases your prosperity.

Method of Distance (MOD): this is the one card whose meaning is determined not only by its proximity, but even more so by which side of the PSC it falls on. If it falls to the right (if you read directionally, it needs to be in front of the client's card), there is a connection, union, or agreement. The closer it falls, the more significant this connection is - the stronger it is. This is reversed should it fall to the left. In this case you want it close, as further away shows the worst case scenario. Either way, to the left it represents a possible separation. If it falls in the same column, it indicates a shift. Having it below will at least give the client a little more control.

Compare To: The Heart for a loving connection but with no indication of commitment, whereas the Ring indicates a commitment which may be loving or not. The Anchor for faithfulness, staying-put, and consistency, whereas the Ring indicates the initial coming together or meeting of the minds. The Whip for disjointed repetitive actions, whereas the Ring is a continuous cycle.

Emblem's Meaning: While a ring is nothing more than a circle, the ancient Egyptians viewed it as a symbol of eternity. Egyptian relics dating back 6,000 years include evidence of the exchange of braided rings of hemp or reeds between spouses. The Western tradition of wedding rings dates back to ancient Rome and Greece and were originally associated with the marital dowry and later a promise of fidelity. As a dowry is the transfer of parental property or money from the bride's parents to the groom, this makes a ring a contract of a business deal. According to the Gemological Institute of America (GIA), Roman women wore rings of ivory, flint, bone, copper and iron "to signify a business contract or to affirm mutual love and obedience."

House Meaning: Relationships, commitments, continuous cycles. What are you committed to? What continues? What's going on with your relationships/partnerships? What do you agree with?

Timing: An ongoing commitment that won't end any time soon, cyclical – something will need to change if you want to progress, once agreed or once you commit, twenty-five days, twenty-fifth day of the month.

Well-being: In a health reading, the Ring can indicate a physical contract such as one for surgery or with a health care agency. It can also represent a commitment to taking care of one's health. It may show that more than one person or agency is working together regarding a treatment. With unfavorable cards, it may describe a condition that is chronic or cyclical. Anatomically, it represents the circulatory system (rings are circular). For example, Heart + Ring + Mountain = Atherosclerosis; Moon + Ring = Menstrual cycle; Stars + Whip + Ring = Eczema (Stars = Skin, Whip = Inflammation, Ring = Chronic).

26 BOOK

Number and Name: 26 Book

Playing Card Inset: 10 of Diamonds.

Primary Vibe: Knowledge yet unknown.

Energy: Neutral/Negative

Influence: There's something you don't know or will soon learn.

Theme Group: Work, well-being, communication.

Base Keywords: Knowledge, research, secrets, learning, education, school, courses, confidentiality, lessons, mystery, unspoken or missing information, tuition (with Fish), large files, books, magazines (can also be Letter). A deck of divination cards, a grimoire, the magical arts (especially with Stars).

Basic Concept: The Book is a card of information that is presently unknown, information that you're seeking or weren't expecting, or facts that are hidden from you or are missing. If the client is searching for a job, the Book may indicate a need to brush up on or expand your qualifications. Do you have enough experience or expertise? If asking about returning to school, the surrounding cards will let the client know if it's a good idea or not. It can reference getting the story, gaining an understanding, or writing more in your own book of life.

Broader Concept: While the emphasis of the Book is that of things you don't know or are attempting to learn or find out, it can refer to books in general, major writing projects or compilations of information and its organization. It may indicate investigations or research projects involving the gathering and organizing of a large amount of information. It may indicate filing, archiving, or accounting. It can also represent a library, bookstore, or deck of cards. With Stars and Garden it can represent Facebook.

It can represent facts or truths, learning and education, or intelligence.

In a spiritual reading, the Book can refer to esoteric studies, diving deeper into spirituality or doing shadow work. It may ask you to start daily journaling, which can have a profoundly healing effect! I find it absolutely amazing that simply putting something in writing allows me to release it from my mind. It may ask you to finally study something that you've always wanted to learn, but never found the time for. Or, it may ask you to teach others or even write a book!

In a relationship reading, the Book can describe a partner who's a closed book. It tells you that there are things you don't know. The seriousness of these secrets will be explained by the flanking cards. With favorable cards, it may refer to a secret admirer or a secret rendezvous.

Descriptive Words: Intelligent-looking, studious, bookish, discreet, mysterious and cryptic. May wear glasses and a pocket-protector! Someone you don't know. A closed-book, inaccessible, reserved, doesn't offer any information. Inquisitive, philosophical and deep. May be introverted or at least, selective in who they speak with. A historian, researcher, publisher, author, librarian, educator, curator, database manager, archivist, file clerk, bookkeeper, a bookie, a card-reader, a bibliophile.

Advice: As a pro: Open-up, study/learn, don't be an ostrich – find out the truth. The truth shall set you free. Trust your creativity – maybe it's time to write your own book! As a con: Don't open up that can of worms. Leave things as they are – you don't need to know everything. Don't be a know-it-all! Ignorance is bliss.

Directional Cues: Some directional readers choose to differentiate between which side of the book is facing the PSC. If the spine side is facing, the information will remain unknown. If the side of the book that opens is facing, you'll find out. Others view an inauspicious placement (behind the PSC) as something unknown, while in front says you're about to find out. If you choose to read the Book in either of these manners, set that intention and be consistent for consistent results.

Philippe Lenormand Original Translation (PLOT): THE BOOK indicates that you are going to find out a secret; according to its position, you can judge in what manner; great caution, however, is necessary in attempting a solution.

Game of Hope (GOH): Whoever reads in this Grimoire will by a hex therein be forcefully returned to the Garden in #20. This makes the Book lean toward the negative.

Method of Distance (MOD): The primary meaning is that of unknown information, so we can say that the closer it falls, the more important this is. Unknown information isn't always a bad thing, so don't jump to conclusions until you have all the facts. Check all surrounding cards for the type of information. If far, the Book will still refer to secrets or knowledge to be revealed, but it won't have as strong an impact on the client. You'll still check the surrounding cards to see what it refers to.

Compare To: The Clouds for simply not seeing the truth or a truth that's hidden by someone out of shame or embarrassment, whereas the Book refers to truth that is kept from you either purposefully or because you haven't yet had access to the information. The Letter for a smaller amount of information such as a document or blog post as compared to the Book for a large compilation of information such as a report or book. Compare the knowledge of the Book to the wisdom of the Lily card or the Fox's street-smart reference. The Sun represents being conscious of something, whereas the Book is not conscious of. The Rider can show expected arrival of information, whereas the Book would be unexpected.

Compare with the Coffin for information that's hidden or buried, whereas the Book is simply information you haven't learned yet.

Emblem's Meaning: This emblem is clearly a printed book. The printing press was invented in Germany in 1440, so printed books such as the one pictured on the early decks had long been in circulation during this period. But, what makes this emblem unique is the GOH instruction for this space that calls the book a "grimoire," which includes a hex that sends the player backward in the game. Because the eighteenth century gave rise to the Enlightenment movement that was devoted to science and rationalism, primarily among the ruling classes, those who practice magic and witchcraft had to do so in secrecy. Governments began passing laws and arrested anyone who practiced such things. It wasn't until several years later that an increased interest in folklore in Germany led to a newfound interest in magic and grimoires. The point here is that during the inception of this deck a grimoire was viewed unfavorably and was thought to contain information that was best left unknown. This gives us the meaning of secrets or information that when discovered, may lead to regret. Some things are better left unsaid and I sometimes see this card as something that should be left alone as ignorance truly can be blissful! This, of course, is only one way to use this card. Context, position, and accompanying cards will tell you how to best interpret it.

House Meaning: Knowledge and secrets. What is unknown? What are you about to or need to learn/find out? What is being hidden?

Timing: Timing is unknown or you're not meant to know at this time, once you find out or figure something out, twenty six days, twenty-sixth day of the month.

Well-being: The Book can refer to yet undiagnosed health issues. It can also indicate a need to do research regarding a health condition or medical science in general. It may also refer to a mysterious illness that can't be diagnosed or can't be treated with conventional medicine. Anatomically, it refers to the brain, cognition and memory. As it's the card of the brain, there's also a connection to pain as this is where the pituitary gland resides, which produces endorphins that reduce pain sensations as well as the fact that pain receptors travel from all parts of the body to the brain to produce the "ouch" sensation. Keep this in mind when you're looking for a determination of pain levels in a reading, especially for animals who can't tell us when they're in pain. For example, Book + Scythe = Brain trauma; Book + Mice = Dementia or Alzheimer's disease.

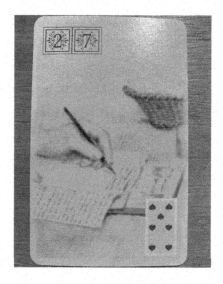

27 LETTER

Number and Name: 27 Letter

Playing Card Inset: 7 of Spades.

Primary Vibe: Information, news, messages, words.

Energy: Neutral

Influence: The primary influence of this card is communication, news, or information that you share, intend to share, or someone shares or intends to share with you. Anything containing words, which includes all forms of communication be it written, typed, spoken, or via sign language or a medium!

Theme Group: Communication, work, well-being.

Base Keywords: Communication, news, information, correspondence, words, vocabulary, reply, invitation, documents, paperwork, texts, emails, faxes, resumes, applications, certificates, bills, examinations, pamphlets, flyers, magazines, notes.

Basic Concept: The most basic concept of the Letter is words. When I see this card, I know there's something to say or read. It can indicate a need to communicate something or a need to put something in writing, as in finally getting it out of your head and committing to recording it. The accompanying cards will indicate what is being done with these words, that is, one's modus operandi of self-expression. If you're waiting to receive word about something, see where the Rider is in relation to the Letter. Always examine the surrounding cards for more details. For example, are you keeping it to yourself (Book), sharing it with others (Garden), official documents (Tower), coming to you (Rider), sending it out into the world – especially for business (Ship), arguments or negotiations (Whip). A combination that showed-up for me frequently before traveling during the 2020 pandemic was the Letter, surrounded by the Tower, Rider and the Clover or sometimes the Child. This told me that the regulations and rules that I was hearing about weren't being enforced but were on paper only. This proved true in every case!

The PLOT for this card is almost identical to that of the Rider, the primary difference being that the Rider is favorable and exciting news, a visitor, or packages that are coming to you while the Letter is neutral and can go either way. This, to me, makes the Letter the general communication card. Along with the fact that the early decks all showed an envelope rather than an actual note or letter (See Emblem's Meaning below). An envelope indicates the conveying of a message from one location to another.

The Coffee card verse wasn't helpful at all. Coffee Card Verse: "You may flatter yourself with good hopes in your enterprise, but act prudently and speak not always as you feel." While it is related to communication, it's more or less telling you to refrain from communicating! The definition for coffee ground reading is more clear. "Communication that is either pleasant or unpleasant, which would be determined by the location the grounds are found in the cup or the surrounding symbols seen in the grounds."

Broader Concept: This is the card of all things related to paper, which includes letters, all types of documents, legal papers, wills, deeds, medical records, bills, resumes or applications, magazines, pamphlets, written advertising materials, emails, faxes, texts, certificates, awards, licenses, even credit cards. Think of anything that you look at that imparts information primarily via words!

When describing a person, one of the terms I saw in my early studies was "superficial". I wasn't sure how this related to the Letter, but in giving it more thought, it makes perfect sense to me now. The word superficial indicates being concerned only with the obvious, apparent, or what something looks like on the surface. Much like a letter. The term, "reading between the lines" refers to digging deeper for meaning. This makes the letters rather superficial unless you read between the lines to catch all the nuances, which would be more indicative of the Book card. Some traditional readers use this card to describe someone who isn't well-spoken, but that never made sense to me! The Letter, to me, says the opposite. It's the card of the writer, author, poet, blogger. Someone with an impressive vocabulary and command of language.

In a reading for a missing object, the Letter may indicate papers, places where writing takes place, or places where you might put paper, where communication takes place.

It may describe anything that is thin, flat, and lightweight.

In a spiritual reading, the Letter can indicate putting something in writing as in making a pact. This may involve a spell where we write an intention and then burn it, bury it, or submerge it in water; or it may involve the use of a "God/Angel/Higher Self Box" where we let go and allow the Universe to take care of our concerns.

In a relationship reading, it can refer to love letters or a need to communicate your feelings. In describing a relationship, it traditionally refers to a superficial, non-committed or "on paper only" type of relationship, though for me, this would require accompanying unfavorable cards. With favorable cards, it tells me that the relationship has been "put in writing" or made official. Ring + Letter can represent a marriage license.

Chakra: Throat/Vishuddha. The throat Chakra governs communication and expression. It relates to all forms of communication, verbal, non-verbal, internal, and external. As the Chakra that connects our lower bodies to our heads, it allows us to take the ideas or revelations from our heads, combined with our creativity, passion, and will from our lower Chakras, and put them together into a tangible and expressible form to send out into the world. When it is open and healthy, we're able to express ourselves clearly and articulately and speak our truths without intimidation.

Descriptive Words: Angular and slim build. Well-spoken, articulate, verbose. May have an impressive vocabulary. Formal, and superficial. Writers, poets, bloggers, journalists, news correspondent, editor, typist, secretary, mail carrier, printer, paper manufacturer.

Advice: As a pro: Communicate, write, record, put it in writing. The squeaky wheel gets the grease! As a con: Don't put it in writing, keep it to yourself. Some things are better left unsaid. Paper trail.

Directional Cues: In a traditional MOD GT, if the Letter falls behind the PSC, the communication is coming from them or being sent. If in front, it's coming to them or being received.

Philippe Lenormand Original Translation (PLOT): THE LETTER, without clouds nearby signifies happiness, which comes to the Person by distant favorable news; but if dark clouds are near the Person, you may expect much grief.

Game of Hope (GOH): Whoever receives this Letter has to pay a fee of two marks for the bearer. While it doesn't send you back, it does cost you something.

Method of Distance (MOD): The Letter refers to news, messages, or information regardless of proximity. The surrounding cards will determine the details. It was traditionally seen as communication that wasn't delivered in person unless it fell with the Rider. If it fell near the PSC, the news was coming from your local environment or we could say that it was personal news. If far, it was coming from a distance or the news was of an official nature. You'll know which by the context of your question.

Compare To: Birds for strictly verbal or informal talk with Letter for any form of communication of a more formal or structured nature. Rider for news or information that's coming to you with the Letter for the news itself, official news, or news you intend to convey. Book for a compilation of information or published material of a more lasting nature as compared to Letter for recorded information of a more transient or superficial nature.

Emblem's Meaning: During the eighteenth century, the written word was the primary mode of communication over distance. This would've come to you or from you in the form of a handwritten letter. While the spoken word could be viewed as hearsay and its recounting often led to alterations of the message based on the receivers opinions and biases, the written word remained intact, making the written word a bit more official or formal. It could be viewed as proof or evidence and carried more weight than a verbal contract.

In the earliest decks, the picture is simply a closed envelope. From this, we get the idea of the conveying of a message, the transporting of it from one place or person to another. If the picture had shown a piece of paper, this could be nothing more than a personal note with no intention of communicating anything to another person.

House Meaning: Communication, correspondence, words. What is or needs to be communicated? What correspondence is being sent or received? What is or should be put in writing?

Timing: Can be rather slow (snail mail), but it's coming (the check is in the mail). You must communicate your need and then wait for a reply, once you're notified, twenty-seven days, twenty-seventh of the month.

Well-being: In a reading for health and well-being, the Letter references any health related correspondences such as appointments, prescriptions and test results. It can relate to literacy – to the ability to read and write. Anatomically, it refers to the hands and fingers because of the aspect of writing, typing, and texting. For example, Tree + Letter + Whip + Mountain = Carpal tunnel syndrome; Letter + Tree + Fish = A medical bill.

28 MAN

Number and Name: 28 Man

Playing Card Inset: Ace of Hearts.

Primary Vibe: The male client or the partner card to the female client. You can set an intention for this card to represent the most significant other person in your female client's life, regardless of gender.

Energy: Neutral

Influence: One of the two people cards that have no other meaning.

Theme Group: People.

Base Keywords: Male client, partner card to female client, men in general, yourself if you're a man.

Basic Concept: There are two people cards in the deck. Actually three if you count the Child, but that card has other meanings as well. There are only two cards in the deck that have only one meaning, and they are #28 Man and #29 Woman. We use them as our significators for whomever we're reading for, choosing one for the PSC and the other for their partner or the other most significant person in their life at the moment of the reading. They have no other meanings so it really simplifies things!

Can we assign other meanings? Of course.

When might we want to?

When we are reading for our inner-selves or our higher-selves, we can view the partner card as our "other" half. If you're using #28 as your significator, then you're either a physical male or resonate more closely with the masculine gender. In that case, #29 would be your feminine side.

What traits are considered masculine?

Masculine traits include strength, courage, independence, leadership, industriousness, competitiveness, assertiveness, logic and objectivity.

Broader Concept: In a spiritual or shadow work reading, you can set your intention to view this card as masculine traits rather than a person. Man kind. Masculinity. Father Time (w/Scythe). Man made.

Descriptive Words: As a descriptor, think about masculine traits. Strength, assertiveness, decisiveness, industriousness, abstract thinker, rational, disciplined, self-assured, goal-oriented, logical, aggressive, and dominant. Traditionally male-dominant occupations include (do not contact me – yes, I know that women can do these jobs too, but still, at the time of this writing, they typically don't) mechanics/automotive workers, loggers, roofers, builders, cement masons, crane operators, electricians, plumbers, tow truck operators, crane operators, metal workers, tool and die makers, construction workers/ heavy equipment operators, firefighters, home appliance repairers, aerospace engineers, software developers, farmers, clergy, aircraft pilots.

Advice: As a pro: Be more sensible, be a leader, be more decisive. Man-up. As a con: Be more sensitive. Are you too authoritarian? Are you too focused on yourself or your ambitions? Let him win.

Directional Cues: In a directional reading, the cards behind are considered inauspicious, that which you don't want to face, or will be more difficult. The cards in front are auspicious, that which you're ready to face, or easier to deal with. In a past, present, future (PPF) reading, the cards behind will be the past and in front will be the future. Cards above and below, if applicable, will be the present.

Philippe Lenormand Original Translation (PLOT): THE GENTLEMAN and THE LADY The whole pack refers to either of these cards, depending, if the person whose fortune is being told is either a Lady (#29) or Gentleman (#28).

Game of Hope (GOH): This Young Gentleman leads on to the brilliant Sun of hope in #31. However, for those who got here by way of the Heart, #24, this does not happen. They wait here for the next turn. I found it interesting that landing on this space sent you to the Sun and landing on the space of the Lady sent you to the Moon as it correlates with the masculine nature of the Sun and the feminine nature of the Moon.

Method of Distance (MOD): The cards that fall the closest are the most significant.

Compare To: Rider for a young man, a lover, or visitor; House for a father, brother, or uncle or a man you live with; Clouds for an ex-husband/boyfriend; Bear for a male authority figure; Child for a male child; Heart for a young man, male lover, or male child if you're using the Child card for a female child; Lily for a father, grandfather, mentor, advisor; Fish for a businessman.

Emblem's Meaning: What we find in all the early decks for both #28 and #29, are well-dressed and well-groomed. The Man is dapper and the Woman, spruce. At the turn of the nineteenth century, who but the wealthy had the time or money to receive readings or play card games? It's important to consider, when purchasing a deck, whether or not they are facing each other. The vast majority of decks produced give you a couple facing one another, but there are some deck designers who failed to consider this, so always check. Another point to consider is what you'll do for same-sex relationship readings. I, personally, have never had anyone object to me assigning the Lady or Man to their partner when I explain when the deck was designed, but I'm happy to say that many deck designers today are including extra people cards so that we can choose two facing females or two facing males. There are even some decks that have non-gendered people cards now, so always do an online image search for all the cards before purchasing a deck online.

House Meaning: Male client or the other person. Masculinity can be chosen.

Timing: When a significant male is ready or around his birthday, twenty-eight days or the twenty-eighth day of the month.

Well-being: In a health reading, #28 will represent the client, his partner, or the most important male in the reading. This might be a doctor, nurse, any healthcare worker or one who plays a significant role in the reading. It can also represent male sexual organs and hormones.

For example, PC + Tree + Clover = Naturopath or Homeopath; PC + Tree + House = General practitioner; PC + Tree + Clouds = Lung specialist; PC + Tree + Bouquet = Plastic surgeon; PC + Tree + Child = Paediatrician; PC + Tree + Moon = Psychologist; PC + Tree + Fish = Dietician; PC + Tree + Scythe = Acupuncturist.

29 WOMAN/LADY

Number and Name: 29 Woman/Lady

Playing Card Inset: Ace of Spades.

Primary Vibe: The female client or the partner card for a male client. You can set an intention for this card to represent the most significant other person in your male client's life, regardless of gender.

Energy: Neutral

Influence: One of the two people cards that have no other meaning.

Theme Group: People.

Base Keywords: Female client, partner card to male client, women in general, yourself if you're a woman.

Basic Concept: There are two people cards in the deck. Actually three if you count the Child, but that card has other meanings as well. There are only two cards in the deck that have only one meaning, and they are #28 Man and #29 Woman. We use them as our significators for whomever we're reading for, choosing one for the PSC and the other for their partner or the other most significant person in their life at the moment of the reading. They have no other meanings so it really simplifies things!

Can we assign other meanings? Of course.

When might we want to?

When we are reading for our inner-selves or our higher-selves, we can then see the partner card as our "other" half. If you're using #29 as your significator, then you're either a physical female or resonate more closely with the feminine gender. In that case, #28 would be your masculine side.

What traits are considered feminine?

Gentleness, empathy, humility, sensitivity, empathy, vulnerability, patience, sensuality, beauty and radiance, intuition and subjectivity.

Broader Concept: In a spiritual or shadow work reading, you can set your intention to view this card as feminine traits rather than a person. Woman kind. Femininity. Lady Liberty. Mother Earth or mother nature (w/Tree).

Descriptive Words: Woman kind. Femininity. Lady Liberty! Female traits include, sensitive, caring, compassionate, humble, thoughtful, attentive, empathetic, thoughtful, intuitive, passive. Female-dominant occupations include, childcare workers, kindergarten and preschool teachers, secretaries, receptionists, dental assistants and hygienists, cosmetologists and hair stylists, social workers, technical writers, compliance officers, nonfarm animal caretakers, bakers, opticians, writers and authors.

Advice: As a pro: Follow your intuition, be more sensitive, don't ignore your own needs. As a con: You're being overly sensitive, don't be a doormat, let her win.

Directional Cues: In a directional reading, the cards behind are considered inauspicious, that which you don't want to face, or will be more difficult. The cards in front are auspicious, that which you're ready to face, or easier to deal with. In a PPF reading, the cards behind will be the past and in front will be the future. Cards above and below, if applicable, will be the present.

Philippe Lenormand Original Translation (PLOT): THE GENTLEMAN and THE LADY The whole pack refers to either of these cards, depending, if the person whose fortune is being told is either a Lady (#29) or Gentleman (#28).

Game of Hope (GOH): The Young Lady leads on to #32 unless one has come here through the Heart. (*See #28 Man)

Method of Distance (MOD): The cards that fall the closest are the most significant.

Compare To: Snake for another woman; Bouquet for a pleasant woman or mother; Bear for a mother or grandmother; Stork for a sister, daughter, or aunt; Ways for a business woman, or an assertive woman; Child for a young female or female child.

Emblem's Meaning: What we find in all the early decks for both #28 and #29 is that they are well-dressed and well-groomed. The Man is dapper, and the Woman is spruce. At the turn of the nineteenth century, who but the wealthy had the time or money to receive readings or play card games? It's important to consider, when purchasing a deck, whether or not they are facing each other. The vast majority of decks produced give you a couple facing one another, but there are some deck designers who failed to consider this, so always check. Another point to consider is what you'll do for same-sex relationship readings. I, personally, have never had anyone object to me assigning the Lady or Man to their partner when I explain when the deck was designed, but I'm happy to say that many deck designers today are including extra people cards so that we can choose two facing females or two facing males. There are even some decks that have non-gendered people cards now, so always do an online image search for all the cards before purchasing a deck online.

House Meaning: Female client or other person. Femininity can be chosen.

Timing: When a significant female is ready or around her birthday, twenty-nine days or the twenty-ninth of the month.

Well-being: In a health reading, #29 will represent the client, her partner, or the most important female in the reading. This might be a doctor, nurse, any healthcare worker or one who plays a significant role in the reading. It can also represent female sexual organs and hormones. For example, PC + Tree + Clover = Naturopath or Homeopath; PC + Tree + House = General practitioner; PC + Tree + Clouds = Lung specialist; PC + Tree + Bouquet = Plastic surgeon; PC + Tree + Child = Paediatrician; PC + Tree + Moon = Psychologist; PC + Tree + Fish = Dietician; PC + Tree + Scythe = Acupuncturist.

30 LILY

Number and Name: 30 Lily

Playing Card Inset: King of Spades. This king is an adult male who is wise, dependable, kind, and helpful. He may be a father, grandfather or older male relative with those traits. He may also be a mentor or advisor.

Primary Vibe: Peace, harmonious/satisfying. Maturity, wisdom, family. Calm, slow-moving, long-term.

Energy: Positive/Neutral

Influence: The first thing I think of when I see this card is Zen. It's influence is peaceful and balanced. It may bring in a sense of maturity, wisdom, calmness, satisfaction and patience to the reading.

Theme Group: Relationships, long-lasting, slow, people.

Base Keywords: Satisfaction, peace, harmony, wisdom, age, maturity, completing something/retirement, experience, patience, calmness, temperance, sensuality, sexual bliss, purity, virtue, honor, integrity, good intentions, contemplative, sabbatical, zen, a long period of time, slow pace, passive, modest, humble, submissive.

Basic Concept: Oy! What on earth does this card mean? The GOH gives us no inkling. The PLOT mentions a happy life, family, and virtue. The Coffee Card Lily says this: "You wish for a virtuous wife, this wish may be granted if you requite the same." This is basically the same as the PLOT, so what we know is that this card is connected to virtue and the state of happiness between a husband and wife. What is virtue? Virtue is defined as a state of moral excellence. What exactly are morals? Morals are defined as our motivations based on what we perceive to be right or wrong. Don't confuse the word virtue with the word chastity. A virtuous person can certainly be sexually active but is adhering to moral standards. So, yes, the Lily can be used as your sex card. Because this deck was intended to be read in a tableau format, the Lily falling above #29 indicated purity or even virginity, while falling below indicated the opposite. (See Emblem's meaning below.) When speaking more generally of virtue, this card can simply refer to doing the right thing or at least having pure intentions. In this way, it relates to morals, or an individual's view of right versus wrong.

When it refers to wisdom, it's important to understand the difference between wisdom and knowledge. Knowledge refers to the collection of information that we've obtained. It's the understanding or awareness that we've gained through study or experience (closer to the Book card). Wisdom, on the other hand, refers to having good judgement or "common sense". It's the ability to discern what's right or true. Knowledge can be obtained from school but wisdom is innate or obtained through time and age.

Broader Concept: Another common interpretation is that of support, a patron or sponsor, or matters pertaining to social welfare. All of these are derived from the court card inset and are perfectly valid. It can also show up to describe contemplating, slowing down, coming to the end of a cycle, or retiring. It may represent an elderly person, a father or a father figure.

In a relationship reading, it can represent honorable intentions, maturity (either physical or emotional), or someone you've known for a long time and are already comfortable with.

In a spiritual reading, it may suggest that we need more "zen" work. A clear head and calm demeanor are indicated. Meditation and quiet time alone will be beneficial. We can then spread this vibe throughout our families.

Chakra: Sacral/Svadhisthana. This is the Chakra of our sensuality, our passions, how we relate to others, and how we express our creativity. It also relates to aspects of the Moon and Heart cards, but in choosing a primary card, I chose the Lily because of this Chakra's primary relationship to sensuality and the pleasure we gain from relating to those we are closest to. When this Chakra is open and healthy, we are free to express ourselves creatively and passionately with no fear of being unique or different. It's very much a card of pleasure, satisfaction, and bliss in simply being ourselves while allowing those around us to do the same.

Descriptive Words: Mature, gentle, calm, balanced, wise, experienced, relaxed, restrained, passive, family-oriented, conservative/traditional, peaceful, fatherly. An elder, judge, justice of the peace, arbitrator, mentor, guru, zen master, yoga instructor, meditation instructor, patron, retiree, veteran.

Advice: As a con: It's time to speed things up. Don't be so complacent. Look for someone younger. This may not bring satisfaction today, but it will in the long-run. Don't be so uptight. As a pro: Value experience. Seek advice from a respected elder. Practice zen. Stay true to your values. Slow down and take a breath. Stay calm. Learn from your past mistakes.

Directional Cues: Above shows virtue and happiness, below indicates unhappiness at the least and immorality, corruption, or dishonor at the worst.

Philippe Lenormand Original Translation (PLOT): THE LILIES indicate a happy life; when surrounded by clouds, it signifies a family grief. If this card is placed above the Person, they indicate the same as being virtuous; if below the Person, the moral principles are doubted.

Game of Hope (GOH): N/A

Method of Distance (MOD): Traditionally seen as one of the three cards of providence or divine guidance (the other two are the Bouquet and Child), this is a card that you want nearby as long as it falls above the PSC. Falling directly below infers that the client is doing something morally questionable or will be in for an unhappy or difficult period. In a small spread, the Lily at someone's back is similar to the Lily beneath them in a GT. Instead of trampling the Lily, they're ignoring or walking away from it. Because the Child card represents innocence and goodness, finding it next to the Lily when below the PSC will greatly neutralize its meaning. You could then say that the client may be doing something wrong, but it's unintentional. In the far position, it will bestow its virtuous meaning upon the card below it but will be too far from the PSC for your client to smell its sweet fragrance.

Compare To: Compare to Bouquet, which represents appreciation, gifts or invitations that are offered or given which bring joy. The Bouquet comes from outside of you, while the Lily is a bliss or perfect happiness that comes from within when you are virtuous and exchange that goodness with your environment. The Lily is a deeper and longer-lasting joy, while the Bouquet is temporary. Compare the Book for knowledge, while the Lily is wisdom. Child is immature and Lily is mature.

Emblem's Meaning: There's a very good reason why the Lily picture is almost always white and that is due to its association with purity. New readers may be confused by this, thinking that being "pure" is only related to abstinence with regards to sex. But if you read the following section, "Sex: The Lily or the Whip," you'll understand that purity and virtue were associated with the sex that takes place in a loving and committed (aka marriage traditionally) relationship. The Lily's connection to sex is also due to fact that it prominently displays its sexual organs, the pistol and stamen, in plain view.

While the Lily symbolises a variety of things according to different cultures, wisdom and maturity aren't among its meanings. These meanings have been derived from the playing card inset of the King of Spades.

Its reference to winter, snow, or coldness also stems from its white color.

House Meaning: Satisfaction, zen, wisdom, experience, sexuality. What is or will bring satisfaction? Where can you find peace/what do you need for peace? What about your family harmony or sex life?

Timing: A time related to an elderly significant person. A long time, be patient, go slow, at a satisfactory time, later in life, thirty days, thirtieth of the month.

Season: Winter.

Well-being: As the card of zen, it may suggest a calm and passive reaction to what's going on. This can be healing on many levels. It may indicate a more passive treatment as opposed to an aggressive one. As the card of virtue, it may recommend finding a mature and trustworthy care-giver. As the card of sexuality, it may connect to sexually-transmitted diseases (especially w/Moon or Whip). As the card of maturity, it may refer to ailments of age or elder care. As a slow card, it may indicate a slow recovery. As it relates to family, it may refer to hereditary disorders (especially w/Ship for inheritance or Tree for ancestors). As always, it's the correlation among the cards that will give you the answer. Anatomically, it stands for the genitals and the endocrine system, which includes the thyroid and adrenal glands. For example, Moon + Lily + Mice = Chlamydia.

31 SUN

Number and Name: 31 Sun

Playing Card Inset: Ace of Diamonds.

Primary Vibe: Energizing, empowering, and thriving. Optimistic and confident. Light and warmth. Big success. Big happiness.

Energy: Positive

Influence: This is the card of big luck. Clover is the small luck card. Just as the Clouds can darken any reading, the Sun will brighten it up.

Theme Group: Well-being, big, high.

Base Keywords: Energy, vitality, optimism, determination, enthusiasm, confidence, joy, victory, warmth, illumination, clarity, seeing the light, consciousness, awareness, awake, obvious, shining, glowing, vitality, health, a good omen.

Basic Concept: The Sun adds energy. It's the source of energy (Bear is how you wield it) and adds positive growth. It always brings improvements and makes everything warmer, brighter, and happier. Goals and desires will be realized when the Sun card appears. Because it indicates optimism and happiness, having this card far from the PSC can indicate the opposite as when someone isn't looking on the bright side of things or their light has been dimmed, especially when Clouds and possibly Coffin are near them. This arrangement can certainly indicate depression. Just as the Clouds has the ability to lessen the positivity of surrounding favorable cards, the Sun has the ability to lessen the negativity of surrounding unfavorable cards.

Broader Concept: This is a card of exposure where secrets are revealed and everything is seen clearly. The Sun will show the truth. It can represent heat, electricity, any power/energy source, summer, daylight, a sunny, warm, or tropical location, lights, heaters, stoves, fire – anything that produces energy or heat. It's important to remember that the meanings of all cards depend on the question asked and the surrounding cards. Can the Sun show something unfavorable? Of course. Too much sun or heat can be dangerous. Fire can lighten the darkness or provide life-saving heat but it can also burn our skin and burn down houses. Allow each card to act as part of the overall story. The entire story is composed of all the cards together answering the question asked.

In a relationship reading, the Sun is a sign of a warm, passionate, successful, thriving and fulfilled relationship that is harmonious and happy.

In a spiritual reading, the Sun may ask you where you need to heat things up in your life. Where are you putting your energies? It may ask you to adopt a more sunny and optimistic outlook in general or to work on your solar plexus Chakra.

Chakra: Solar Plexus/Manipura. This is the Chakra that relates to our personal power and how we're radiating it into the world. It's the center or our will, independence, confidence, standing-up for ourselves, and taking control of our lives. When it is open and healthy, we're able to step out into the world and share our truth with no fear of being wrong. It allows us to courageously be who we were meant to be!

Descriptive Words: May be blonde, with a bright and clear complexion, they're the picture of health and energy. Optimistic, radiant, warm, bright and glowing personality, lively, happy, someone who loves the limelight.

They radiate joy, success, and confidence. A leader, a mover and shaker, this is someone who lights up the room! Their energy is contagious and they have great influence. A charismatic extrovert. Many keyword lists include the word, ego. This can be confusing because we tend to view that word in a negative way. Ego is Latin for "I" and it refers to looking out for ourselves, acting out of self-interest, and pursuing one's own goals. This is a necessary part of a healthy psyche and is only negative when it is out of balance. If the Sun appears as part of a cluster of unfavorable cards regarding a question of someone's personality, it can refer to someone with an inflated ego, especially near the Tower card. A cheerleader, self-empowerment speaker, one who works in power and electric, heating and cooling, nuclear physicist, solar-energy occupations, tanning booth owner/worker.

Direction – South.

Advice: As a con: Too hot, sunburn, dehydration, conserve your energy. Don't fear the darkness – you can't see the stars without it! As a pro: Give it all you've got! Look on the bright side, shed light on it. Make hay while the sun shines.

Directional Cues: N/A

Philippe Lenormand Original Translation (PLOT): THE SUN, lying near, points to happiness and pleasure as its beams spread light and warmth; far away, it indicates misfortune and sorrow as without the Sun's influence nothing can grow.

Game of Hope (GOH): Interestingly, landing on space #28 Gentleman sends you here, while landing on #29 Lady sends you to the Moon. This makes sense if we consider assertiveness and logic to be masculine traits and receptivity and intuition to be feminine traits. (See Emblem's meaning below.)

Method of Distance (MOD): As the most intense card of the three luminaries, the Sun is a card that you always want to see close by, particularly above, up in the sky where it can shine its light down. The cards surrounding it will receive light, warmth, and positive energy. When far, you may have no success, no courage, or no energy. You'll still check the flanking cards to see where the positive energy is going. I think the most important thing to realize is that this is an extremely positive card, so it's energy will intensify the beneficial effects of all positive cards near it and it will lessen the negativity of any surrounding unfavorable cards. For example, if it sits above the Clover, the Clover's small luck becomes huge luck and will be lasting. Sitting above the Tree when near the PSC, it doesn't increase the negativity of that card (as it pertains to health), but instead, shows that you will have the energy to deal with whatever illness the Tree is indicating.

Compare To: Sun adds positive energy and increases, compared to Mice, which takes away and reduces in a negative way. Tree which shades, slows growth, and stunts energy; Sun makes things thrive and increases growth and energy. Clover is small luck and success, whereas Sun is big luck. The Sun increases the luck and success of a situation, while the Coffin buries or stops a situation. The Mountain blocks, hinders, or delays a situation. The Cross adds a depressing heaviness that you must endure to the situation.

Emblem's Meaning: The emblem's meaning is consistent with the general symbolic meanings of the sun. The sun has been a symbol of power, growth, energy, health, vitality, passion and the cycle of life in many cultures and religions throughout time. It has the ability to create and sustain life and without it, we would all perish! In Chinese culture, it is a "yang" symbol associated with heat and masculinity. This correlates with the GOH rules mentioned above. Many see the sun as a representation of the cycle of life because of its cycle throughout the day. It rises at dawn with the beginning of life for the day and eventually must "die" or set. It's no wonder that this is considered by many to be the most favorable card in the deck!

House Meaning: Energy, growth, confidence, success. Where should you put your energy? What will grow and flourish? What victories or successes can you expect regarding this situation?

Timing: During the day. In the afternoon. Thirty-one days or the thirty-first of the month.

Season: Summer

Well-being: In a health reading, the Sun brings energy and success. It's certainly a card you want to see in a reading regarding recovery! It may refer to a need to gain clarity on the situation. Anatomically, it's my primary card for recovery and relates to our store of Vitamin D. It may also represent burns or burning sensations, dehydration (w/Fish), dry skin (w/Stars), heat stroke (w/Scythe), sun poisoning (w/Snake). In questions regarding diagnostics or treatment, it can refer to X-rays, CT scans, MRI, or radiation therapy with the Key card. For example, Heart + Sun + Mice = Heartburn; Tree + Sun + Mice = Vitamin D deficiency.

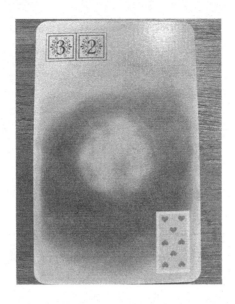

32 MOON

Number and Name: 32 Moon

Playing Card Inset: 8 of Hearts.

Primary Vibe: Attention, impression, work/career.

Energy: Positive

Influence: The Moon is a mirror and tells us how our light is being reflected outward. How do others see us? How are we standing out? With regards to our identities, such great emphasis is placed on our careers, so the Moon card is a logical choice for use as our primary work card. I see the Moon card as a big spotlight or a magnifying glass. It's placement and the question will determine if the seeker is under the spotlight or holding it. But, the meanings of this card go much deeper. Through introspection, the Moon can reveal the truth about ourselves. It gives us a deeper insight and allows us to recognize possibilities. On its own, it's a positive card, which can indicate respect and adulation when it is near our card or a positive outcome regarding the question asked. It's not just an indication of our reputation and the validation we receive from others, but our own self-image and level of self-efficacy.

Theme Group: Work, relationships, big, high.

Base Keywords: Social success, reputation, accolades and possibly fame, as in, you have risen! Achievement, awards, attention, admiration, regard, distinction, prestige, celebrity, career (if you choose). Perception, image, self-image (how others view you), self-esteem (how you view yourself), identity, pride, public status.

Basic Concept: Reflection, as in how we're viewed, how we view ourselves, or how we view others all belong to the Moon card. It is my card of the psyche because our deepest thoughts, feelings, and beliefs about people or situations determine how we view them, and likewise, how others view us. Strongly tied to identity, the Moon can indicate a well-known, famous, or highly-regarded person. It indicates that one is proud, with a high regard for themselves and is held in high esteem. It can also indicate how we impress and how things are impressed upon us. I see the Moon as a spotlight. Is it shining on you favorably? The Moon can only be seen as a result of the Sun's light reflecting off it. It does not produce any light of its own. So, the moon is simply reflecting the light it receives. This is why the Moon card represents how we are perceived or how we are perceiving. As the card of reflection, it's important to view the accompanying cards to see what we're receiving attention for. With other work cards, we're known for our careers. With the Stars and/or Book, we're known for our mystic/psychic talents. With the Letter or Book we're known for our writing or teaching.

On its own or accompanied by favorable cards, the Moon is a card of success! It shows that we're in the spotlight and being acknowledged. Others are admiring us. We're getting a lot of "likes" in social media posts (which is nice as long as we don't put too much stock in it).

While the PLOT relates this card only to honors, fortune, and fame, the GOH connects it only to the Lady card. Once again, I went to the Coffee Cards. Here, the Moon says this: "The liberality of your mind will always rather increase than lessen your prosperity; it will also daily endear you more to your friends." Here we have a mention that being open-minded (psyche) in how you view things will lead to prosperity and social success. Now, I was getting somewhere. The mind is mentioned, as is material and social success. Honor is nothing more than public recognition that affects our success in life. When we are honored we have risen as the rising of the moon.

If the light of the moon is a reflection of the sun's light, then the sun's light can be seen as the energy we put into something, while the Moon then reflects upon us, showing that we're being noticed for our efforts. This light is what we all want to shine upon us. As a card of social success, it references popularity and emotional satisfaction. It's a "feel-good" card that indicates being selected or honored. (Are you noticing the references to feelings and emotions? See below.) It can show that you're standing out in the crowd.

Broader Concept: If you've read many different books or online keyword lists, you'll see everything from romance to intuition, from dreams to adulation, from your job to your unconscious mind. While I found this utterly confusing initially, I came to realize that the Moon can relate to all these things in the presence of appropriate cards and with the right context. What's important to keep in mind is that you begin each reading with the primary vibe for each card and then adjust the meanings according to the question, the context, and the correlations you see among the cards in the spread.

How exactly does the actual moon affect us? To sum it up briefly, the moon affects the tides via its gravitational force. Humans are, on average, 60 percent water. No matter how you slice it, the moon affects us all. So it's a small wonder that there are so many ways to view this card. Let's see how they all connect to the primary vibe.

How is the Moon card connected to romance? Via admiration from another in a dreamy and mysterious sort of way as well as the aspect of night. Romance is defined as the mystery involved with love and can anyone really explain why others feel romantically toward us? I believe the phrase, "love is blind" confirms that it's quite mysterious! The night is also often defined as romantic via its mystery. How does it connect to creativity? Creativity comes from deep within ourselves and flows in tides. It's connected to our subconscious. Self-esteem is necessary in order to allow our creativity to flow. If we're too afraid of being wrong, we'll never give our creativity that freedom. How is it related to our careers? Success and recognition are often gained via our careers. I believe that those who are happiest and most successful in their careers are those who are allowed to express their creativity.

The Moon is also connected to our dreams as what are dreams but impressions? How does the Moon relate to personality? Our psyche, or inner self, is how we perceive ourselves through our deepest feelings, thoughts, and beliefs. It represents our disposition, temperament, and behavioral norm. It is the subconscious to the Sun's consciousness. It's said that the Sun affects our spirit while the Moon affects our souls. This truly makes the Moon more of an "inner" card, while the Sun is an "outer" card. This brings us to the idea of intuition. How does the Moon relate to intuition? Intuition is the impression or insight gained via an innate ability to know or understand something without proof or reasoning. So, intuition is nothing more than an impression. It's the voice of our higher selves – of our souls. But, if intuition is your primary vibe for this card, then this card is virtually useless. Is there ever a time that one shouldn't follow their intuitions? I live by mine and always have. I can't imagine ever telling someone not to listen to their intuitions so I certainly don't need a card to represent this. To me, it would be like having a card to tell me to breathe! Or when readers see the Coffin at the end of a spread as saying that the day will simply end. Really? So, if the Coffin wasn't there, would the day continue indefinitely? The cards always have a message and they don't show up for no reason. Let them speak!

I think you can see that I'm stretching the limits of what this card can stand for now. This is why we always start with a primary vibe, lest we get lost in a forest of alternate meanings!

Many use the Moon as their primary card of emotions but I see that as belonging to the Heart. Consider first that feelings are conscious and emotions are unconscious. Emotions are intense and powerful, with passion being one of the most intense. We can be just as passionate about hate as we are about love and the Heart card covers all of these, even though on its own it refers to the positive emotion of love. We don't need two identical cards in this small deck, so differentiating between the primary vibes of these two cards is important. Emotions, passions, strong feelings, love – they're all connected and you won't have to think very hard if you stick with the Heart card for this topic. On the other hand, if you include all of these concepts with work, social success, and the ideas of acknowledgement and reflection, you may have to struggle with the meaning of the Moon every time it shows up. For this reason, when it comes to emotions, my primary card is the Heart. The Heart is naturally connected to feelings and emotions via passion, and as such I don't have to stop and think about what it means. The surrounding cards and the context within the spread will describe it further.

For example, in a general reading, the Moon with the Heart will give me the idea of feelings, romance, and being admired. The Fish with the Heart would also give me the impression that the seeker's primary concern or reason for coming to me is related to emotions and feelings. But, if I draw the Fish with the Moon, I now see a different picture. What do these two cards have in common? Fish = Money and Moon = Career, so the seeker is probably concerned with their job. Now, what if the question is, "How does she feel about me?" and you draw the Fish and Moon. Well, you already have a theme built into your question, so in this case, we have an abundance of feelings and a deep attraction. (See the section on questions.)

The Moon represents all lenses as the eyes are the mirrors of the soul. It may indicate glasses, camera lenses, videos and photos – captured images as seen through a lens. With the Stars it may indicate Youtube or Instagram.

In a business reading, the Moon may refer to advertising and publicity.

In a relationship reading, the Moon may indicate attraction or an opportunity for romance. There's chemistry between you!

In a spiritual reading, it may reference your dreams or a need to dig deeper for the truth. It may suggest not fighting natural cycles. As it relates to social success, it may suggest that we not put so much stock in how others view us and put more stock in who we really are. Could it be that our idea of recognition from others is just an illusion? Is it lunacy? Isn't what's inside of us and how we see ourselves most important?

Descriptive Words: One who is or looks like a well-known, famous, or highly-regarded person. One who's proud, with a high regard for themselves. They may be charming and enchanting. The Moon person craves the spotlight and needs a lot of validation for everything they do. They may work in public relations or publicity where they work to improve how a business or company is recognized. In relation to the psyche, occupations include psychologists, therapists, night-workers, somnologists, oneirologists, mattress designers/makers, movie stars.

Advice: As a con: You're not going to receive the recognition you deserve, you're not viewing things clearly. Tarnished reputation. Consider how this will make you look. You're imagining it. Things aren't always as they seem. Are you viewing others fairly? This isn't the right career for you. As a pro: This will get you noticed in a good way! It's your turn to be in the spotlight – enjoy it!

Directional Cues: N/A

Philippe Lenormand Original Translation (PLOT): THE MOON is a sign of great honors, fortune and fame, if the card lies at the side of the Person; if at a distance, it means grief and misery.

Game of Hope (GOH): Interestingly, landing on space #29 Lady sends you here while landing on #28 Gentleman sends you to the Sun. This makes sense if we consider assertiveness and logic to be masculine traits and receptivity and intuition to be feminine traits.

Method of Distance (MOD): As the last of the three luminaries, my description of the other two (Stars and Sun) holds true for the Moon also. You want this card near and preferably above. When it's close to the PSC, they're being recognized, noticed, appreciated, respected, or at least seen. When near, it can also indicate the tangible rewards of being honored. With the Fish or Ship, you may be in for a pay raise, increased business, or a company car! When far, it's possible that you're being overlooked. If far from the PSC, and the PSC is surrounded by unfavorable cards, this was traditionally seen as a risk to one's reputation.

In a relationship reading, finding this card far shows that they just don't "get" you.

Compare To: Moon is night (as is Stars), while Sun is day. Compare to the Clouds card for the illusion of appearances. Compare to Stars for following your intuition while the Moon might indicate the impression you get from your intuition. The Sun for seeing things clearly while the Moon is our impression of things. Compare to Bouquet for a tangible offering of recognition.

Emblem's Meaning: While many associate the moon with emotions and intuition, the intention of this emblem, based on the PLOT and Coffee Cards is that of honor and respect. The moon has a long association with honor and fame due to the fact that it reflects the light of the sun down to us. We only have to consider astrology to understand this concept. While your sun sign shows how you express your identity as in how you shine your light into the world, your moon sign relates to your inner world, or who you truly are. To be recognized for your authentic self is the highest honor anyone can receive! The moon is connected to an unconscious magnetic force that pulls us toward something that screams to be acknowledged. But, possibly the most obvious reason why this meaning was given to this card is based on the fact that the deck's inception was in Catholic/Christian Europe and the Bible states that the moon was created for the purpose of giving light to the Earth. So, we can say that unlike the sun, it has no purpose of its own. It simply shines the sun's light upon us – acknowledging us. It's actually a very lovely concept!

House Meaning: Career, recognition, reputation, social success. What about your career? How are you being viewed? How are you viewing the situation?

Timing: Night. When you're recognized for something. Within twenty-eight days (a lunar cycle). During a full moon or an eclipse, during high tide, in your dreams.

Well-being: In a health reading, the Moon may refer to a prominent hospital or doctor. It may describe the patient's ideas of their illness and how it may be perceived by others, which may cause them to hide it. As the work card, it can represent health care careers or work-related diseases, injuries, or illnesses. As the card of the psyche, it can refer to the client's self-esteem or self-confidence. Anatomically, it stands for female hormones and menstrual cycles.

For example, Tree + Woman + Moon = Gynecologist; Woman + Moon + Scythe = Severe menstrual cramps.

33 KEY

Number and Name: 33 Key

Playing Card Inset: 8 of Diamonds.

Primary Vibe: Solutions, certainty, importance, success.

Energy: Positive

Influence: The key brings importance and assurance to a reading. It's where we look for openings and answers.

Theme Group: Relationships, well-being.

Base Keywords: Solutions, strategies, security, opening doors, closing chapters, to hold the key, opportunity is knocking, yes, go ahead, success is within your grasp, unrestricted, liberation, certainty, permission.

Basic Concept: It's the card of answers, finding solutions, fulfilment, gaining or controlling access and locking or unlocking. It can be a way in or a way out. Falling near the client's card it represents having the key to something but it's up to them to use it.

Think of all the phrases related to keys: The key to success; you hold the key; something significant is termed as "key". It's traditionally seen as showing success, but I see it as success that's in your hands. In other words, you can't gain access if you don't pick up the key and use it. It isn't success that you stumble upon like the Clover and it isn't the big general success of the Sun, which may shine on you without any effort on your part. It's success that is gained by opening a door or closing one (if that's beneficial to you) – either literally or figuratively. It's a card of security. It's the exclamation point of the Lenormand deck and sometimes shows an "aha" moment! Following the Book, it may indicate a major revelation.

Broader Concept: It can represent actual keys, key codes, locking, unlocking, anything with a lock, security, surveillance, having control over a situation or possessing mastery.

In a relationship reading, the Key may speak of solutions, so falling near or in a small spread, it may indicate that there is a solution to your problem. It may also suggest a key, important, or karmic connection.

In a spiritual reading, the Key may ask you to open the door – now's the time! This is a key moment. It may suggest work on your third-eye Chakra.

Chakra: Third-Eye/Ajna. This Chakra governs our intuition, imagination, and foresight. It is the center of clairvoyance as well as clairaudience and all psychic abilities. As it falls between the Crown and Throat Chakras, it relates to our comprehension of stimuli and the perception of what we receive from our higher consciousness with the ability to intuit it correctly. When it is open and healthy, we're able to perceive – either externally or internally – all things as they truly are. We will see the answer in the cards. We will see the truth. As a born mystic, it is where I access this state. (I believe that mystics are naturally drawn to divination. Do an online search for "how to tell if I'm a mystic" and see if this describes you!) It allows us to clearly discern all that comes to us through the Crown Chakra (Stars).

Descriptive Words: Lean and with an air of importance, a "key" person. Self-confident and intelligent. They bring answers and solutions to our problems. They are analytical leaders that offer valuable insights. They may open doors for us, literally or figuratively and offer us security. As the card of certainty, Key people are very self-assured. They have strong opinions and personalities and are most likely indifferent to anyone else's point of view. Key-holders, security people, decoders, strategists, any therapist or life-coach who helps you find answers, diagnosticians, mathematicians, statisticians, engineers, jailors, security officers, locksmiths.

Advice: As a con: Lock 'er up! Deny access. Don't be so sure! Not the right solution. Don't turn in your key yet! Don't open a door unless you're fully prepared to see what's on the other side. As a pro: Recognize the importance, you hold the key – use it! Figure it out. Keep an open mind. Say yes!

Directional Cues: Cards to the left of the Key (behind it) receive a yes answer to the question asked. Consider that the cards behind are holding the key.

Philippe Lenormand Original Translation (PLOT): THE KEY, if near, means the certain success of a wish or a plan; if distant, the contrary.

Game of Hope (GOH): On receiving the Key, one receives two marks. In other words, you were rewarded. You were given the key!

Method of Distance (MOD): Falling near, it shows that ventures will go well and success is within reach through the efforts of the seeker who has access to the Key. When far, especially when accompanied by unfavorable cards, it can indicate failure of your ventures or dreams. As when you lose or simply don't have a key.

Compare To: Compared to the Sun, which shines or it doesn't, you have no control over it; the Clover, which grows wild and you're simply lucky if you stumble upon it; the Bouquet, which is given to you; the Key requires a hand to use it. Compared to the Stars, which says, "look here, this is where you're meant to go," the Key says, "look here, this is what you have access to or can make happen on your own".

Emblem's Meaning: To hold is key is to have power. Keys unlock as well as lock. They allow or deny access. But a key has no power on its own. It requires someone to pick it up and use it. For this reason, the emblem signifies the power to access answers or areas or to control these things, providing us with safety and security. In art, you'll find everyone from Christian saints and medieval kings to pagan gods holding keys, which symbolize their earthly or spiritual power. For the rest of us mere mortals, they represent our ability to access things that are important to us, whether material or spiritual.

House Meaning: Solutions, answers, what's important and certain. Where can you find the solution? What's certain? What needs to be opened up in order to move forward?

Timing: Now – it's a card of importance so take action before the opportunity evaporates. Certain – can show that something is already put in motion.

Well-being: In a health reading, the Key can represent solutions/cures or diagnoses. Being a positive card, it will be a welcome sight! It infers that a solution has been or will be found and healing will take place. Anatomically, it refers to our store of vitamins, minerals, and trace elements including iron. For example, Tree + Key = A solution has been found.

34 FISH

Number and Name: 34 FISH

Playing Card Inset: King of Diamonds. This king will show up as an adult male who is confident, independent, wealthy or striving to be. He knows what he wants and how to get it. He may be impulsive and unpredictable. Can be a businessman.

Primary Vibe: Abundance, fertility, exchange, independence.

Energy: Positive

Influence: Abundant, plentiful, flowing, value, increase.

Theme Group: Work, movement/change, low, fast, relationships, people.

Base Keywords: Prosperity, abundance, plenty, value, increase, quantity, affluence, luxury, money, cash, profit, income, acquiring new assets, cashflow, transaction/exchange/trade. A large quantity, independence, deep, flexible, profuse, adaptability, flowing, unrestrained, slippery, elusive, entrepreneurship, financially independent.

Basic Concept: I think that two words sum up the meaning of this card perfectly if we consider their full meanings. Abundance and fertility. Abundance is defined as a large quantity of something, a plentiful state, having all that you want. This can refer to money, love, friends, recognition, etc. It denotes value and enrichment. Fertility refers to a state of being fertile or fruitful. It refers to the quality of producing in abundance, multiplying, fecundity, or productiveness.

On its own, it's a card of successful endeavors that bring in remuneration. It can indicate things that add value or pay off, as well as cash-flow, exchanges, and transactions. A large quantity of something, a plentiful state, freedom of movement, adaptability, and flow. Going deep, deep feelings. Flowing freely and unrestrained. With unfavorable cards, it may refer to something fishy or elusive.

Broader Concept: Its reference to deepness can indicate indulging and excess. This card references both food (fish) and water/beverages (ocean). There's an obvious reason that many readers use this card to represent emotions while others use the Moon and still others only use the Heart. The Fish is a water card, which tarot readers, astrologers, or anyone familiar with the four elements of fire, air, earth, and water will equate with emotions. It's a card of deepness and flow, which both relate to emotional states. It's important to remember here that the Lenormand system is based on applying simple fundamental meanings to each card so that you can read them in relation to each other as you'd put words together to form a sentence. For this reason, you don't want to give your cards too broad a meaning base as you may do with Tarot. It's the combination of these cards that give broader meanings. The individual cards need to be kept simple, each having only one or possibly two core values. Therefore, if your question is about or related to emotions, the Fish will describe them as deep, a large amount, and free-flowing or fluid. But on its own, the Fish is the card of finances and more specifically, abundance.

This card can refer to all bodies of water, especially the ocean with the Anchor; waterside locations, seafood, restaurants in general, aquariums, places where money is exchanged such as shopping areas, banks, the stock exchange.

As it refers to water, it represents all liquids, and alcohol.

In the right context or when it falls with unfavorable cards, the Fish can relate to greed, materialism, valuing quantity over quality.

In a relationship reading, It refers to an abundance of free-flowing feelings, having all that you want, deepness of emotions, a valuable and enriching relationship. With unfavorable cards, it may suggest someone who's still moving freely among the many fishes of the sea!

In a spiritual reading, the Fish may suggest a need to free yourself and open yourself to bringing more of something into your life. Have you stagnated spiritually? Have you overfished your current pool? Are you finding value in the spiritual aspects of your life? Have you become too focused on materialism? Maybe it's time to allow yourself to freely exchange with others. This card can also refer to water in a spiritual reading. So drinking more water, having flowing water such as fountains in your home, or practicing water-scrying may be indicated.

Descriptive Words: Blue-eyed and flashy. Fish people exude wealth and may be ostentatious in appearance. They'll wear expensive clothes, jewelry, and accessories. Manicured and well-groomed, they'll also drive a prestigious car. They may be quite materialistic, putting great emphasis on comfort. They tend to be workaholics as they can never have enough money. Value quantity over quality. With relation to water, they may be quite sensitive and capricious. They're not easy to please as they always think there are more fish in the sea. They may not complete projects as they're too wishy-washy. Lovers of water and the beach, they enjoy travel. Bankers, financial consultants or analysts, accountants, investors, loan-sharks or money launderers. Fisherman, fishmonger. Oceanographer, sea mammal trainers.

Direction: East.

Advice: As a con: You're too wishy-washy or moving in too many directions. You're spending too much money or the money/income won't be there. Avarice is the root of all evil. Don't value quantity over quality. As a pro: Go with the flow. Stay independent. Complete the purchase, make the transaction, go for it! Dare to swim against the tide.

Directional Cues: N/A

Philippe Lenormand Original Translation (PLOT): THE FISHES, if near the Person, point to the acquisition of large fortune by marine enterprises and to a series of successful undertakings; if distant, they indicate the failure of any speculation, no matter how well projected or planned. From this we can see that this card relates to business and making money. Notice the phrase, "large fortune and series of successful undertakings". This gives us the meaning of quantity and money. The Game Rules were of no help, so I again turned to the Coffee Cards to provide more information. The coffee card verse says, "Don't let yourself be caught with baits like the fish; circumspection is very necessary especially on a long journey." This relates to being careful in your business dealings, so it's another connection to finances.

Game of Hope (GOH): Reaching the Fish, one has to pay two marks. I found this interesting; it takes money to make money. While I and many other readers classify the Fish as a positive card as it pertains to wealth, in looking at it as a large quantity of something or one's cash flow, it can be positive or negative. So you'll see some readers placing it in the neutral category. For me, on its own, it is positive.

Method of Distance (MOD): The closer this card falls to the PSC, the more stable their financial situation will be. If it's near but surrounded by challenging cards, your attention is required to sort out the issues, but this is still considered a better placement than far away. A far placement indicates lean times, financial losses, unforeseen expenses, poor financial planning, or financial difficulties that will be explained further by the surrounding cards. This is valuable information in any tableau. Consider that this card falling near the client's card indicates affluence, as in an abundant flow or supply of something, whereas the card when falling far infers austerity or a need for restraint regarding the satisfaction of one's appetite (whatever the client is hungry for). Austerity refers to being frugal, practicing restraint or constraint, or displaying discipline or self-control. You can see that the far placement provides information that's just as important to the reading as a near placement.

Compare To: Fish shows the flow of your resources and the Bear is a need to protect them. Ship is going out and getting them. Fish is the deepest while Stars is the highest. Fish is flowing and Tree is fixed.

Emblem's Meaning: Fish symbolize many different things in different cultures, but we have to remember that the intended meaning is related to eighteenth century European thinking as is evident from the PLOT. The abundance of fish in the sea is recognized as a symbol of prosperity. The first mention of this is in the Bible at Genesis 1:22, which relates, "And God blessed them saying: Be fruitful and multiply, and fill the waters in the seas."

House Meaning: Finances, plentitude/abundance, deep and flowing. What's affecting your income or how is your financial state affecting the situation? What freedom do you have to bring abundance into your life?

Timing: Will take several months. During fishing season. February/March. When you're independent, and when you can afford it.

Well-being: In a health reading, the Fish can relate to finances, but also anything that adds value or enrichment to one's health or the treatment of a condition. It references fluid levels, fertility issues, or drug and alcohol issues. Anatomically, it refers to the urinary tract and the detoxifying organs: Kidneys, bladder, liver, spleen, gallbladder. As the card of liquids, it can indicate blood, sperm, urine or stool, sweat, or gastric juices. For example, Bear + Mice + Fish = Nervous diarrhea; Lady + Stars + Moon + Fish = Menopausal night sweats.

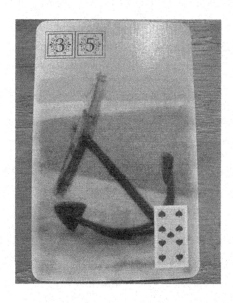

35 ANCHOR

Number and Name: 35 ANCHOR

Playing Card Inset: 9 of Spades.

Primary Vibe: Goals, hopes, stability and steadfastness.

Energy: Positive

Influence: Anchor shows where you have or want to drop your anchor – what you're striving toward or where you're staying put. It represents safety, stability, and perseverance.

Theme Group: Work, relationships, fixed/resistant to change, low, big, long-lasting.

Base Keywords: Hope, goals, intentions, stability, faithfulness, reliability, dependability, steadfastness, perseverance, tenacity, determination, grip, firm foundation, constant, consistent, safe, secure, grounded, focused, centered, balanced, not being swayed, longevity, anything that anchors you in life, your regular routine.

Basic Concept: The Anchor represents Hope and in the Game of Hope, it is the winning space. It's important to understand what hope really refers to.

It differs from desires in that it indicates a feeling of expectation that what you want will be obtained. When we have hope, we tend to be unwavering in our quests. This is the card of your long-term goals and the hope you have of reaching them. It indicates being focused and not being swayed or going off course. The coffee card verse is: "A person as honest as you in his dealings will never want a rich harvest of gain; your wishes too are likely to be accomplished." From this verse, we see that it refers to a person as being reliable/stable (honest in their dealings) and there's mention of success as in "rich harvest of gain" and reaching one's goals as in "wishes are likely to be accomplished". This gave me a more thorough understanding of what the PLOT referred to. When I combined this with the game rules, it was easy to create a meaning of having reached a goal or steadfastly persevering toward reaching a goal without being swayed. It shows that one is determined and hopeful in getting there. Consider the phrase, "Safe Harbor," that which we put our faith and hope in and where we find safety and security. So, with favorable cards around, it shows that your hopes will be fulfilled and with negative cards, you're left with only your hopes and no certainties! The Anchor stands for stability – something lasting. Be it your business, relationship, or job security. The closer to the SC, the stronger it is.

Broader Concept: The Anchor shows perseverance. You're going to stick to it because you truly believe that you'll make it. If it's followed by Cross you may have to endure something arduous. It can indicate being stationary or immovable. Preceded by the Heart will show what you have your heart set on. It may refer to being someone's "anchor," staying on course or arriving at your destination.

As it pertains to the sea, it can refer to anything related to the ocean.

Some choose the Anchor as their primary work card. To be honest, it was my first work card but I quickly switched to the Moon simply because the Moon's meanings confused me so much that I wanted to give that card a simple primary meaning!

In a relationship reading, it will describe a safe, secure, and dependable relationship. It may show durability and being settled with no intention to leave.

In a spiritual reading, it may indicate a need to commit to something such as a consistent spiritual practice or to ground yourself through earthing.

Descriptive Words: Stable, strong (Popeye), and solid in appearance. They may have a military tattoo, especially referencing the Navy. They are dependable, diligent, and unwavering, enjoying the peace and quiet that comes with being securely anchored in calm waters. They tend to be balanced, steady, resolute, and put great emphasis on work. Very much goal-oriented, they persevere until they reach their destination. Insurance, public safety jobs, steel-workers, news anchors, anchorites.

Advice: As a con: It's time to lift anchor or you've dropped your anchor in the wrong place. Are you clinging to the wrong thing? Don't drift aimlessly. Have you become the "old ball and chain"? As a pro: Solid as a rock. You've found a safe port. Perseverance will get you there. Your goal is worthy of your effort. Hold on!

Directional Cues: N/A

Philippe Lenormand Original Translation (PLOT): THE ANCHOR is a sign of a successful enterprise at sea, of great advantage in trade, and of true love; but distant, it means a thorough disappointment in ideas, and inconstancy in love. Here we have success and advantage in both business and love mentioned.

Game of Hope (GOH): This is the most important sheet (space/house) of the whole game, insofar as the one who comes to stay on this picture of Hope has won the game and draws the whole cash-box or deposit. So, this was the winning space and the first person to reach it won the game. That makes the Anchor a very positive card and drives home the idea of it referring to reaching a goal.

Method of Distance (MOD): The nearer to the PSC, the stronger its meaning of stability is, so you want to see it surrounded by favorable cards. Because it traditionally referred to both business and love when in the near position and favorably surrounded, your personal or business endeavors are secure and sound. It shows that you have a good grip on the situation. When near but accompanied by challenging cards, you may have dropped your anchor in the wrong place or too soon. Look at those other cards to see what they're telling you. In the far position, the stability of the Anchor is out of your reach or you may have a long way to go before reaching your goals.

Compare To: Faithful is Anchor and loyal is Dog. What's the difference? Loyalty refers to committing to someone or something for a mutual benefit. On the other hand, faithfulness is more like integrity, which is a step above loyalty. It represents loyalty and righteousness at the same time. Loyalty is being devoted, while faithfulness entails firm determination and belief above everything. Mountain can show being stuck and Anchor (with unfavorable cards) can show that you've dropped your anchor in the wrong place. Mountains aren't of your making – they're external obstacles. The Anchor is yours to drop where you see fit. So, because the Anchor refers to staying, it can refer to a decision to not leave, unlike the Mountain which may be an enemy that prevents you from leaving.

Emblem's Meaning: As we know, this deck was designed in eighteenth century Catholic/Christian Europe. If you look at an anchor, you can see a cross within it. It was used as a symbol instead of the cross during Roman persecution. It was chosen because it holds a ship safely in port during storms and was seen as a symbol for safety and strength. It's a symbol of steadfastness, as in not being swayed because we're firmly anchored in our beliefs, or that we should remain anchored as success will follow. Why is this card associated with "hope"? The archaic meaning of the word hope is "trust". The Biblical meaning: "Hope" is commonly used to mean a wish. Its strength is the strength of the person's desire. But in the Bible hope is the confident expectation of what God has promised and its strength is in His faithfulness. So, we can say that relating this card to hope is saying that it shows your faithfulness and confidence in what you desire.

House Meaning: Goals, where you drop your anchor, stability, perseverance. What are your goals or what's affecting them? What gives you stability? What are you certain of in life? Where are you placing your hopes for security or what is giving you hope for security?

Timing: A year, a lifetime, lifelong, forever, when stable.

Well-being: In a health reading, the Anchor brings hope to the reading and indicates that a treatment is safe or with favorable cards, that there will be a stable recovery. Anatomically, it stands for the hips, pelvis, and tailbone. For example, Tree + Anchor + Scythe = Broken hip; Tree + Key + Anchor = A safe treatment.

36 CROSS

Number and Name: 36 CROSS

Playing Card Inset: 6 of Clubs.

Primary Vibe: Burdens, suffering, pain.

Energy: Negative

Influence: As a card of hardship and grief, it adds a heavy vibe to a reading.

Theme Group: Fixed/resistant to change, slow, long-lasting,

Base Keywords: Despair, hardship, heavy weight, strain, suffering, pain, struggles, grief, burdens, devastation, misfortune, sacrifices, guilt, remorse, unpleasant things that must be endured – duties, responsibilities, the crosses we bear in life, something inevitable or fateful. Religion, dogma, martyrdom, ideologies, absolutism, convictions that one is helpless to overturn.

Basic Concept: This is a card of pain, burdens, grief, sacrifice, oppression, martyrdom, hardship, distress, suffering, trials and tribulations, ordeals, worry, remorse, or bad luck. As one of the three "Stop" cards (Coffin and Mountain being the other two "Stop" cards), it indicates a situation that you'll have to endure. No one carries a cross unless they have no choice, or at least, they think they have no choice! When reading left to right, you certainly want to see a favorable card to the right, or following the Cross.

The PLOT, GOH, and CC all give the same meaning. CC: "There is no misfortune, however severe, that does not produce some good; hope therefore all will be for the best." Hope is mentioned again as it is in the PLOT, though in the latter, the card must fall nearby. It can represent what is fateful or necessary or a period of being tested. I see the keyword, "endings," in many lists for this card but you need to be careful with that. Because this card first and foremost relates to burdens that must be endured. If an ending is favorable or will bring relief, then the Cross isn't indicating an end. It will, however, represent the suffering that accompanies endings or an enduring hardship because of an ending.

Broader Concept: The Cross also represents organized or man-made religions (as opposed to Stars for spirituality). With this comes the dogmas and beliefs of that religion as well as devotion, sacrifice, and martyrdom that goes along with it. If asking a question about religion, different combinations can indicate different religions. For example: Cross + Tree = Paganism; Cross + Moon = Islam; Cross + Stars = Judaism; Cross + Snake = Hinduism; Cross + Fish = Protestantism; Cross + Tower = Catholicism; Cross + Ring (Dharma Wheel) = Buddhism.

Many view this card as representing Karma (capitalized), which is associated with rebirth in many Indian religions such as Buddhism, Hinduism, Taoism, Sikhism, and Jainism. When the word isn't capitalized, it refers to the theory of karma, which refers to the spiritual principle of cause and effect based on intent and actions of an individual (the cause), which influence their future (the effect). Karma is something that isn't forced on us, but that we bring about ourselves through good intentions and actions. It simply happens just as we automatically get water when two molecules of hydrogen meet one molecule of oxygen. When viewing the Cross as Karma, being a negative card of burdens and grief, I'd view it as enduring the suffering that you believe you deserve. Along the same line of thinking as religious dogma, we can use the Cross for any strongly-held beliefs and principles that we take very seriously.

In a relationship reading, the Cross refers to an unhappy relationship. It may indicate a prearranged marriage or a couple who stays together out of a sense of duty. It can refer to a period of trial and tribulation.

In a spiritual reading, the Cross asks you to consider what you've been enduring that is draining you spiritually. Are you struggling needlessly? Are you stuck at the intersection between victim and victor? Are you carrying a lot of pain in your neck, shoulders and back? If so, it's time to put that cross down and go look for a four-leaf clover!

Descriptive Words: Heavily-burdened, stern, and downtrodden are the typical Cross characteristics. They tend to be troubled and pessimistic. A person who suffers and is weighed-down with responsibilities. A martyr or someone who sees life as a quest or pilgrimage, regardless of the hardship that entails. They may be quite saintly and selfless. This is also the card of religious (all religions) persons, who may not exhibit the aforementioned characteristics. Occupations include all religious vocations, non-profit humanitarian careers such as the Red Cross, Habitat for Humanity, Peace Corp, or United Nations Volunteers. Careers where one puts others welfare before their own safety such as rescue workers.

Advice: As a pro: Keep the faith. Things will work out for the best. Pick up your cross and take responsibility. As a con: You're far too hard on yourself. Don't be a martyr. Don't be so dogmatic.

Directional Cues: The card to the left is diminished in importance while the card to the right gains in importance. The card below in a tableau is in the worst position as the Cross is stabbing or pinning it down. There are some traditions that view the card above the Cross as being lifted up by faith. It often appears before a card as a warning or after it to show that one's fate is sealed.

Philippe Lenormand Original Translation (PLOT): THE CROSS is always a bad sign; if very near the person, you may hope that the misfortune will not last long.

Game of Hope (GOH): So near to the luckiest field, the player is cheated as against his will he has to advance one step too far to the figure of the Cross, where he has to remain until another player takes this burden off him or he throws a double. When we examine this statement, we get the feeling of helplessness. "Being cheated as against his will," tells me that this is something that must be endured. The word "burden" is mentioned as well as being stuck here for a length of time, that is until another player lands here and frees him or he throws a double. From this, I adopted the idea that the Cross is a burden that you can't walk away from and it must be endured for a period.

Method of Distance (MOD): Another challenging card that is more favorable in the near position (the other is Mice) because you at least have some control over the situation and it shouldn't last long. This didn't sit well with me when I was learning. I couldn't imagine wanting to see that card close to mine. But as I began to work with GT's, I began to realize that it was going to fall somewhere no matter what – unless I removed it from the deck! It's going to touch at least three other cards no matter where it falls. The reasoning in having it close is that you are showing up and able to handle whatever it's bringing your way. If it's far and behind you, you could say that you're avoiding the issue, which will only make things worse.

As a card of misfortune, grief, and suffering, this made no sense to me initially. Why would I want it near my card, I wondered? But in giving it a lot of thought, I realized that no matter what, our lives contain both joy and sorrow. Being able to deal with that sorrow effectively makes all the difference. You can view this as suffering of a short-term nature or the client is being tested in some way when this card falls near. Other than near, you also want it to fall under the seeker's card so that it isn't weighing down on their heads. In the far position, the problems that the Cross brings are out of our control and of a more lasting nature. Check which cards are around the Cross and especially directly underneath as these will receive the worst the Cross has to offer. When I lay a GT, the best placement I can think of for the Cross is not very near, but near and below, while the PSC is surrounded by favorable cards.

Compare To: Coffin for severe illnesses that you'll either recover from or not, whereas Cross says you'll have to endure it for a length or time or permanently. Also, Coffin for ghosts and Cross for angels. Stars for spirituality, whereas Cross represents organized religions. Cross is heavily-laden, while the Clover is carefree.

Emblem's Meaning: The cross depicted in all early decks is an empty Latin cross. A Latin cross, or Crux Immissa, is one with a long staff, crossed near the top with a shorter bar. While the Latin cross normally contains the crucified Christ, I imagine that was a bit much for a card game! But the intended meaning of this card relates to crucifixion rather than the empty cross's meaning of resurrection. The Latin cross is favored by the Catholic and Orthodox churches as a reminder of Christ's sacrifice.

House Meaning: Burdens, pain, religion. What hardships/trials/challenges will you face? What burdens must you endure?

Timing: Religious holidays – Easter or Christmas. A very long or indefinite period of time as it's the card of enduring something. Something that's been happening for a long period of time and will continue.

Well-being: In a health reading, the Cross represents long-term suffering and a depletion of energy. It may indicate setbacks in healing or feelings of helplessness and a loss of hope. Anatomically, it refers to the arms and shoulders and intervertebral discs especially the lumbar region. For example, Tree + Tower + Cross = Long-term back pain; Cross + Scythe = Shoulder pain.

IT'S ALL ABOUT
THE QUESTION

As card readers, we've all heard about the importance of context. For those who aren't sure what context is, it's the circumstances surrounding the situation that you're inquiring about. It's the known facts that set the stage regarding the atmosphere or climate of the situation. It's your frame of reference regarding the subject. Basically, it's your starting point. From this context, you must formulate the right question in order to get the information you're looking for from the cards. The question is of the utmost importance. To quote Camelia Elias, "Without a question, there is no reading. There's only people looking at cartoons." I'd like to take that a step further and add that without asking the correct question, you only have people making guesses. Therefore, if we want accurate answers, we'd best ask accurate questions. Here are some basic rules:

1. Be as specific as possible. Vague questions give vague answers. In fact, vague questions will give you vague cards. You could replace, "How will the meeting go?" with "How will my proposal be received at tomorrow's business meeting?" Include all those details in your question! I recently saw a question online, "Is he good for her?" The cards that showed up were generic. Think about all the things this question could mean. In what way is he good for her? Financially? Romantically? Emotionally? Spiritually? Good for her children? Will he make her happy? Other

than the obvious fact that this is a yes/no question (keep reading!), this question is too vague to give you any usable information. If you're posting online, get specific or you'll be left with a bunch of people reading cartoons or simply guessing.

2. REMAIN NEUTRAL! Be open to unexpected answers. If you have your heart set on a specific answer, you may be inclined to try to find that answer in the cards or rephrase the same question and redraw to try and get the desired answer. One of the reasons we consult the cards is to broaden our scope and introduce us to new possibilities. Allow the cards to show you alternate pathways and situations. This is how we grow and improve ourselves and our lives.

3. Here's the big one! Use open-ended questions rather than yes/no (closed questions) for compound situations. It is human nature to ask yes/no questions, and frankly, the Lenormand deck is one of the most suitable card systems for this type of question. But, they're only suitable for simple inquiries. When we're trying to formulate our questions, yes/no are usually the first that come to mind, but are they helpful? I agree that sometimes they're perfectly legitimate and can save time and energy. When asking them, the most important rule is to always phrase them in such a way that there will be no confusion about the positivity or negativity of the answer. If you ask, "Will my boyfriend leave me?" and you get positive cards, is that a yes to your question or are those cards showing you that everything will be fine? Instead, if you asked if the two of you will stay together and you draw positive cards, there will be no confusion about the answer. Therefore, always ask your yes/no questions in the positive so that there will be no question about what the negative cards are saying. What are the problems with yes/no (closed) questions? Yes/no answers are black and white, but life is a big shade of gray. Yes/no answers are simple, but life is complicated. If you consider that these questions are based on a 50 percent probability, wouldn't you prefer better odds? Conditions are always changing. We have free will and I believe that few, if any, things in life are set in stone. So asking

a yes/no question regarding a future happening can be problematic. I believe that readings are a snapshot of the energy surrounding a situation at the present moment. This is why so many readers question where they went wrong in a reading that gave them a yes but the answer turned out to be no. The cards weren't wrong and their interpretation probably wasn't wrong either. Circumstances changed or there were simply too many variables involved in the outcome that weren't taken into consideration. It's better to ask how you can stack the odds in your favor for the desired outcome rather than simply asking if the desired outcome will come to pass. Or, my favorite method is to ask what the likelihood is of something coming to pass if the querent continues on their current path. Lenormand is a language and wants to tell us a story. Its greatest strength lies in showing possibilities and probabilities. If we ask closed questions, we just ended the conversation before it even started. Getting a no when we want a yes can be disempowering and lead us to give up on something that we may have been able to change. Getting a yes can make us complacent or overly confident to the point that we no longer try and this can lead to a change in circumstances that will ultimately change the outcome. In other words, our yes will become a no through our own actions or lack thereof. Closed questions tend to be passive (Will I?) or desperate (Should I?). Both are unhelpful and disempowering. Passive questions simply lead to more questions and the answers leave us standing on shaky ground. They give us no actionable advice. Desperate questions show that we're not taking any responsibility for our own actions or their consequences and won't show us the different options and opportunities available to us.

4. Brainstorm a little to hone in on the real issue that you're asking about. So often, the first question that comes to mind isn't really what we want to know. For important and detailed topics, draw a mind map. Once you have your question, WRITE IT DOWN! I can't tell you how many times I forgot the question once I got involved in drawing the cards. Write it down and continue to refer back to it as you interpret the cards.

When you're interpreting others' cards online, follow the same practice. Be certain of what the question is really asking and keep referring back to it. Enough of the don'ts. Here are some dos: Do start your questions with what, how, or why. Instead of "Will I get a divorce?" ask "How can I avoid divorce?" or "How can I make my marriage work?" or "What will the outcome of my marriage be if I ... ?" Instead of "Is my boyfriend cheating on me?" ask "What will the outcome of my current relationship be if we continue on our current path?" or "What do I need to know about my current relationship?" or "How can I strengthen the bond between myself and X?" Instead of "Will I get the job?" ask "What can I do/what should I focus on to improve my chances of getting this job?" In other words, let's use the cards to give us ideas. Let's put ourselves in charge rather than being passive observers of our own lives. Lastly, I'd like to touch on timing questions. Certain Lenormand cards have an essence of timing built into them. We can look for fast cards such as the Rider or Clover, slow cards such as the Lily or Tree, beginning cards like the Child, and ending cards such as the Coffin to give us an idea of timing. The position of the cards can also show us the sequence of events, as in what follows what. While there are several proposed methods of determining timing available to us through books and websites, my own personal experience has left me turning away from all of them. My method of choice is to set up a tableau spread and use the columns to represent days, weeks, or months. A 9-square, Petit Tableau, or a Grand Tableau are my go-to's for timing. I can then tell the querent when something will likely occur based on which column the related card falls in as well as by reading the series of events that will take place before the event happens. Some of the problems with divining for exact time frames include the following: Timing questions assume that the event will happen at all. If someone asks when they will sell their home, they're assuming that they will sell it. They may not. Life is always changing. They may decide not to sell it, or not until the seller's market improves, or their reason for wanting to sell may change, or they may decide to keep it and rent it, etc. Lenormand, while specific, really shines when we ask conditional questions. It loves to tell us stories. Try asking questions such as, "If I do X, what will likely happen?" If you don't like the answer, then you can move right to questions such as, "What steps can I take to stack the odds in my favor that X will happen?" Let the cards give you more ideas than the single one that's lodged in your head! For questions concerning major life events, I believe that the cards prefer conditional questions because there are no set destinies. They prefer to show us a series of events, experiences, and conditions that need to align in order to make something possible. As diviners, we need to recognize our own agency and ask what we can do to make certain things happen rather than asking when something will happen and sitting back with our fingers crossed, waiting. I think it's best to focus on the here and now and ask what we can do to improve the likelihood of something happening in the future rather than asking if it will (closed question) or when it will (assuming too much and subject to change). Remember that the choices we make today shape our tomorrows, so let's focus on today. Now, I understand that fortune-telling, in general, is based on future predictions, but there are ways of improving the odds of an event occurring. The first thing I've noticed over the years is that the closer the event, the more accurate your prediction will be. I imagine that's because over a shorter time period there are fewer chances for condition changes. Also, you can ask first what the likelihood will be.

Yes/No Questions

Ah, the ever popular yes/no questions! They're the most used and misused questions we ask because they require little thought and let's face it, it's human nature to ask them! Let's start by looking at how yes/no questions differ from other types of questions and how we can best handle them.

1. Yes/No questions leave no wiggle room for interpretation – there's no gray area. They are black or white, when in reality, life is full of the gray

stuff! Life is fluid and ever changing. Time can change outcomes as can human free-will. This is why questions asked in close proximity to the event asked about will likely give more accurate answers. I discovered this during my first year in card divination when my husband was asking me which soccer team would win in upcoming matches. What I discovered was that asking about matches that wouldn't take place for a month gave me inaccurate answers, while asking about the outcome of matches that would be played that day or the next drastically increased the accuracy rate.

2. Another problem is that the answer itself may be gray – there may be no absolute yes or no but the answer may lie somewhere between. This is especially true when asking about feelings. If you ask if someone will enjoy something, you have to choose a yes or no, but they may enjoy part of the event and hate other parts.

3. Why do we think that we always have to say yes or no? The word, "maybe" exists for a reason. Sometimes answers truly lie somewhere in between. Neutral cards may be trying to tell us something!

4. Always ask in the positive. Asking questions in the negative makes it very difficult to interpret negative cards for the answer. Double negatives are very confusing. For example: Is my beloved hamster going to die from this illness? Cards drawn: Mice and Coffin. Oh no! Nibbles is going to die! Are you sure? You asked a yes/no and got 2 negative cards. That would be a no – wouldn't it? Now, change the question from negative to positive and ask, "Is my hamster going to survive this illness?" You pull Mice and Coffin. Now, you have a clear no. This is especially important for health readings regarding illnesses and diseases. You want to ask about the person or animal's recovery (positive) rather than the progression or "health" or the disease (negative). For example, if you ask about the progression of cancer and draw the Sun, that would be a card of positive growth for the cancer. It would be difficult not to be

confused by seeing positive cards regarding such a disease! Ask about the client's body/constitution or the healing, not the disease.

5.   5. Probability counts too. If you're asking if you're going to receive mail, and you've been receiving mail daily for twenty years, then you'd have to get very negative cards to give you a no answer because the probability is so high. For example, 1-21-2 could tell you that your mail will be late but you'll still get it. But, if you rarely get mail except for bills, then this could very well be a no – delivery is blocked – no news is good news!

6.   How did you intend to interpret the cards for the answer? An intention must always be set. When you're shuffling your cards, you not only give the cards your question but you also tell them how you'll be drawing, laying, and reading them. You do this either consciously or subconsciously. If your system for answering yes/no questions is to look at the insets (something that can cause a lot of problems as most readers have a hard time ignoring the cards themselves) – red versus black, then that's ALL you'll consider for your answer. Others choose to answer according to the number of positive versus negative cards. In order to use this method, you must first assign positive, neutral, and negative values to all the cards. Again, this is the only thing you'll consider. The other option is to interpret the cards as you'd do for any other question.

All of these methods can give you a different answer. For example: If you ask if you'll get the job and you draw 21-14-9. Based on black/red insets, 3 blacks = No. Based on positive/negative, 2 negatives = No. Based on interpretation, you may have a yes! There was a challenge (21), something went wrong (14), or you've chosen fox as your work card, but in the end, you are offered another position (9). BUT, this could also be read as the odds were against you from the beginning (21), things went from bad to worse (14), and you were simply given a "thanks for applying" at the end of it (9). This last case scenario may seem like the most improbable, and yet I've seen it play out this way more than once.

7. Drawing too many cards. If you intend to interpret the spread as with any other question, the issue with too many cards is this: The more cards we draw, the more of a story we'll start to form from those cards and this can be a problem in that we are veering off from a simple yes or no answer. Yes and no is black and white. The longer the story, the more shades of gray come into the picture. In another example, we set our intention to answer our yes/no question based on the positive/negative value of the cards. We draw the first card and it's positive. Why then would we need to draw another card? Mostly, because we want confirmation, or because the card doesn't connect to the question. So we draw another. Now we get a negative card. So, we draw a third and it's neutral. Now what? What I've found that works for me is this: If my question is a simple one such as "Will I get mail today?", I simply draw one card, look at it for a moment, and I'll get an immediate feeling as to whether it's answering my question or not. We want to see some connection to our question or simply a card from the positive list (Bouquet, Star, Sun, etc.) or the negative list (Coffin, Scythe, Whip, etc.) to show up to give us a confident answer. A card from the neutral list will require another card or two.

8. Is a yes/no question suitable for the information you're seeking? Using yes/no questions for quick and simple answers is very efficient. Will my package arrive today? Will my husband come home for lunch today? Will my dog finally graduate from obedience school this session? Those are all clear-cut and basic. A question such as "Will I ever meet my soulmate?" is completely unsuitable. The word "ever" is a problem. What if you get a yes and you meet your soulmate 5 minutes before you pass at age ninety-seven? What if you meet your soulmate after you pass through those pearly gates? What if you get a no? Will you be satisfied with that answer? Could it simply mean that most of us may fall in love but maybe that person really isn't our soulmate? Could it be that the term, "soulmate" has no true meaning? Does anyone really know what a soulmate is? Hmmm.

9. Give this a try: Every time you think of a yes/no question, write it down, give it a look, and consider if there's a better way of gaining the information you seek. Consider using open-ended questions rather than yes/no (closed questions) for compound situations. It is human nature to ask yes/no questions, and frankly, the Lenormand deck is one of the most suitable card systems for this type of question. But, they're only suitable for simple inquiries. Try a little brainstorming to determine exactly what information you or your querent really seeks. Brainstorm a little to hone in on the real issue. So often, the first question that comes to mind isn't really what we/they want to know.

10. Stay away from "Should I" questions. Why on earth would you place a decision in someone else's hands? Why would you want to give your power away? Be an active participant in your own life and don't just sit back and let it happen to you. Ask the cards how you can make things happen, not if they will or should happen.

A QUESTION SAMPLER

WHAT:

1.   What can I expect if I ___?

2.   What is my best course of action regarding ___?

3.   What will be the outcome of ___?

4.   What am I overlooking regarding ___?

5.   What is the best way forward regarding ___?

6.   What will the most likely result be of this decision?

7.   What do I need to know about ___?

8.   What are some potential problems with ___?

9.   What is the biggest obstacle I'll face regarding ___?

10. What is it about ___ that causes me to ___?

11. What do I need to be aware of today?

12. What lesson am I meant to learn from this situation?

HOW:

1.   How can I do ___?

2.   How are things progressing with ___?

3.   How can I better relate to ___?

4.   How can I improve ___?

5.   How can I best resolve this issue?

6.   How did this issue begin?

7.   How can I better communicate with my boss?

WHY:

1.   Why is ___ upset/leaving/not calling?

2.   Why is my dog behaving badly when my friend Jill comes over?

3. Why is the earth round? Seriously, have fun when you play with your cards and see what comes to mind!

WHERE:

Where questions can be asked for missing objects, planning vacations, ideas for venue locations, etc. You'll view the cards as descriptors when you ask "where" questions. For example, the Sun could indicate south, tropical, or near a heat or light source. Coffin could be in a box, in the ground, or at the funeral home. (See the Broader Concept and Descriptive and Descriptive Words sections of the Card Meaning pages.)

WHEN:

These are timing questions which are covered in the Timing section of this book.

WHO:

Who questions can be answered based on the descriptive meanings of the cards. You can also use the court card insets.

SHOW ME:

I'm a "show-me" kind of girl. I'm very visual. I think that card readers in general are probably like me which is why they choose to read cards in the first place. When I use the cards I'm asking them to paint me a picture or draw me a diagram that will trigger the correct response in my mind and lead me to the appropriate answer. I find the show-me technique particularly useful in converting yes/no questions. It changes the black or white one-word answer with no wiggle room into a complete story that uses both sides of your brain, giving you a more fluid and confident interpretation.

QUESTION IDEAS BY THEME:

CAREER:

1. What steps can I take now to advance in my career?

2. Show me if now is a good time to change jobs.

3. How can I get on my boss's good side?

FINANCES:

1. In what area of my life do I need to curtail my spending?

2. What's holding me back from making the money I feel I deserve?

3. What steps can I take right now to decrease my debt?

FAMILY:

1. How can I improve my relationship with _____?

2. What am I not seeing clearly regarding _____?

3. Show me the long-term result of limiting contact with ___?

LOVE:

1. What does my partner need most from me right now?

2. How will our relationship progress over the next week/month?

3. How can I improve my love life?

4. What steps can I take now to find love?

HEALTH:

1. What does my body need more of/less of now?

2. What steps can I take to improve my overall health right now?

3. Show me how my healing will progress over the next week/month.

REPHRASING COMMON QUESTIONS:

Rephrasing questions in order to receive the most useful information can make a world of difference in your readings. Here are a few suggestions to change disempowering questions into empowering questions.

1. Will I ever meet my soulmate?

2. Better: What steps can I take to find my soulmate?

3. Should I quit my job?

4. Better: What will the outcome be if I quit my job?

5. Must I go back to school for another degree?

6. Better: What will the result be if I choose not to get another degree?

LENORMAND TIMING

I was in an online practice group one day and noticed a posted question with many conflicting responses from other readers. The poster's question reminded me of one that I had journalled. The issue was timing.

We run into trouble when we ask a question and then try to interpret the cards for timing in addition to interpreting them as an answer to the actual question asked.

Here is the question I had journaled. Someone asked: Will she finally start a serious relationship this year? This reader laid a 5-card line and proceeded to narrate a story from the cards as well as reading the cards for specific timing (day and month). For the cards they had assigned timing meanings to, they chose not to read them as part of the answer. The problem is that what the reader asked was a yes/no question and rather than using all the cards to answer that, they used some to answer a question that they didn't even ask. That of "when". Because of this, they misinterpreted the line. Here it is:

Question: Will she finally meet her soulmate this year? Scythe-Clover-Ring-Stars-Crossroads.

The reader chose to see the three center cards as a yes answer and then chose to read the first and last cards for timing. This was not a predetermined intention. They simply noticed that two of the cards had timing references and decided at that moment to interpret them that way. Their answer? Clover-Ring-Stars = Yes, you'll finally get lucky and connect with your soulmate. Scythe and Crossroads they read as Scythe = Autumn and Crossroads = The 22nd. Their final answer was yes, on November 22nd (it was already October when the question was asked). When they updated with feedback, they were asking for help in figuring out where they went wrong. What this line actually said is this: No, you'll miss an opportunity to connect with someone as your intended path took a detour.

So, how exactly can we effectively handle timing questions? There are a few different ways to handle them.

1. Say we want to know when we'll be able to move back into our main home, which is being renovated. We can lay a Grand Tableau and set our intention for a particular time period, such as 8 months when using an 8x4+4 format. We'll set our intention for the Stork to represent moving back into the house. We then lay the spread and see what column the Stork lands in. We'll also read the cards around the Stork

to get more details as well as checking the house of Stork to see what falls there and see how it connects to the Stork card. I also check any cards/houses that relate to the question. So, in this case, I'd also check the House card/house and see how it connects to the Stork. If the Stork lands in the final column and has problematic cards around it, the move most likely won't happen within the 8 month period. I would then ask a specific question about this and lay a small spread. This is my primary timing method and it works better than any other I've tried. Give it a try and see how you like it. If it doesn't resonate with you, try the other methods until one clicks.

2. If we're using small spreads, we can establish that something will take place by asking a specific question such as, "Will he ask me out again?" If we established a yes answer, we can pick up the cards, shuffle again, and ask when. The new spread will only answer the timing question. (See #6 below.) In order to use this method, you have to have timing meanings assigned to all your cards. There are several sources online and you can also find this information in books. I'm including my personal list below. Use mine if it resonates with you or make your own. Just be consistent.

3. You can include timing right in your question. For example, "Will I receive my check on Thursday?" A nice simple yes/no question. Or, "How will the party go on Friday night?" While this isn't a specific timing question, I want you to get an idea of how to include time frames in your questions.

4. We can also get an idea of when things will happen based on the active/ passive, fast/slow nature of the cards themselves. If we ask, "How will my current work project go?" and we draw Tower-Child-Rider-Dog-Anchor. We know from the first card that this is going to take some time. Tower is the "longevity" card. It's an immobile card that shows many steps to get to the finish line. We then have Rider facing Child telling us that we have a new burst of energy, new ideas, or maybe a little help from someone, especially with the Dog following. In the end,

we'll reach our goal (Anchor) by remaining faithful to the task (Dog). While we have one "fast" card here (Rider), it's surrounded by immobile or slow cards.

5. We can choose to ask a timing question and then read the cards as a narrative to show us what will follow what, or what must happen in order for something to occur. For example, we ask, "When will my book finally get published?" and we decide to interpret the spread as a narrative. We draw Ring-Letter-Sun-Stars-Clover. If we stay committed to this writing project, put a lot of energy into it and stay focused, it will happen sooner than we think.

6. Lastly, we can lay a specific spread only for timing and set an intention while shuffling to read for a general season or use the numbers of the cards to represent a particular date or month. For example, if you decide to read for a general season, the Coffin would represent Winter, but if you set your intention to use the card numbers to represent a monthly timing, you will use the number 8 to represent the eighth month which is August, or the eighth of the month. If you choose the numbers to represent a smaller time frame, it may be eight hours, days, or weeks. As you can see, it's all dependent upon your intention. Get organized and be sure the cards know exactly what your intention is before you lay them. I also use this method for specific dates and I follow this procedure:

A. Choose your theme card such as the Heart for love, Ring for a contract, Stork for moving, Moon for a promotion at work, etc.

B. Focus on your intention to search for that card as you shuffle and tell the cards that you'll be taking the two cards in front and the two behind the focus card. Of these four cards, you're going to look for a correlation. For example, one of my clients asked when they'd find the right dog last July. I drew: Anchor-Letter-Dog-Scythe-Stork. Anchor wasn't specific but inferred that it wouldn't be for a while. Letter fit with Anchor as it's a slow card, so already I felt that it wouldn't happen soon. Scythe, then became the fall/autumn. And, the Stork fit in with the other cards to indicate the change of seasons. At this point, putting it all together, I make the Scythe October as that is the change of season to autumn where I live.

Why are so many timing predictions wrong? If you spend a period of time in any of the practice groups online, you'll come to see that certain questions are harder to answer correctly on a consistent basis than others. This is a frequently discussed topic. The most difficult questions seem to be yes/no and timing. Please see the section on handling yes/no question for more information on them. As for timing, I see two issues.

First, we're asking the Universe for a specific time when something will happen, but we're asking using man-made timing. Clocks and calendars are a human invention and don't exist outside of the here and now of our physical existence. What the Universe understands is seasons based on the rising and setting of the sun and lunar cycles.

The second issue is free-will can change everything. When we interpret the cards to predict timing, we have to consider that this will only come to pass if the current trajectory is continued. This is why I tell my clients that nothing is set in stone, and if they don't like the outcome of their current trajectory, they can most likely change it. For anyone who predicts the outcome of sporting events (something I'm constantly asked by my husband to do!), you'll know that the closer in time the event is, the more accurate your prediction will be. The reason is simple. There's less chance of anything changing regarding a game that will take place in a couple days, but if it's a month away, a lot can change between now and then.

When someone asks me a "when" question, I will use one of the methods above and will give them an answer based on the order in which certain events will take place, leading to the desired outcome. If they press me for a specific date and time, I'm happy to do that but I always include this statement: "The event will most likely happen on this date if everything continues to move along on its current course." While the predicted dates are very often correct, what's always correct is the prediction of what needs to happen in order for something to take place. The part about "X will happen, followed by Y, which will lead to Z" is what always holds true. It's easy, then, for the client to look back at the reading if something predicted doesn't take place and realize that one or more of the necessary ingredients didn't take place. Something changed along the way which changed the outcome. Nice and neat. You'll always come out smelling like a rose!

Timing assignments:

Rider – Soon, next, one day, week, month, first of the Month, January, on a Visit, it's on the way.

Clover – Unexpectedly/when you least expect it, by chance, fast, February, two weeks, days, months, second of the month.

Ship – when things start to move in a certain direction, on a Trip, March, three weeks, days, months, third of the month.

House – Evening. Not soon, you're too comfortable, when at home, April, four days, weeks, months, fourth of the month.

Tree – Slow growth that takes years or only if its needs are met, May, five days, weeks, months, fifth of the month.

Clouds – It's currently unclear/uncertain, when it's raining or overcast, June, six months, weeks, days, sixth of the month.

Snake – Whenever the enemy decides to make their move, during a negative event, July, seven days, weeks, months, seventh of the month.

Coffin – Winter. It's done, over, not meant to happen, never, after a death or ending, August, eight days, weeks, months, eighth of the month.

Bouquet – Spring. Once you deserve it, September, nine days, weeks, months, ninth of the month.

Scythe – Fall/Autumn/harvest time. Suddenly and often before you're ready! Very fast, strikes when you least expect it, October, ten days, months, weeks, tenth of the month.

Whip – After something repeats, it may happen more than once, during a difficult time, November, eleven days, weeks, months, eleventh of the month.

Birds – Morning. A time of year when the birds migrate (Spring or Fall), during a stressful time or stressful conversation, fast, December, twelve days, months, a year, annual, twelfth of the month.

Child – Dawn. A small amount of time, on a new day, when something is new and just starting, related to your child's birthday, during childhood, thirteen days, weeks, months, thirteenth of the month.

Fox – At the wrong time, fourteen days, weeks, months, fourteenth of the month.

Bear – When you take charge and make it happen, fifteen days, weeks, months, fifteenth of the month.

Star – Night. When it's destined to happen, on a clear night, sixteen days, sixteenth of the month.

Stork – When the seasons are changing or when you make a change. In some cases it can refer to nine months. Seventeen days, weeks, seventeenth of the month.

Dog – You'll have to wait, so be patient. On your friend's birthday or when you're with your friends, eighteen days, eighteenth day of the month.

Tower – It could take a long time, in increments, on a government/bank holiday, when in a large building, nineteen days, weeks, nineteenth of the month.

Garden – Afternoon. At the time of an event – wedding, birthday, a large gathering, outdoors, twenty days, weeks, twentieth of the month. Saturday.

Mountain – Winter. Something that will take years or once you tackle the obstacles, when alone, twenty-one days, three weeks, twenty-first of the month.

Crossroads – It won't happen until you make a final decision. When a choice is presented, twenty-two days, weeks, twenty-second of the month.

Mice – After a slow erosion, during an anxious period, after a loss or theft, twenty-three days, twenty-third of the month.

Heart – Early Spring. When in love, around an anniversary or Valentine's Day, twenty-four days, twenty-fourth day of the month.

Ring – An ongoing commitment that won't end any time soon, cyclical – something will need to change if you want to progress, once agreed or once you commit, twenty-five days, twenty-fifth of the month.

Book – Timing is unknown or you're not meant to know at this time, once you find out or figure something out, twenty-six days, twenty-sixth of the month.

Letter – Can be rather slow (snail mail), but it's coming (the check is in the mail). You must communicate your need and then wait for a reply, once you're notified, twenty-seven days, twenty-seventh of the month.

Man – When a significant male is ready or around his birthday, twenty-eight days or the twenty-eighth of the month.

Woman – When a significant female is ready or around her birthday, twenty-nine days or the twenty-ninth of the month.

Lily – Winter. A time related to an elderly significant person. A long time, be patient, go slow, at a satisfactory time, later in life, thirty days, thirtieth of the month.

Sun – Summer. During the day. In the afternoon. Thirty-one days, a month, thirty-first day of the month, Sunday.

Moon – Night. When you're recognized for something. Within twenty-eight days (a lunar cycle). During a full moon or an eclipse, during high tide, in your dreams. Monday.

Key – Now – It's a card of importance so take action before the opportunity evaporates. Certain – Can show that something is already put in motion.

Fish – Will take several months. During fishing season. February/March (Pisces), when you're independent, when you can afford it.

Anchor – A year, a lifetime, lifelong, forever, when stable.

Cross – Religious holidays – Easter or Christmas. A very long or indefinite period of time as it's the card of enduring something. Something that's been happening for a long period of time and will continue.

START WITH THREE CARDS

Now that you've learned the meanings of the cards, and you've read about how card divination works, you're finally ready to ask a question. Because your purpose is to formulate a complete sentence or statement, you want to draw three cards rather than two. You have a few different ways you can interpret the line and you'll need to decide that before you lay the cards.

The Line of Three:

1. You can either read the line as a narrative or story, as in this happens and then this follows, leading to this outcome. In this case, you're connecting each card to the previous one as you do when you read any sentence and the energy is flowing left to right. I'll call this a narrative reading.

2. You can choose to have each subsequent card describe the previous cards. Here, you're pairing cards together so card two describes card one, as an adjective describes a noun. The third card will then further elaborate on or modify the message of the first pair. I'll call this a paired reading and the energy has an overall flow to the right but it bounces back and forth as you use subsequent cards to modify the previous ones. This was the first method I learned and yet it never quite resonated with me and I immediately began reading the lines as a narrative or description. The back and forth reading process breaks my flow and it

appears choppy to me. The only time I perform paired readings is when I have no question and I am simply trying to get a feel for why a client is coming to me. In this case, the first card will give me a subject and the next card will explain further and so on through the line.

3.   You can choose a center card as a focus card that can be preselected (charged) or you can allow it to fall naturally. I'll call this a focus-card reading, which is a descriptive reading. You can perform descriptive readings without a focus card also where every card laid will describe the subject you're asking about. I generally choose the center card to be the focus. There's one instance when I choose the focus to be the first card and that's when I have no question. (*See first card focus reading below.) With a center card focus spread, the energy is all flowing toward the center card. If you choose a first card focus, the energy is flowing from right to left as each card is modifying or describing the first card.

4.   A Past-Present-Future reading. I call this a PPF. Let me say from the start that this is the reading I perform least. In most cases, I wouldn't waste my time asking the cards to describe something that's already happened or tell me something that I already know. The only instances in which I'll read for the past is when I'm trying to determine where something from the past went awry, causing a present problem or in consulting the cards for a reason why there is a current issue as in a cause and effect reading. I'll often use these to answer my "why" questions. The energy flow is naturally from left to right as you lay past-present-future. There are times that I'll perform an all-past mediumship reading as well.

Let's look at examples of each type of reading.

A Narrative Reading:

This is no different than reading a story or a comic strip. You will decide on your question as usual, but won't charge any cards. You simply lay out a line of three cards and read them as a sentence using your base meanings.

Example:

How will today's meeting go? You draw Sun-Cross-Tree. From this, you will read the line across and say that it will start with energy, positivity, and enthusiasm. But you then hit a snag with the Cross. Things turn heavy and troublesome and you know at this point that it won't end well (as the Cross is an enduring pain). The Tree at the end of the line tells you that the meeting will end in a deadlock (stagnation).

Paired Reading:

What makes a paired reading different from a narrative or a focus card reading? As I already stated, a narrative reading is one where you read the line as a story. Each subsequent card adds the next layer to the story, all leading to the final card that is the ending or outcome of the story. The first card may or may not represent the main subject but is simply where the story begins. This happens, which leads to this, and ends with this. In a focus card reading, every card in the line is describing or elaborating on the subject that was chosen by you or fell naturally by setting your intention to make a particular card the subject or focus, as in the first or middle card. In a paired reading, the first card is the subject and the second describes or modifies it. The third card then modifies the pair. If you're using a line of five or seven, the additional cards are all modifying what comes before them.

Example:

How will my blind date go tonight? You draw Book-Fish-Lily. In pairing rather than reading a narrative, each subsequent card modifies what comes before it, making the first card the focus or noun. So, in this line the Fish will modify the Book. The Book is the subject, and how appropriate for a blind date as it's the card of yet unknown information or secrets being revealed. (How do we know the secrets will be revealed? Because the card showed up in a small spread, which means that we use the near meaning of the card.) Because we're asking how the date will go, it will start out like a closed book as you enter yet undisclosed territory. Next, we have the Fish that is going to act as an adjective describing the noun. Fish is our financial card as well as the card of abundance, so we could say that there will be an abundance of unknown. This pair could also refer to financial information coming to light, so we need to view the third card for clarification. The third card modifies the first pair and the Lily is a very nice card to see in a date question, so we can now eliminate any ideas of a negative interpretation of the first pair. The Lily represents satisfaction, harmony, maturity, and family. It's important throughout the entire process to constantly refer back to the question, because we're tempted at this point to say that we'll discover our date is wealthy (old family money). But that isn't answering the question of how the date will go. At its simplest, this paired line will read, many satisfying secrets will be revealed. Had this been a center card focus question, the focus would more likely be on money. In that case, we could read this as satisfying financial information will come to light. Had this been a narrative question, we could say that the date will start out with many unknowns but will end in a harmonious and pleasant way.

Charged Focus Card:

Probably the simplest way to get started is to "charge" a focus card. This method naturally places the focus card in the center. You'll see the word charge used a lot amongst card readers and it simply means that you focus your attention on a particular card that is the crux of what you're asking about. For example, if I'm asking about my finances, my focus will be on the Fish card, which represents cash flow. If you're looking for romance, charge the Heart card. If you're asking about an existing relationship, be it personal or business, charge the Ring card. If your concern is school, charge the Book card, or in the case of a particular test or paper you're writing, you could charge the Letter. Charging a card is nothing more than placing your focus and attention on it as you shuffle the cards. Once it's firmly set in your mind, start thinking about your question. All the while, you're shuffling those cards! Once you feel ready to begin (you'll simply know when the deck is ready – trust your intuition!) turn the deck over and search for your charged card. Because you've already established that you'll be reading a line of three before beginning, you'll simply take the card behind and the card in front of the charged card and lay them in order. If the card you've charged lands at either end of the stack, take the card next to it and the card at the other end of the stack is then the third card. There's your line of three with a center card focus that you preselected. When you choose a center card focus, you'll be reading the line as a description rather than a narrative as you already chose the center card, the other two cards that fell naturally will simply describe it. Example:

What will my next dog be like? That's a descriptive question, isn't it? You decide to focus on (charge) the dog card and lay it as the center card, taking the card on either side of it as the descriptors. You shuffle well while concentrating on your question and then turn over the deck and search for the Dog card. The cards on either side of the Dog card are the Key and the Tower. Key-Dog-Tower. The Key tells you that your next dog will be lean, smart and confident. This will be an important dog in your life. The Tower says the dog will be tall and thin. That corresponds with the Key's reference to leanness so you'll keep that. The Tower also suggests a proud dog with an air of importance. It will be independent and not clingy or too needy. A "top dog" type. This also corresponds with the meaning of the Key so there's no question as to the personality of your next dog.

Uncharged Focus Card Reading with Middle Card Focus:

In this case, you'll still be viewing the center card as a focus card but you'll allow it to fall naturally. The other two cards will describe it. When I perform a focus card reading, I lay the focus or center card first, followed by the left and then the final card to the right.

Example:

How will I like my new exercise class? You draw Book-Birds-Coffin (remember that the center card was laid first). As the focus, the Birds tells you that this class will be exciting but a little stressful and a bit chaotic for you. The Book describing the Birds shows that you'll feel that you don't know what you're doing (you may feel like everyone else is in the groove and you're simply out of the loop). The Coffin describing the Birds shows that all of this activity will be exhausting. Remember that in this type of reading, the Coffin is describing the center card, which makes the line different than if you'd chosen a narrative. As a narrative, this line would read as, what you'll learn will be hectic and stressful and lead to exhaustion and you'll wind up down for the count! The slight difference is that you're not explaining how things will end with a descriptive reading as you do with a narrative.

Focus Card Reading with First Card Focus:

Example:

Why has this silent client come to me today? (this is an actual reading from my journal). I drew the Key. They're looking for a solution. A solution for what? I then drew the Letter. A solution regarding communication. What type of communication? The next card to show was the Garden. The client wanted to find a solution for an issue regarding communicating with others. What type of others? I drew the Stars. Others online, possibly. What is the issue with the others online? I then drew the Mountain. She had enemies or others were challenging her and she wanted to find a solution. Bingo! When I asked her if this is why she'd come to me, her jaw dropped and there was no sound but the crickets outside! She finally gasped and asked how I knew? She's been a regular client ever since. Telling a client something about their present situation (or past) will astonish them from the start and I find that they tend to listen more intently and not question or doubt the rest of the reading. Give it a try!

Past Present Future (PPF) Reading:

In a three card line, the first card as the past, the middle as the present, and the final card as the future.

Example:

Why didn't he call me after our first date like he said he would? In this case, the past card will describe the date, the present is what he's thinking now, and the future will let you know if he'll still call or if you should stop being so pathetic and stop staring at your phone. Sorry. You draw Mice-Cross-Clover. The Mice tells you that for him, the date was a loss. It didn't go well and he felt drained afterward. He currently feels dragged-down and heavy at the thought of calling you. But, the future card shows a twist of fate and it tells you that he'll most likely be desperate enough for your draining company to call you again. As there are no cards here telling you that he really cares and simply hasn't called due to work or being in a coma, my advice would be to remove him from your contacts and move on. Don't be a doormat – you can do better – have some pride!

Try the three methods and see what's most comfortable for you. You'll discover with practice that different types of questions will elicit the need for one method over another. What I've discovered personally is that pairing isn't my thing. I always choose a narrative or a focus reading and the question determines which one I choose. If I'm asking how something will turn out, that's a narrative. If I'm trying to describe something such as the personality or physical traits of someone, that's a focus card reading.

Lines of Five and Seven:

The line of five is read exactly as you'd read a line of three, but you get more details. The line of seven is where I start to depart a bit from the standard small-spread line methods as now we have two 3-card spreads joined by a central focus card. This gives us some new possibilities for interpretation. We can read the line as a cause and effect PPF, where we overlap the third and fifth cards. In this case, we'll read cards 1-3 as the past, 3-5 as the present, and 5-7 as the future. You can also read cards 1-3 as a description of a current situation, the center card as the primary issue or a suggested action (as per the intention you set beforehand), and cards 5-7 as the outcome of the issue or result of the action. We can use a line of seven to give us a lot of details in describing a person or animal. We can assign the first three cards to describe the physical traits, the center card can be preselected to stand for the subject or you can let it fall naturally as an indicator of compatibility. The last three cards will describe personality traits.

All lines can be doubled to give you houses for the cards. In the case of a line of three, you will set an intention to draw the houses first and lay out three cards. You then draw three cards for the second row to represent the cards that fall in the houses.

HOUSES AND MULTIPLE DECKS FOR SMALL SPREADS

Now that you're comfortable with small line spreads, let's have some fun with adding houses and multiple decks.

Using two decks:

I shuffle two decks together when I lay multiple lines for a single question, such as asking for advantages vs disadvantages or outcomes of two or three options. By combining two decks, each of the lines you lay will have access to a full deck.

Example:

A middle-aged man asks if he should accept the offer to receive extra training at work. I shuffle two decks together and lay an outcome spread for accepting or not.

Outcome if he accepts training: **Key-Man-Bouquet**

Outcome if he doesn't: **Cross-Child-Coffin**

Light deck is "Whisper Lenormand". Darker deck is "Unforgettable Lenormand", both are mini decks by Teri Smith.

We can immediately see that accepting the offer looks better. Man is facing Key telling us that this training will give him the key to open doors. The Bouquet shows appreciation, luck, and offers to come his way. For the second line, the poor Child is stuck between the Cross and the Coffin! He'll regret not accepting this offer (Cross). It will keep him small and inexperienced (Child). He'll be boxing himself into his current position with no chance of advancement and could even lose his job (Coffin).

Houses in small spreads:

You can easily lay a line of 3, 5, or 7 with houses and it's one of my favorite techniques. The houses will be viewed precisely as in a GT. They ask a question or set the stage. The card that falls in the house answers the question or elaborates on the situation. Because I prefer that every card be available for use as a house or the card within it, I often shuffle two decks together when using this technique. In this way, a card falling in its own house will accentuate its importance. Identical cards falling in different houses within the same small spread can also provide different meanings for that card, such as the Child might mean something just beginning in the house of Rider but may infer an appearance of immaturity in the house of the Mountain.

Example:

A young woman asks, "why won't he tell me he loves me?"

Houses: **Mountain-Fox-Bear**

Cards: **House-Fox-Scythe**

The houses are the first thing I consider because they tell me what the primary issues are. The Mountain tells me that something (other than himself) is blocking him from saying it. The Fox says that he's hiding something. The Bear shows that he's trying to protect something. I then look at the cards to explain the houses. The House in Mountain says that the obstacle is at home. The Fox in Fox is a big exclamation mark! He's acting wrongly in hiding something (as opposed to hiding something with good intentions). He's lying and tricking her. The Scythe in Bear shows that he's protecting himself from a cut or decision that's irrevocable. What he has is in danger of being divided or removed. It appears that he has a wife at home who is being lied to as well. She has no idea he's cheating or that there's anything wrong with their marriage.

THE ART OF TABLEAU READING

T ableau-style reading is all about positions – what's on top, below, auspicious and inauspicious, what leads to what, what is weighing down on what, what is supporting, where are you coming from and where are you going, diagonals, etc.

Where did it begin? According to my research, most early card readers couldn't afford Tarot cards as they were very expensive and not mass-produced as they are today, so they used regular playing cards. Because each card didn't contain all the information that individual tarot cards offer, it was the combining of the playing cards that provided meanings. All the cards would be laid out in rows and the reader would then note which cards fell together and how they related to each other via techniques such as counting and pairing.

So, while Tarot cards may contain such a vast array of meanings and correspondences within each card, cards with limited and basic meanings such as Lenormand and Gypsy cards require groupings to form full meanings.

When I look at a tableau, I see a puzzle or a map. It never ceases to amaze me how the cards fall together to paint a picture which gives me the answer to my question. All tableaus from the 9-card box to the grand tableau are maps by which I follow different roads or paths that lead to my answers.

All positions influence the other cards in unique ways. Cards above influence down on those below. Cards below are supporting the cards above. Cards behind are pushing the cards in front. They are the reasons, the causes, the issues, the motivations for forward propulsion. The cards in front are what the cards behind are striving for, trying to reach, looking toward. The diagonals, as they flow toward the end of the tableau are showing the results of all of this motivating, influencing, and striving.

The cards in a line of sight of the PSC show the current story. This is the horizontal row that the card lands in. I use the column for the partner card. All cards immediately touching any SC give you the details of that card. Moving further away, and you have layers of cards that are influencing the influencers or adding more details to the detail cards. Keep moving out layer by layer and the impact of the cards is diluted.

Where the PSC falls in a tableau gives immediate information. Because the flow of energy moves from top to bottom and left to right, the best position for the client's card is to the left and near the top. In this position they have the least amount of cards weighing down on them or inauspiciously placed behind them.

The client's card is:

Landing high: In control and on top of things.

Landing low: Too much on their minds or out of their control. Under a lot of pressure.

Landing left: Looking ahead and ready to take things on. In a PPF, this indicates little or no past cards indicating that the client may be leaving the past behind or wants to. They may also be overly focused on the future or heavily focused on it at the time of the reading due to a major life change.

Landing right: Many inauspicious cards implies more difficulty in dealing with the cards behind (even positive cards) or the client will be passive regarding them. In a PPF, there would be mostly "past" cards and little or no future cards indicating unresolved issues, not letting go, the future is still undetermined, or the client is about to make major life changes that aren't set in stone yet.

VARIATIONS OF A BASIC CROSS SPREAD

How to Read a Basic Cross:

In any cross spread, you will see that there is a diamond around the center card. Just as you do in a box spread, you can read the diamond in a cross as the outside influences or what is surrounding the main theme. This will be applicable if you don't preselect the center card.

You can lay the outer cards first and set your intention for the final card to be the outcome card, which you then place in the center. If you are reading the horizontal row as PPF or a progression, then the final card in the row will be the outcome.

You can set an intention for the top card to represent thoughts, intentions, or aspirations while the bottom card will represent your foundation, as in what you already have control over, or it can represent what manifests via the top card's intentions. Another variation is for the bottom card to show the reason for the issue and the top card to represent the potential. The horizontal row will then show the current progression of the issue.

5-card cross variations with a preselected significator card (SC):

1. Past/present/future (PPF) or simply a progression of an event or circumstance. The center column would then be the present. With a preselected SC, the card below would represent the temporary present while the card above – carrying more weight – would represent the longer-lasting present as it is influencing down.

2. You can also view the card above (5) as thoughts/ideas and the card below (4) as the present situation the SC is standing on. Card 2 is then the past and card 3 is the future or outcome.

3. You can view the card above as thought/ideas/what's on your mind and the card below as what you're ignoring or not seeing. The center row represents the present circumstances.

4. Another method that is a nice choice for relationship readings is to read the card above the SC as their thoughts, the card below as their feelings, and card 2 is what is difficult or unfavorable and card 3 is what is easy or favorable.

5. Impact/Control Cross. The center row will show the current happenings. If the center card is preselected or shows up as a significator card, the card to the left can represent what is inauspicious to the SC, while the card to the right will represent what is auspicious to the SC. The card above represents what has an impact on us or is bearing down on us that we have little control over. The card beneath represents the control we have or will have over the situation. (*Keep in mind that the center horizontal row will be affected by directional cues.)

6. The intersection of two stories. In this method, you'll read the vertical column as a progression from top to bottom and the horizontal row as a progression from left to right. The center card will be the intersection point and shows how the two stories come together.

The 9-card cross:

You can easily turn the 5-card cross into a 9-card by adding 2 more cards to the horizontal row and 2 more to the vertical column.

You now have a vertical column, a horizontal row, and two diagonal lines.

Let me number the cards as follows:

$$1$$
$$6\,7$$
$$4\,2\,5$$
$$8\,9$$
$$3$$

You can see that card 6 connects 4 to 1. Card 7 connects 1 to 5. Card 9 connects 5 to 3. And, card 8 connects 3 to 4.

You can follow any of the guidelines above for reading a cross spread, but now you have connecting cards that will show the relationship between the cards. You also have a 4-card diamond, a 4-card square, and two diagonal lines. Laying the cards in this fashion differs from the 3x3 box in that you have above and below energies (cards 1 and 3) that are separate from the rest of the spread and can represent one's intentions and their foundation or what is out of their control and what they have control over. I read the square as the closer influences on the center card theme and the diamond as the indirect influences.

EXTENDED CROSS SPREAD

This is a 13-card spread that is a step beyond a box spread for me.

There are several different ways you can tackle this spread. These are the steps I use.

To explain the steps, I'll number the cards 1-13 starting with the top card, moving top to bottom, right to left. The way I lay the cards is to lay the row of five across, then complete the horizontal column from top to bottom, followed by filling in the last four cards beginning with the top two and then the bottom two.

1. Check the mix of cards that fell. Mostly favorable? Unfavorable? A mix?

2. Look at the focal point – the center card to see what's at the heart of the matter. This can also be a preselected SC.

3. Read the primary cross. The horizontal row of 1-5, and the vertical column of 6-9. This will give you the overview of the present situation. Summarize what you see here and put it into a sentence or two. Remember that cards above influence those below. If you've chosen a preselected SC, the two cards above can be viewed as out of the SC's control and below as under the SC's control. Above can be thoughts and below feelings. Above can be conscious thoughts and below can be uncon-

scious thoughts. This is entirely up to you depending on the reading you're doing. You simply have to decide this before you lay the cards.

4. Read the inner diamond 2, 7, 4, 8 to see what's floating around the focal point.

5. Read the 4 corners of the inner box. (Yes, there's a box spread in there!) Just as with any box spread, these 4 cards are framing the issue/answer.

6. Now, read the outer diamond 1,6,5,9. This will show another wave or layer of what's floating around that central issue (the center card).

7. Now split the spread into two sides that are flanking the biggest string of cards – the vertical center column. Because I always see the energy of spreads moving from left to right and top to bottom, how does the left side move into the right side? What do the cards around the horizontal line cards tell you?

8. How does the top half of the spread move into the bottom? What's on top of this issue? What's at its core? What's it based on?

9. Another way to view this spread is by simply seeing the center 5-card row as the current situation and what you're facing. The cards above can represent what is out of your control and weighing down on you. The cards below will show what you have control over and what you can do to effect the cards that are out of your control.

Example:

Jim is a research analyst who was having trouble adjusting to working at home and contacted me for a reading. I preselected his card for the center. Looking at the vertical column, I see that what he has no control over is the government and corporate changes that have forced him to work from home (Stork and Tower). What he has control over is his career, the reputation he has built, and the money he makes (Fish and Moon). His inauspicious cards show that he feels stuck at home. He's stagnating there and it's gnawing at him. The kids are always underfoot and he doesn't know how to be at home and be unavailable at the same time. He was so upset at this unhealthy situation that he couldn't think of a way out. I then saw the Book and Key in front of him. He needed to put a lock on the door and become inaccessible – like a closed book. I looked at the Ways above and saw a house split in two. He needed to take charge (Bear) and make the decision (Ways) to lock himself in a secret room of the house (Book mirrors House) during working hours. He needs to become incommunicado and his family needs to understand that while he's physically in the house, he's not accessible to them just as if he were still at the office. Looking at the 9-square, I saw the Tree in the hidden issue position and told him that everyone in the family needed to allow time to adjust to this new scenario. I also saw the Moon under him and asked if he had a spare bedroom that he could convert into an office. He said he did but it was his wife's sewing room. Because she hadn't sewn anything since the third child was born, he decided that it would be better served as his office for the time being.

BOX/PORTRAIT SPREAD

The box spread is the smallest tableau. It's a complete tableau if you consider that all the positions are present – you have three columns, three rows, and two diagonals giving you cards of influencing, supporting, present situation, pushing, receiving, anterior, posterior, and even a center focus card! It's also a little chunk of a Grand Tableau (GT), and once you get comfortable with it, you're all set for Grand Tableau reading!

As with any other spread, your first step is to consider what information you're seeking and formulate a question. You then want to decide if you wish to view past influences, in which case, you'll lay a past, present, future box using the columns from left to right. This will be useful if you want to see how a situation came to be. While it's most common to see the vertical columns dividing the time frame of the spread, I've seen some people use the horizontal rows for past, present, and future with the past on the bottom. If you like to view the bottom as the foundation as you do with a pyramid spread, go ahead and read your boxes the same way for consistency. It's completely up to you!

Beyond viewing the columns or rows as these time frames, you'll follow all the other steps as usual.

You can also use the box as a timing spread, in which case you'll set your intention for each column to represent a day, week, or month and then read the columns.

Other than viewing rows or columns for timing, you can choose to read the top row as what's in someone's head, the middle row as what they're currently dealing with, and the bottom row as what they have control over or what they've already started.

You'll then use the columns to provide more information regarding your rows.

Whether you set an intention for timing or not, my method for reading tableaus is to follow the flow just as I do in a sequential/narrative line spread (3, 5, 7 card lines). I'm basically starting the story with card one and following the story through the box to card nine. The center card is the heart of the spread – the crux of the story – as every other card touches it.

The following are my standard box-reading steps. I approach the reading of a box the same way every time and by adhering to this system, the cards know exactly how to fall and the reading progresses smoothly and quickly. I always lay the cards in order from 1 to 9, starting in the upper left-hand corner and moving from left to right, top to bottom.

The spread will look like this:

1-2-3

4-5-6

7-8-9

Interpretation Steps:

1. My first step is to give the spread a quick scan to see if the primary significator card (PSC) showed up and what theme cards have appeared (that is, work, relationship, finances). This is critical to your answer. For example, if you're asking how the person you're currently dating feels about the relationship and you receive the Heart, Ring, Anchor, Moon, Sun, Dog, Lily, Bouquet, and your own card, well, there's no doubt that YOU are the one and they're quite serious, in love, committed, and the Universe is smiling upon this union! Does it even matter in which order those cards fall? No! The scan is also to check the general energy of the spread, that is, how many beneficial cards, how many problematic cards, how many action cards, and which cards relating to my question didn't show up. Following the example above, you draw the partner card with the Ring to their left, Lily, Dog, Clover, Ways, Cross, along with the Moon and Heart. What you see here is that you still have the Heart, Ring, Moon, Lily, and Dog, but the addition of the Cross, Ways, Clover as well as the fact that the partner card showed up rather than the client's card and the placement of the Ring in relation to their card changes the entire story! You now see that this person has feelings for you but

is already attached to someone else and the Clover, Ways, and Cross are indicating that your relationship won't last. Even if that Ring wasn't there, the addition of the unfavorable cards will change the answer. Don't assume that the Heart appearing equals living happily ever after. This person may love you with all their heart but that's where it may end. Just as the Dog shows loyalty, it doesn't indicate a commitment/contract (Ring), nor does it indicate that the goal has been reached (Anchor). Do you see where I'm going with this? It's the clusters of cards that give you the complete story, not the individual cards. Do you really have to go any further? Sometimes, you won't. Other times, you'll need to analyze further to get your answer or you'll simply want more details. Following are my detailed steps.

So, what is the first thing to do? Notice or write down the favorable cards versus unfavorable. Take note of the center and final (9th) cards. Look for theme cards and note how many you have from any theme group. Take note of important cards that are missing. Did the client's card show up and if so, where? Did the partner card appear?

2. My next step is to check my primary 3 cards, which form the main diagonal of 1, 5, and 9. I can often answer my question with this line alone and the other cards will provide more details. I may also add the cross and the other diagonal line (together they form the X) and read nothing more. But, let's consider what all the placements represent and look at all the steps, which together, will give you a very detailed reading with only 9 cards!

3. Card #1 shows where the story begins. This can show the cause of the issue you're asking about or what is pushing things forwards. You can view it as the primary influencer. It's also known as the trigger card.

4. The center card (#5) is the heart of the matter. All cards touch this card. It's the main theme – the focal point. Take note of what's bearing down on it and what it's standing on. Consider how card #1 is affecting it.

5. The last card (#9) is the exit card. It tells you where the story winds up. Now, you can see why 1,5, and 9 form my primary line. Card 1 affects card 5, which is the heart of the matter, which leads to the result shown in card 9. But, there's a lot more information here, so let's continue.

6. At this point, I like to check card #7. It's hiding at the bottom of the spread in the corner and often shows me the underlying issue regarding what I'm asking about.

7. Next, I check the corners to see what's framing the heart of the matter. Here, I combine cards 1, 3, 7, and 9. This is where I start to form a story. I first read cards 1 and 3, and then 7 and 9, and write down what they're telling me. I then combine them diagonally, 3 with 7 and 1 with 9. I now start getting a story that I connect to my question. I consider how they affect the main theme card (#5) and how they connect to the primary influence card (#1).

8. Now, I check the cross. Cards 2,5, 8 and 4, 5, 6. As you can see, both of these lines intersect the main theme card (5). If you consider that the middle row (4,5,6) is the center of this spread, then the middle column intersects that. You can view cards 4 and 6 as describing or providing more information regarding the center theme and card 2 shows what's influencing that, while card 8 is the result of that influence. Put this information together with your 4 corners, and you have your base answer.

9. I now look at my other diagonal line (3, 5, and 7) to give me my X. Diagonals, because they skip cards in the forward flow of 1 to 9, give you indirect influences or chunks of information, as opposed to rows and columns which show direct influences/information.

10. I check my rows and columns now for more information but at this point, they generally repeat what I've already extracted. I use this step more as confirmation of what I'm already seeing.

11. Lastly, I knight any significant cards. For example, if I'm asking about the querent's boyfriend, and card #28 shows up in position #7, I want to pay attention to his knighted cards (2 and 6) as they generally show hidden influences (cards above) or motivations (cards below if you're knighting a middle or upper card).

12. The Diamond can also be checked. This consists of cards 2, 4, 6, and 8. Because I always read the cards in the order I laid them, I read it as 2 to 4 to 6 to 8 – not the way I'd draw a diamond. Some people choose this as a primary technique. I may only check it as confirmation.

13. Another technique that many use is to look at the mirrored cards for some cause and affect information. The mirrored cards are 1 and 3, 4 and 6, 7 and 9, 1 and 7, 2 and 8, and 3 and 9. This is another technique I rarely consider, but many do.

14. If you still aren't satisfied with the information you've received or want further confirmation on what you're seeing, you can perform a counting round to extract a line of 5. You can also use this as a final message for your querent.

Start with the center card as it's the focal point of the reading and remove it. You then count and remove every second card. You'll then have cards 5, 7, 9, 2, and 4 to lay in a line of 5. You can now read this as a narrative.

To wrap things up, I'd like to mention a couple more techniques. You can pre-select your center card if you are looking for specific information relating to one particular topic or to read around an SC as you would in a GT.

You can also set your intention to assign specific meanings to the rows or columns as is commonly done in a cross spread. How you do this will depend on what information you seek. The center row is typically the now – the reality of what's happening, the most likely path, or what's actually going on with the person or animal you're asking about. Above, can represent what's weighing down on them or what is on their mind. Below can be what they have control over or what they're ignoring. If you choose the entire spread to describe someone, the center can be physical or personality traits, above can be mental processes, and below can be emotional processes.

Mastering the box is the key to understanding GT reading and as a small spread, can provide you with a wealth of information. Give it a try! Here's an example:

A BOX SPREAD EXAMPLE

A Man asks why his dog is suddenly afraid of his leash. I laid a box spread. My leash card (Snake) shows up under the Tower and Whip. I ask if he is taking the dog to a trainer and he says no. Hmmm. My hidden issue card is the card of visitors and movement. With Dog and Stork above, I asked him if he's had a house guest or someone different that has taken the dog out for a walk. Bingo! He hired a new dog-walker. Whip and Book told me that this person probably is or wants to become a dog trainer, though they're using harsh methods (Tower – with Fox facing, sitting above Whip and Snake facing Cross). Upon questioning the dog walker, he discovered that she indeed was taking a course to become a dog trainer but it was taught at a school specializing in police and military dog training. Absolutely unsuitable for most pet dogs! Case solved.

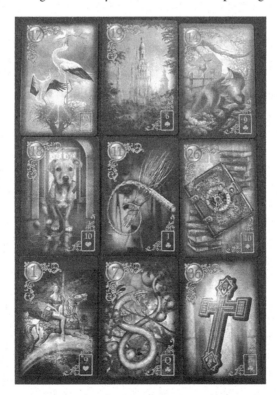

THE PYRAMID SPREAD

The pyramid simply gives you another way to view a tableau. Its shape will naturally prompt you to view it from a multi-card base to a pinnacle card, or vice versa as it can also be laid in an inverted fashion. Your decision as to which way to lay the cards will depend on the information you start with and the answer you seek. Here are a few variations and how to tackle them.

CAUSE AND EFFECT PYRAMID:

When I want to see what past events have led to a current situation and how it will progress, I lay a pyramid spread, which contains ten cards. This is read from the bottom up to the top. If you prefer to always read top to bottom, reverse the spread – invert it – so that cards 1-4 are on the top.

When I look at a pyramid spread, I see one big pyramid with six small pyramids within it.

First, I will explain how I view the levels.

1. The bottom level of four cards lay the foundation. This is where it all started. It's the root cause of what led to the current issue.

2. The next level of three cards give us more information on the bottom four cards. Now we're getting more details on the reason why something is happening.

3. The third level of two cards is the next layer of information that is garnered from the root cause below and leading to the primary influence above in card ten.

4. The top level is card ten and shows the ultimate effect, outcome, or result.

Steps:

1. Read the bottom row as a narrative.

2. Read the second row as a narrative and then start bridging the first row to the second. So, read cards 1 and 2 with 5, cards 2 and 3 with 6, and cards 3 and 4 with 7. Now you can start to see the smaller pyramids.

3. Now, do the same for the third level. Read cards 8 and 9 as a pair and then read cards 5 and 6 with 8, and cards 6 and 7 with 9.

4. Next, read the top card as the ultimate answer.

So, you can read this as bottom to top – past to future. In this way, the top will be the future outcome.

PRESELECTED SIGNIFICATOR PYRAMID:

This is still a 10-card pyramid but with the addition of a significator card (SC). Perfect for seeing what options the querent has when considering an issue. Pre-selecting the SC is perfect when you want to see where the other cards will fall in relation to your querent's card.

Explanation:

1. Cards 1-5 form the bottom row. This is where the reading begins. It shows the past and the events that led to the present circumstances.

2. The next row contains your significator card. The cards on either side are in closest proximity and therefore carry the most weight. You can say that they are most relevant in the present as they are closest to the querent's consciousness.

3. The two cards above the significator's head will show the choices they have.

4. The top card, also called the summit card, represents the final outcome. This is going to be the final outcome, if the querent only follows the path of least resistance and nothing else.

Steps:

1. Read the bottom line as a 5-card narrative, which explains how the situation began.

2. Read the cards on either side of the SC using their near meanings (for those who understand the Method of Distance). Also consider the direction the SC faces if applicable. This line shows you the present circumstances and how they're impacting the querent.

3. Read the two cards above the SC and see if they relate to a single option or do they describe two completely different options.

4. The summit card will represent the outcome of the single choice below, or will represent the outcome of choosing the option of least resistance if two options are indicated by the 2-card line. This is something that has to be determined for each reading.

THE PYRAMIDAL YES/NO SPREAD:

I developed this spread when my husband asked me to draw cards regarding whether next year will be a good year to move. The spread contains six cards.

Steps:

1. The bottom row of three represents the foundation of your question. What you're currently standing on or where you're at right now.

2. The 2-card row shows the progression of the action taken on the bottom row.

3. The summit card is your ultimate answer. So why do we need the other cards, you may ask? Because the answer card isn't always a strong positive or negative and doesn't always answer the question on its own.

Example:

My question was, "Is this an optimal time to sell our primary home?"

My interpretation:

While we have the energy and resources to look for an opportunity to do this, they will be met with complications. This row has even deeper meaning as it was the end of the summer when I asked this question. The Sun represents summer and the Clover following shows that the window of opportunity is small. This leads to the next row, which shows that this journey is heading toward the card of patience and calmness. The Lily is also my card for winter, which is what we're heading for. The answer card is a no card, but also confirms the Lily card indicating a delay or no movement forward at the present time.

THE INVERTED 11-CARD "WHEN" PYRAMID:

I developed this spread to show what needs to take place in order for something to occur. This isn't a spread to give you an exact date but it may show that something most likely won't occur at all or at least, it will show you the level of difficulty or ease you face in making something happen.

I read this from top to bottom, so all the cards influence those below.

Steps:

1. The top row gives you the baseline for your answer. It will show you where you need to start to put your plan in motion. I like 5 cards in this line so that I have a focus card (center).

2. The 3-card row shows the effects of the top row and leads into the next tier. Take note of these cards. Are you moving in the right direction if you follow the advice of the top row? If not, you know that you'll be laying more spreads asking for alternatives. If so, keep going.

3. The third tier, containing the 2 cards, will show you whether you're getting closer or further away from your intended outcome.

4. The bottom single card is the ultimate outcome. Take note of whether this is a positive, negative, or neutral card as well as considering its meaning. Also take note of whether this is a fast, slow, or no movement card.

Example:

My question for this spread was, "When should I open my first website?"

1. Looking at the top row, I love that my card (#29) showed-up as the focus. It's completely up to me! Isn't that nice. The cards on either side of me are perfect – Anchor for reaching my goal and Bear for success and power. Reading the line as a focus-read gives me that I need to make some definitive decisions to reach my goal, assess my strengths and determine the complications that I'll face.

    Snake mirroring Ways tells me that I should consider taking an alternative approach or direction. Bear mirroring Anchor shows that I need to concentrate my focus and protect myself by keeping my work to myself until the right time.

2. Following this advice gives me the key to a successful website.

3. The next tier slows things down a bit by indicating that patience will still be needed as this site will be new and need time to mature.

4. The final card tells me that this will happen. It will happen soon, and also that the site will require ongoing input to maintain the forward momentum.

MY SIGNATURE SPREADS

1. My Extended Box.

This Petite Tableau is a box spread with a frame of cards placed around it to provide more information. This spread is read exactly in the same way that you're accustomed to reading a box spread, but each peripheral card now has an additional card to further describe it or show you what the cards of the inner box are leading to.

Explanation:

While this may just look like 5 rows of 5 cards, this is in fact, an extension of a box spread. The 16-card frame around the box are cards that further describe the box's message. Look at this frame as the next wave of cards around a 9-square in a Grand Tableau.

Steps:

1. Set your intention and shuffle the cards for a portrait spread.

2. Lay the box/portrait as you normally would.

3. Now, set your intention for more information on the cards contained in the box.

4. Starting in the upper left corner, lay a frame of 16 cards around the outside of the box. I prefer to leave a small space between the outer cards and the box, which helps me to separate the box from the outer cards.

5. If you find this many cards too distracting, simply keep the 16-card frame upside-down until after you've interpreted the box spread. Then, turn over the other cards to give you more details.

If you want to ensure that one or both people cards (significator cards = SC) show up, you can do that. There are times when you'll want to let all cards fall naturally to see who is a predominant player or how much control or presence someone will display during the timeframe of the spread. In other cases – especially if you read directionally – you'll want to ensure that your SC or both land in the spread. In this case, you'll want to remove your SC from the deck and set it aside. Shuffle the cards while setting your intention for the 23 or 24 cards you'll need to add to the one or two SC's to give you the 25 card total. Instead of laying the spread, simply lay the cards in a pile. Now add the SC's and shuffle them into the pile. You now have 25 cards total with your SC included. Lay the spread as you would normally.

Example:

This is the spread that gave birth to the idea for the extended box spread. A young woman came to me for a reading about an elderly dog that she was thinking of adopting. Her boyfriend thought she was crazy for wanting to adopt a senior dog with health issues, but she was drawn to this dog for reasons she couldn't explain, other than the fact that it looked like a dog she had for a very short time as a child. I decided to lay a box with a preselected focus card but also wanted a way to have descriptor cards attached to the box. I thought of how we read the layers of cards that surround any SC and decided to lay a frame of descriptor cards around the outside of the box. This is the story that the cards told.

Question asked: Why is this woman so drawn to this dog?

Interpretation: The primary diagonal line of the inner box told me that this dog would bring a satisfying end to the goal the woman was trying to reach. The card beneath the dog is the decision card (Ways) but also shows a split between the woman and the dog. The Fox facing the Ways told me that something was wrong. The key was hinting at finding a solution. The Dog was searching for a final home (Stars+Coffin+House) that involved a long journey to be recognized (Ship+Moon). I then asked the woman about her mother and what had happened to her childhood pet. She told me that her mother had passed when she was very young and she had been raised by her father and stepmother (whom she never cared for). The cards were now completing the story. The stepmother was the enemy in this story (Mountain+Bear). She had wrongly removed the dog from the home and placed it in a shelter (Scythe+Clouds+Mice+Tower+Book). She had fabricated a lie and the truth of her wrong deed had been her secret (Book+Snake+Fox). The young woman's card is facing the Ring and Child indicating a contract to adopt and give the dog a fresh start, but I suddenly saw the Ring+Child+House as a reuniting with a dog from her childhood. My eyes then went to the Stars+Key as an internet or computer related solution, with the Sun+Moon+Coffin, I saw a scan of an ID microchip. I told the client to ask if the dog had a microchip and for its information. Yes, as you've probably guessed by now, this was indeed the dog that had been taken from her as a child and placed in the local shelter, where 10 years later, it was returned only to be reunited with its original owner! Amazing!

2. The Party No-Table Reading.

This is a fun reading that I developed when my hairdresser asked if I would barter card readings for my haircuts. Because I had no table as I sat in the chair, I used a method I had learned from a Tarot group years ago.

There are two variations.

A. For those who have no question and just want a fun reading, I fan out the deck in my hand or hands and ask the querent to feel through the cards while considering any part of their lives or they can ask, "What message does Spirit have for me today?" and choose a card. If they aren't near you, choose for them. Look at and discuss the meaning of the card, place it back in the deck and shuffle. Take the card or two in front and behind the focus card for a quick answer.

B. For those who do have a specific question and if I have a table to work at, I will expand on the above method a bit while still keeping it to a small, fast reading. I follow as above, searching for the SC and taking the card in front and the card behind and laying them into a line of three. I now randomly choose a card to place above the SC to see what is weighing down on it or influencing it and a card to place below the SC to see what the foundation is, or what it's really all about. I now have four random cards to read that will describe the SC. I'll read all the cards as descriptors of the SC and can then read the diamond as a narrative.

These are so much fun and have become my party-piece that I use at all social gatherings. Give it a try, have fun with it, and see how popular you will become!

Example:

Sui Generis Lenormand deck by Ciro Marchetti

This was a reading I did while getting my hair cut. My stylist had no question so I simply fanned the cards out in my hand and said, "Let's see what's on your mind, girl!" She drew the House. I said, well, it's something to do with your home or personal life and she said, well that could mean anything. True. I replaced it in the deck and decided to draw the two cards on either side after a thorough shuffle. I drew the Woman and Stork behind and the Whip and Man in front. You can see that the couple is facing apart with the Whip between them. I said, it looks like you want to move but your husband doesn't agree. Bingo! That led to a lengthy dissertation of her issue with wanting to move back to the city, while her husband is adamant about staying in the country. If you're ever at a social gathering where the conversation is lagging, just get out your cards and give this a try!

3. The Conflict Resolution Spread.

Life is full of conflicts and they generally have two sides. For these kinds of questions, I like to do a spread with a double line of five or seven. That allows me to see what is going on from two different points of view. We can assign one line for the first party involved in the conflict, and the other line for the other party. The first two or three cards of each line represent the current situation. The middle card is what needs attention, and what should be focused on. The last two or three cards of each line show where the situation is headed or possible solutions. After reading each line separately, I combine the two lines together, which allows me to compare and contrast the two different points of view in order to help the client possibly arrive at a mutual understanding.

Example:

This is a follow-up to the reading above. I set my intention for the top row to show her side of the story and the bottom row to show her husband's side. I lay the cards in order, one for the top row and one for the bottom. I chose a 5-card line. The center cards show what they both need to focus on and he got his own card while she got the card of recognition. This told me that he needed to stick to his guns while she needed to recognize his side of the story. The first two cards give us the current situation and her row shows her feeling of being stuck somewhere that she's not meant to be. His cards show that he's not budging! This was an ancestral home where he has deep roots and he fully intends to live out his days there. The final two cards recommend the solution. Her cards indicate that she looks on the bright side and put energy into beautifying the home and adding her own decorating touches to make herself happier there. His cards show that he should look for a lot of little opportunities to make the home more inviting to his wife. Also, to open her eyes (Key + Sun) to the beauty of living amongst nature (Clover + Bouquet).

4. Quick and Easy Options Spread.

I use this for "which one should I make for dinner – fish or chicken?" type questions, not life-altering decisions. This is a charged focus card spread using card #22 Ways. You can make it a five or seven card spread. Find the Ways card and focus your attention on it as your option card. Place it back in the deck and while you're shuffling concentrate on your two options. Tell the deck which option will be to the left of the Ways and which will be to the right. I write this down to avoid confusion. Now, shuffle until you feel the deck is ready and search for the Ways. If you planned to lay a five card spread, take the two cards behind and the two cards in front of your charged card. For a line of seven, take the three cards from each position. Lay the cards out as you found them.

Example:

Jill asked if she should allow her "outlaws" as she calls them to come for the weekend. I focused on the Ways and set an intention for the two cards behind to represent the outcome of inviting them, while the two cards in front will show the outcome of not inviting them. We both laughed at what turned-up! If she invites them, peace will reign in the home and she'll be well-recognized by the outlaws as being family-minded and recognizing the needs of the older generation (Moon + Lily). If she doesn't invite them, she'll be inviting discord with her husband (Whip + Man). True! Her husband felt that an invitation to them was long overdue.

5. A Quick and Easy Cross Spread.

I love crosses and boxes because they give you vertical as well as horizontal card interactions. While I occasionally use an extended cross of 13 cards, I'm much more likely to lay a simple 5 card cross. This is the smallest and simplest one that I use. You can lay 2 or 3 cards for each position if you prefer.

Explanation:

I use this very simple cross when I want to find out a little more about a person, animal, or situation. I pre-select the center card to represent that which I want more information on. The format of the spread is based on directional reading.

Steps:

1.   Consider what information you seek and decide which card represents your significator. For example, you can select Man, Woman, Dog, Rider (for horse), Fox (for a cat), Fish (for your finances), Ring (for your relationship), etc.

2.   Place your SC in the center. (Card 1)

3.   The card above will represent the greatest impact on the SC. It can also show what the PSC is seeing clearly and correctly about the situation. (Card 4)

4.   The card below will represent what you are ignoring. This may be something favorable or unfavorable, but either way, you haven't considered it. (Card 5)

1.   The card to the left of the SC is inauspicious to your SC and will show what will be difficult or require attention or effort. (Card 2)

2.   The card to the right of your SC is auspicious and will show what will be easy or beneficial. (Card 3)

The cards are numbered as follows:

4

2 1 3

5

Example:

This is a reading I performed for a friend's daughter who wasn't sure if she should accept an invitation for a blind date. I placed the Bouquet in the center to represent the date offer. The card above (Tower) showed that the greatest impact on this date would be that these two have nothing in common – they're miles apart. The card below told me that he was too old for her but the evening would be a peaceful one. The card to the left said that the most difficult part of the date would be dealing with him! The card to the right showed that the easiest part of the date would be that they'd both recognize that this isn't a good match or you could say that the easiest part of the date would be saying goodnight. She decided to go on the date despite the reading and found the cards to be accurate. As she put it, nothing ventured, nothing gained. Interestingly, the man was retired from a corporate job, which also showed itself in the cards (Tower + Lily). After that night, she decided that she was finished with blind dates!

Sui Generis by Ciro Marchetti

SPREADS FOR ANIMAL COMMUNICATION

A basic 4-position pet spread:

This is a perfect little spread for inquiring about a specific situation. The cards will be read from your pet's perspective. You can lay 1-3 cards for each position.

1. Position 1 – How your pet views the situation?

2. Position 2 – What are the pros or benefits of this situation?

3. Position 3 – What are the cons or disadvantages of this situation?

4. Position 4 – What advice or feedback would your pet like to share?

Example:

A female client asked how her cat felt about her new boyfriend who was spending a lot of time at their home.

Position 1: The cat viewed this situation as a need to be sneaky and hide. The cat was indeed hiding for quite a while.

Position 2: The pros in this situation were that the boyfriend, not knowing anything about cats, was interested in learning more about cats and wanted to understand her cat in particular.

Position 3: The cons were that the woman's attention would now be divided between the cat and the boyfriend. All of her decisions would involve both of them.

Position 4: The cat clearly wanted them both to know that she was there first and was in charge! That's such a cat thing!

Physical and Personality Traits Spread

This spread is ideal if you are considering adding an animal to your household. The center card was pre-selected and represents the animal. The 3 cards to the left describe the physical traits the animal will possess. The 3 cards to the right describe the personality traits the animal will possess. These cards were drawn for someone wanting a pet cat. Using the descriptive meanings of the cards, we can say that the ideal cat will be female, white or gray with round features, and physically fit. The personality cards show that it will be easy-going, calm, mature, and sociable.

Compatibility Spread

I use this spread to check the compatibility of an animal you're considering bringing home with any human or animal members of the household. In this case, the dog was already in the home and the dog's human was considering adopting a cat she saw at the shelter.

The positions:

1. The cards above the animal's heads represent their conscious thoughts. These can be shaped and changed but they'll show you what you have to work with.

2. The cards below them represent their subconscious tendencies. These are deeply ingrained and difficult to change.

3. The cards to the left and right describe personality traits and behaviors.

4. The center pair is the ultimate answer regarding the compatibility of the two.

In this example, there's an existing dog in the home and the client wants to know if he'll accept a new cat. Both the dog and the cat had both lived with the other species previously. The spread on the left with the card from another deck represents the cat and the spread on the right represents the dog. What we can tell from this spread is that the dog has an underlying easy-going nature but is a thinker and doesn't miss much. In other words, he'll be very interested and focused on the cat. He's active and loving. As for the cat, I had to laugh because the cards are so typical! Her underlying tendency is to be elusive and she'll do whatever she has to so she gets what she wants. She'll be rather hard to read initially and will be a bit nervous and flighty. I also suggested that she be checked for fleas, ticks, and parasites (Mice) and she was indeed treated for them. This reading could've gone either way based on the descriptor cards for each animal, but the center pair told me that it would work out. And, it did! Knowing upfront what the new pet would be bringing into the home can make a big difference. Because the client expected the cat to require some patience and TLC, she gave her the time she needed to become comfortable with a new dog and a new home. Likewise, she gave the new dog time to become comfortable with the cat. Without this reading, the cat's initial behavior may have sent her back to the shelter!

A Grand Tableau for Animals

My GT's for animals generally contain extra cards. Consider the fact that pet readings are a combination of animals and people. Pets have human caretakers. So, if I'm assigning #28 and #29 to humans, but the animal or animals are the primary significators, then I need to add extra cards and houses to accommodate them. Here's an example of a GT for three dogs and three people. Here's a great example:

This was a dog adoption reading I performed two years ago. Because there were three dogs to consider, I used two extra dog cards and houses. The primary deck used is the Whisper Lenormand by Teri Smith. The potential adopter's dog is represented by the Dog card of that deck. There are two dogs being considered for adoption. Dog #1 is represented by the large dog card from Teri's Her Legacy deck. Dog #2 is represented by the Dog card in Teri's Unforgettable Lenormand deck.

The scenario:

A Westie breeder had two dogs who were littermates and had never been apart. They were returned to her after their owners got a divorce so that she could rehome them. The potential adopter was a mature husband and wife with an adult child in the home and an older adult Westie from the same breeder.

The question:

Show me how the relationship among all three dogs and all three people will play out if the dogs are adopted by this family.

The first thing I notice is that the Book is in Clover telling me there was something unknown regarding this opportunity. The Ship is my card/house for where the journey is heading and we had Bear in the house of Ship, Ship in the house of Coffin, and Cross in the house of Bear. I then saw that Whip was in the house of Cross with Dog #2 sitting above. Are you seeing a possible problem? I then saw that the Ways landed in Dog #2's house with Mountain above it. But, Dog #2 sat in Lily, so I knew I had to dig deeper to figure this all out. Bear in Ship told me that there was a need to take control somehow. Ship in Coffin suggested a problem, a buried issue, or a possible end to this transaction. Ways in the dog's house suggested a tough decision. But that dog sat in Lily which told me that it wasn't a bad dog. Let's look to see if we can figure out what the issue might be. The Mountain led me to the woman as she sat in its house. I wondered if she really only wanted to adopt the other dog. I then looked at the other two people and found that the man and woman were facing apart and she landed in a difficult house whereas he landed in the house of the Bouquet. It was looking like she was the problem. The Child was in Ring and Stars landed in her house, so she wasn't an issue. I then checked on the family's dog and found it in the house of Garden and Anchor was in its own house. The cards around their dog suggested that it would take some time to adjust to the change, but there would be no issue. So what was going on with the woman? I set that thought aside for a moment and focused on

Dog #1. It lands in its own house with all favorable cards touching, so there was no issue there. Because Dog #2 has the most unfavorable cards touching his card, I decided to perform a counting round to get a line of five. Now, stay with me! I got Bouquet, Coffin, Garden, Clouds, and Heart. Because I relied heavily on houses for this entire reading, I wanted to connect those cards to their houses. The Man lands in Bouquet, the Ship in Coffin, and the family dog in Garden. There was going to be a problem with the man and dog. But Clouds lands in Stars and the Heart lands in Ways which lands in Dog #2's house bringing me full-circle. If they give this dog a chance, it will work out. Don't forget that he landed in Lily with Heart above his head. Now look what sits in the house of Heart. Lily! The Snake landing in the house of Clouds shows initial complications but they, like the clouds in the sky, will pass. Because this reading was performed almost two years ago, I'm happy to report that they did adopt both dogs and everyone is living happily together!

Whisper Lenormand, Unforgettable Lenormand, and Her Legacy
Lenormand by Teri Smith

SPECIFIC TYPES
OF READINGS

For the most part, readers use cards to answer questions for themselves
and other living humans. But the cards can be used to read deceased
loved ones and other spiritual beings, animals—both living and passed—as
well as for specific topics such as spirituality, physical and mental health,
crime-solving, or finding missing objects. For all of these subjects, you simply
need to follow a few basic steps.

1. Set a clear intention on who you'll be communicating with.

2. Consider how the cards will answer your specific questions. For exam-
    ple, if you're reading for a spiritual question, the House card may repre-
    sent your root chakra rather than personal success or your home. If
    you're trying to solve a crime and reading for the perpetrator, the Scythe
    may represent a weapon, or the Anchor may tell you that something or
    someone is underwater.

3. Determine all your significator cards before you begin. This is especially
    important in animal readings where you need significator cards other
    than 28 and 29. Pet readings are a combination of animals and their
    humans, so you'll need extra SCs. (See the section on how to perform
    animal readings).

4.   Brainstorm to determine exactly what information you seek and clearly form your questions beforehand. I always write them down.

5.   Decide on your spreads and how you'll interpret them.

On the following pages, you'll find the chakra and health meanings quick reference sheets, a spread for connecting with a Spirit, and the animal communication information.

CONNECTING WITH THE SPIRIT WORLD

To connect with a Spirit, you simply need to decide if you're connecting with a known Spirit or trying to determine what Spirit or Spirits are around you or your client. Connecting with a known Spirit isn't very different than connecting with a living person when it comes to the questions, spreads, and card interpretations. Trying to determine what Spirits may be around you is a bit different. Think about what you want to know. Is it a male or female ancestor? Maternal or paternal? Is it someone who was physically alive during your lifetime? Did they pass when they were young or old? How did they die? What type of personality did they have? What do you have in common with this Spirit? You can then move into the questions that you have for them, such as what type of sign will you send me when you're with me? What area of my life can you help me with? What legacy has been handed down to me? Why are you with me now? What message do you have for me?

Example:

I primarily work with ancestors and wanted to know which ancestor was near me at the moment. I laid four 3-card spreads/lines to determine which ancestor was present.

Questions:

1.   Which ancestor is closest to me right now? I laid Sun-Ways-Birds. The Queen of Diamonds tells me that it is a female.

2. Are you from the maternal or paternal side of my family? In this case, the Man came up, so I knew for sure that the Spirit is paternal, but I also got the Lily (grandfather) which told me that she is from my father's side of the family. The Snake also has a court card inset but doesn't represent a family member, and this is an ancestor reading, so only blood relations will be represented.

3. What part of my life are you here to help me with? Moon-Bear-House. The first card told me that she's here to help with my career. The Bear and House refer to my career bringing prosperity into my personal life.

4. What message do you have for me? Because I've already laid nine cards, I wouldn't ask much more without adding another deck or picking all the cards up and reshuffling. I drew Whip-Dog-Lady. I loved that my card (#29) showed up for the message because it clearly shows that the message pertains to my own thinking or efforts. As I have no one helping me with my current career efforts, the Dog represents loyalty. The Whip clearly indicates that I continue to fight my way through all my current challenges and keep working hard to remain loyal to my plan and not allow anyone to distract or dissuade me. Wonderful advice, indeed, and exactly what I needed to hear at that moment!

PERFORMING HEALTH READINGS

Before embarking on a health reading, here are a few tips:

1. When interpreting a general Grand Tableau, we may provide very basic health information to our client by reading around the Tree card and how it connects to our client's card. If we want to get more specific, we can lay a spread solely for health. It's important to include a disclaimer if you plan to do this to cover yourself legally.

2. Never draw cards to answer, "Should I go to the doctor?" If they're asking, then they need to go.

3. Valid questions include asking about alternative or complementary treatments as well as asking if a second opinion or change of doctor or treatment might be helpful.

4. Other valid questions include asking about a possible misdiagnosis as well as asking about possible underlying or hidden issues that may be compounding a current illness or disease.

5. Reading for chakra issues is safe and can be very helpful.

Examples on how to use the cards for a health reading:

1. Ask if the client has any current health concerns that should be addressed and lay a simple line of five or seven cards. Look for a theme amongst the cards. For example, did you draw two or three work-related cards such as Moon, Anchor, Bear, Fox, Fish? Work-related stress may be an issue that needs addressing. If you have a grouping of Moon-Heart-Fish, that would indicate an emotional issue for me. Add in the Birds and the Dog, and you may have to distance yourself from stress-inducing gossip. Did the Rider, Stork, Tower, and House show up? All relate to the skeletal system. What about Fish, Mice, and Bear? All relate to eating and diet.

2. Specific questions regarding a known disease or illness can be answered using small spreads as with any other type of question.

3. A GT can be laid solely for health. In this case, you'll be looking primarily at the Tree C/H as well as the cards around the client's c/h as well as checking the proximity of all of them. The worst-case scenario would be the Tree card touching the client's card (PSC) with unfavorable cards surrounding it. Should the Tree have unfavorable cards around it while falling far from the PSC, then the issue isn't of immediate concern.

MY HEALTH AND WELL-BEING MEANINGS

1. Rider – Shows general improvement, news coming to you about healing, a visit from or to a healthcare professional, or your overall mobility and horsepower. Anatomically, it represents the strong legs, knees (see Stork), feet, paws, hooves. For example, Rider + Scythe = Broken leg; Scythe + Rider = Knee surgery.

2. Clover – Shows progress and improvement, a pick-up of mood or energy. It refers to greens and vegetables. Temporary illnesses. Holistic herbal or homeopathic remedies. Cannabis. May describe a vegan or vegetarian. For example, Tree + Clover + Clouds = Medical marijuana.

3. Ship – The Ship may refer to illness or disease from foreign travel, motion sickness or vertigo, or a fear of travel. In its relation to money, it may refer to extra money that comes in from insurance or possibly a lawsuit related to an illness. Anatomically, it refers to the liver/spleen/pancreas/gallbladder. As it relates to motor vehicles, it may represent an ambulance. For example, Ship + Stork + Tree = Medevac.

4. House – In a health reading, the House may refer to small health-related businesses such as a doctor's office, clinic, or treatment center. Anatomically, it stands for the bones of the skeleton and when near speaks of a strong and solid constitution. Because it was originally one of the "Tree" cards (*See Well-being for #5 Tree), it could somewhat offset the negativity of the Tree card when landing near the PSC as it's a card of security and a strong foundation. For example, Tree + House + Dog = Veterinary office.

5. Tree – It is the card of well-being and represents one's overall health as well as oxygen, vitamin C (fruit) and genetic disorders (family tree). Appearing near the PSC, it will indicate that some element of physical, mental, or spiritual health isn't at its full potential. In a general reading, falling with the House card, it refers to physical well-being; with the Stars, it will refer to spirituality; with the Clouds, it will relate to mental health. In a reading specifically about health, these cards have their own

health references. Tree with the Snake = Allopathic/conventional medicine, with the Ways = Alternative approaches, with the Clover = Herbal medicine, the Bouquet = Homeopathic or Bach Flower Remedies. Keep in mind that as with any specific small-spread question, the primary theme card does not have to show up as it is built into the question, so if we're asking about someone's health, the Tree card, in a small spread, doesn't always appear. If it does, it's needed to explain the flanking cards or it may reference one of its more specific meanings of oxygen or a genetic disorder that the other cards and context will explain. For example, Tree + Tower = Hospital.

6. Clouds – As always, the Clouds may refer to confusion or uncertainty in a health reading. Anatomically, it refers to the respiratory system including the lungs, trachea, chest, and bronchial tubes. It references breathing, airborne diseases, smoking, intoxication, air pollution, bronchitis, asthma, pneumonia, respiratory viruses and colds. With the Snake, it can refer to intestinal gas. With the Birds, it may indicate vision problems – add the Book and you need reading glasses. If the other cards indicate, it may refer to hidden addictions or mental illnesses. Any inhalation intoxications or respiratory diseases. For example, Tree + Garden + Clouds + Mice = Rhinoviruses, influenza viruses.

7. Snake – The standard meaning of the Snake may apply to treatments or diagnoses in a health reading. Being the card of deception, it may indicate false disease as in a false pregnancy (more common in animals) or imaginary disorders as with hypochondriacs (w/Clouds). Anatomically, it represents the lower gastrointestinal tract of the intestines, bowels, to the rectum; the umbilical cord, and vein problems such as spider veins. It may represent poison, worms/tapeworms, or dry skin. In the right context and with favorable cards, it may point to seeking an alternative approach. For example, Snake + Mountain = Constipation; Snake + Fish + Mice = Diarrhea; Bear + Snake + Ways (going a different way) + Scythe = Projectile vomiting.

8. In a health reading, it can refer to a loss of money or courage as well as health. It can indicate chronic illness, depression, severe headache, pain, fatigue, exhaustion, terminal disorders, or claustrophobia. Things that make you bedridden. Don't jump to a conclusion of death when you see this card in a health reading. It rarely indicates that. In my personal readings, the Ship, Stork, Stars, and Lily are generally involved when death is imminent. To claim that you see death is to play God and even with many cards pointing to death, I NEVER use that word as it will take away all hope and I've seen miraculous reversals happen. Instead, I may state that things look grim, recovery will be extremely difficult, things have taken a turn for the worse, etc. It ain't over till it's over! An MRI. For example, Tree + Mice + Coffin = Cancer. '

9. Bouquet – Always a great card to draw in a health reading, it represents the gift of recovery or healing. It may indicate flower essences or allergies. Anatomically, it represents the face, general appearance and coloring/pigmentation. It may recommend bringing flowers or any display of care and concern for another who's ill. For example, Tree + Bouquet + Fox = Cat allergy.

10. Scythe – Always a card that indicates danger, it's not one you want to see in a health reading. It can refer to surgery including laser surgery, injections, biopsies, fractures, accidents, stabbing pains, cuts, trauma, and surgical tools. For example, Garden + Clouds + Scythe = Flu vaccine; Mice + Scythe = Dental extraction.

11. Whip – The Whip generally refers to recurring health conditions that you're fighting, relapses, fever, and back-and-forth pain. It can signify inflammation, which is the body's localized reaction to tissue irritation, fever, infections, muscle aches (especially from overuse), stiffness, or stretch marks; rheumatic disorders such as Osteoarthritis, Fibromyalgia, or Lupus; hoarseness or stuttering, OCD. Male fertility (female is Moon). It may refer to a medical dispute that the client will have to fight. It's more serious if found with the Tree near the PSC. Anatom-

ically, it relates to the muscles as well as the throat and vocal chords. With Clouds, it can indicate addictions that will be further explained by the other cards such as Fish for alcoholism or bulimia, or Snake for a drug addiction. For example, Mountain + Whip = Arthritis; Man + Whip + Mountain = Male infertility.

12. Birds – The Birds brings transitory stresses, tension, and agitation to a health reading. It may indicate hyperactivity, impulsivity, or ADHD. Anatomically, it represents the nervous system and the eyes (think of bird's eye or hawk-eye). With the Sun it may indicate hot flashes, with the Heart it may indicate high-blood pressure (low blood pressure is Heart + Stars). For example, Tree + Birds = Vision problems such as myopia. Add Book and you need reading glasses.

13. Child – Generally, it will indicate a disease or ailment that is in the early stages as well as just starting a new treatment or medication. It may refer to childhood diseases such as measles or chickenpox, things that decrease in size such as rashes or tumors, congenital disorders, dwarfism or growth issues, or diseases that manifest as a return to child-like behavior such as dementia. Anatomically, it refers to the immune system. For example, Tree + Book + Child = Dementia; Tree + Child + Stars = Diaper rash.

14. Fox – As with any reading, the Fox indicates that people or situations are misleading or intending to manipulate you in some way. Proceed with caution and get a second opinion if possible. The Fox may indicate a misdiagnosis or an ailment that is masked by another. This card may infer issues with medical deontology. Anatomically, it stands for the nose and sense of smell. Because it's the card for the cat, it may refer to toxoplasmosis or with the Bouquet, a cat allergy. For example, Fox + Scythe = A broken nose.

15. Bear – In a health reading, the Bear will offer its usual strength, support, and courage. As a person, it may signify a strong and helpful woman who will play an important role in the reading, be it a doctor, nurse,

mother, or grandmother. It can reference obesity issues, sleep patterns, or your own strength to fight a disease or illness. Anatomically, it stands for the stomach and hair. For example, Heart + Birds + Bear = High blood pressure due to obesity.

16. Stars – It's an overall healing card as it's a card of hope and success. Anatomically, it refers to the cells, the skin/pores, pills or tablets (w/ Snake = Allopathic or Bouquet = Homeopathic). As it relates to the skin, it can indicate anything from rashes, rosacea, acne, moles, psoriasis, eczema, candidiasis, herpes, shingles to measles or dermatitis herpetiformis (a sign of Celiac disease). For example, Tree + Rider + Stars = Athlete's foot; Stars + Mountain = Clogged pores.

17. Stork – In a health reading, the Stork refers to change, which will require other cards to elaborate on. If it's with all neutral cards, you can expect some improvement in the condition asked about. It may refer to pregnancy and all that's related to it. Anatomically, it stands for weak limbs – both the legs and knees as well as the elbows. In determining pregnancy in a reading, my general rule is that I need to see the Child card nearby. Add the Birds and there's nervous talk about it or possibly a premature announcement. With the Letter, there is a confirmed birth announcement. For example, Tree + Stork + Whip = Tennis elbow; Child + Stork + Scythe = Cesarean section.

18. Dog – As a card of someone who's helpful and supporting, the Dog can refer to anyone who provides assistance and care during an illness. Anatomically, the Dog refers to the ears as well as the tongue/mouth/breath. For example, Tree + Dog + Mice = Ear infection; while Dog + Mice = Hearing loss.

19. Tower – Because the Tower refers to longevity, where it lands will have great impact. If it lands next to the Tree, it indicates a long-term health condition. Landing near the PSC in a health reading and far from the Tree, it indicates long life expectancy. It may indicate health related buildings such as hospitals and medical universities. It's my quarantine

card. Anatomically, it references the spine and neck. For example, Tree + Tower + Dog = Veterinary hospital.

20. Garden – Being the card of people, it may refer to any group of people who play a role in a health reading. It's one of the traditional "tree" cards, so you want it close to the Tree as it shows there will be support. It's the card of contagion, public diseases and infections, and pandemics. It's connection to fruit (Garden of Eden) says that it may refer to a need for more fruit, vitamin C, or an allergy. It may indicate recovery through fresh air, rest, relaxation. A spa or retreat. For example, Tree + Garden = Patients; Tree + Tower + Garden = Hospital staff.

21. Mountain – The Mountain is a card of blockages and obstacles, so this can pertain to the treatment of a disease as well as the disease itself. It refers to blockages in the body such as constipation, large swellings such as tumors, abscesses, hemorrhoids, are any abnormal growths. It can also indicate hardening, stiffening, or compression, so consider hardened or blocked arteries, arthritis or rheumatism. It may also refer to any type of resistance in the body. Anatomically, it stands for the head, skull, and breasts. For example, Whip + Mountain = Muscle stiffness; Snake + Mountain = Constipation; Snake + Stars + Mountain = Medication resistance.

22. Ways – As the card of alternatives and choices, it may refer to a need to make an important choice regarding an illness. It's another "tree" card and with favorable surrounding cards, it can indicate having options or it may suggest alternative health care or getting a second opinion. Anatomically, it stands for the lymphatic system, veins, arteries and all transport pathways in the body in general. For example, Coffin + Ways + Clover + Sun = Choosing a holistic treatment leads to a brilliant recovery.

23. Mice – As the card of loss and damage, this isn't a card you want to see in many health readings. While it's true that the Mice can gnaw away at something such as a tumor or indicate needed weight-loss (after

the Bear), there will still be a mess to clean-up such as side-effects or unhealthy end results. You'd need a card of success or healing following to show a truly positive result. The Mice card represents regrets, damage, and worries in general. It's the card of metabolism, deficiencies, nervous tics, decay, infections, parasites, bacteria, and viruses. Anatomically, it represents the teeth. For example, Mice + Scythe = Dental extraction; Clouds + Whip + Mice = Anorexia/bulimia.

24. Heart – The heart is the hardest working muscle in the body. It never stops! It's like an engine that never runs out of gas. The Heart card may refer to compassion and care received or given during an illness. Anatomically, the Heart card can represent the heart itself as well as the blood. For questions about specific health issues, it may indicate any cardiovascular disorders such as abnormal heart rhythms, congenital heart disease, aorta disease, heart valve disease, cardiomyopathy, pulmonary embolism, heart attack, or stroke. For example, Heart + Scythe = Heart attack; Tree + Tower + Scythe + Heart = Heart surgery; Heart + Birds = High blood pressure; Heart + Cross = low blood pressure.

25. Ring – In a health reading, the Ring can indicate a physical contract such as one for surgery or with a health care agency. It can also represent a commitment to taking care of one's health. It may show that more than one person or agency is working together regarding a treatment. With unfavorable cards, it may describe a condition that is chronic or cyclical. Anatomically, it represents the circulatory system (rings are circular). For example, Heart + Ring +Mountain = Atherosclerosis; Moon + Ring = Menstrual cycle; Stars + Whip + Ring = Eczema (Stars = Skin, Whip = Inflammation, Ring = Chronic)

26. Book – The Book can refer to yet undiagnosed health issues. It can also indicate a need to do research regarding a health condition or medical science in general. It may also refer to a mysterious illness that can't be diagnosed or can't be treated with conventional medicine. Anatomically, it refers to the brain, cognition and memory. As it's the card of the brain, there's also a connection to pain as this is where the pituitary gland resides which produces endorphins that reduce pain sensations as well as the fact that pain receptors travel from all parts of the body to the brain to produce the "ouch" sensation. Keep this in mind when you're looking for a determination of pain levels in a reading, especially for animals who can't tell us when they're in pain. For example, Book + Scythe = Brain trauma; Book + Mice = Dementia or Alzheimer's disease.

27. Letter – In a reading for health and well-being, the Letter references any health related correspondences such as appointments, prescriptions and test results. It can relate to literacy – to the ability to read and write. Anatomically, it refers to the hands and fingers because of the aspect of writing, typing, and texting. For example, Tree + Letter + Whip + Mountain = Carpal tunnel syndrome; Letter + Tree + Fish = A medical bill.

28. Man – In a health reading, #28 will represent the client, his partner, or the most important male in the reading. This might be a doctor, nurse, any healthcare worker or one who plays a significant role in the reading. It can also represent male sexual organs and hormones. For example, PC + Tree + Clover = Naturopath or Homeopath; PC + Tree + House = General practitioner; PC + Tree + Clouds = Lung specialist; PC + Tree + Bouquet = Plastic surgeon; PC + Tree + Child = Paediatrician; PC + Tree + Moon = Psychologist; PC + Tree + Fish = Dietician; PC + Tree + Scythe = Acupuncturist.

29. Woman – In a health reading, #29 will represent the client, her partner, or the most important female in the reading. This might be a doctor, nurse, any healthcare worker or one who plays a significant role in the reading. It can also represent female sexual organs and hormones. For example, PC + Tree + Clover = Naturopath or Homeopath; PC + Tree + House = General practitioner; PC + Tree + Clouds = Lung specialist; PC + Tree + Bouquet = Plastic surgeon; PC + Tree + Child = Paediatri-

cian; PC + Tree + Moon = Psychologist; PC + Tree + Fish = Dietician; PC + Tree + Scythe = Acupuncturist.

30. Lily – As the card of zen, it may suggest a calm and passive reaction to what's going on. This can be healing on many levels. It may indicate a more passive treatment as opposed to an aggressive one. As the card of virtue, it may recommend finding a mature and trustworthy care-giver. As the card of sexuality, it may connect to sexually-transmitted diseases (especially w/Moon or Whip). As the card of maturity, it may refer to ailments of age or elder care. As a slow card, it may indicate a slow recovery. As it relates to family, it may refer to hereditary disorders (especially w/Ship for inheritance or Tree for ancestors). As always, it's the correlation among the cards that will give you the answer. Anatomi-cally, it stands for the genitals and the endocrine system, which includes the thyroid and adrenal glands. For example, Moon + Lily + Mice = Chlamydia.

31. Sun – In a health reading, the Sun brings energy and success. It's certainly a card you want to see in a reading regarding recovery! It may refer to a need to gain clarity on the situation. Anatomically, it's my primary card for recovery and relates to our store of Vitamin D. It may also represent burns or burning sensations, dehydration (w/Fish), dry skin (w/Stars), heat stroke (w/Scythe), sun poisoning (w/Snake). In questions regarding diagnostics or treatment, it can refer to X-rays, CT scans, MRI, or radiation therapy. For example, Heart + Sun + Mice = Heartburn; Tree + Sun + Mice = Vitamin D deficiency.

32. Moon – In a health reading, the Moon may refer to a prominent hospi-tal or doctor. It may describe the patient's ideas of their illness and how it may be perceived by others, which may cause them to hide it. As the work card, it can represent health care careers or work-related diseases, injuries, or illnesses. As the card of the psyche, it can refer to the client's self-esteem or self-confidence. Anatomically, it stands for female hormones and menstrual cycles. For example, Tree + Woman +

Moon = Gynecologist; Woman + Moon + Scythe = Severe menstrual cramps.

33. Key – In a health reading, the Key can represent solutions/cures or diagnoses. Being a positive card, it will be a welcome sight! It infers that a solution has been or will be found and healing will take place. Anatomically, it refers to our store of vitamins, minerals, and trace elements including iron. For example, Tree + Key = A solution has been found.

34. Fish – In a health reading, the Fish can relate to finances, but also anything that adds value or enrichment to one's health or the treatment of a condition. It references fluid levels, fertility issues, or drug and alcohol issues. Anatomically, it refers to the urinary tract and the detoxifying organs: Kidneys, bladder, liver, spleen, gallbladder. As the card of liquids, it can indicate blood, sperm, urine or stool, sweat, or gastric juices. For example, Bear + Mice + Fish = Nervous diarrhea; Lady + Stars + Moon + Fish = Menopausal night sweats.

35. Anchor – In a health reading, the Anchor brings hope to the reading and indicates that a treatment is safe or with favorable cards, that there will be a stable recovery. Anatomically, it stands for the hips, pelvis, and tailbone. For example, Tree + Anchor + Scythe = Broken hip; Tree + Key + Anchor = A safe treatment.

36. Cross – In a health reading, the Cross represents long-term suffering and a depletion of energy. It may indicate setbacks in healing or feelings of helplessness and a loss of hope. Anatomically, it refers to the arms and shoulders and intervertebral discs especially the lumbar region. For example, Tree + Tower + Cross = Long-term back pain; Cross + Scythe = Shoulder pain.

CHAKRA QUICK REFERENCE SHEET

1. Root/Muladhara - **HOUSE.** The Root Chakra is connected to our sense of safety and security. It's what keeps us grounded, practical, and of the earth as it relates to our basic needs while on the physical plane. It's the lowest Chakra that connects us to Mother Earth and gives us our practical sense of self as human beings. When it is healthy and open, it allows us to function comfortably in the world, feeling safe and secure, while receiving and offering practical and useful advice for daily living.

2. Sacral/Svadhisthana. **LILY.** This is the Chakra of our sensuality, our passions, how we relate to others, and how we express our creativity. It also relates to aspects of the Moon and Heart cards, but in choosing a primary card, I chose the Lily because of this Chakra's primary relationship to sensuality and the pleasure we gain from relating to those we are closest to. When this Chakra is open and healthy, we are free to express ourselves creatively and passionately with no fear of being unique or different. It's very much a card of pleasure, satisfaction, and bliss in simply being ourselves while allowing those around us to do the same.

3. Solar Plexus/Manipura. **SUN.** This is the Chakra that relates to our personal power and how we're radiating it into the world. It's the center of our will, independence, confidence, standing up for ourselves, and taking control of our lives. When it is open and healthy, we're able to step out into the world and share our truth with no fear of being wrong. It allows us to courageously be who we were meant to be!

4. Heart/Anahata. **HEART.** Ah, the Heart Chakra! The center of love, compassion, and appreciation of beauty. It governs our emotions, our compassion, our ability to forgive ourselves and others, and our ability to allow ourselves to grieve or feel empathy for others. When it is open and healthy, we're able to feel deeply connected to the Earth and all its inhabitants in a truly peaceful and harmonious

way. It allows us to filter all truths, either sent or received, through a place of love. Without this Chakra in alignment, we cannot perform useful and accurate readings for others with any consistency. Opening this Chakra is the first step in communicating with animals and without it, we won't have their trust or cooperation.

5. Throat/Vishuddha. **LETTER.** The Throat Chakra governs communication and expression. It relates to all forms of communication, verbal, non-verbal, internal, and external. As the Chakra that connects our lower bodies to our heads, it allows us to take the ideas or revelations from our heads, combined with our creativity, passion, and will from our lower Chakras, and put them together into a tangible and expressible form to send out into the world. When it is open and healthy, we're able to express ourselves clearly and articulately and speak our truths without intimidation.

6. Third-Eye/Ajna. **KEY.** This Chakra governs our intuition, imagination, and foresight. It is the center of clairvoyance as well as clairaudience and all psychic abilities. As it falls between the Crown and Throat Chakras, it relates to our comprehension of stimuli and the perception of what we receive from our higher consciousness with the ability to intuit it correctly. When it is open and healthy, we're able to perceive - either externally or internally - all things as they truly are. We will see the answer in the cards. We will see the truth. As a born mystic, it is where I access this state. (I believe that mystics are naturally drawn to divination. Do an online search for "how to tell if I'm a mystic" and see if this describes you!) It allows us to clearly discern all that comes to us through the Crown Chakra (Stars).

7. Crown/Sahasrara. **STARS.** This is the Chakra that connects us to the Divine. It gives us access to higher states of consciousness, allowing us to leave behind all secular concerns and personal preoccupations. It is where we get in touch with the Universe. I guess you could call it our long-distance telecommunications carrier! When it is open and

healthy, we gain an awareness of the higher wisdom of the sacred. It's a connection to all that is, ever was, and ever will be. It's form-less, faceless, and limitless. It is here that we are free from all human limitations and gain full realization of Universal immutable realities.

ANIMAL COMMUNICATION WITH LENORMAND THE BASIC PROCEDURE

When it comes to card reading, animals are nothing more than vibrations. Humans are too, as is the chair I'm sitting on and the computer I'm typing on. These vibrations are caused by billions of kinetic electrons that contain a lot of empty space, but group together so tightly that they form the illusion of solid mass. What differentiates some masses from others is a level of consciousness, better known as the soul. While everyone agrees that humans possess consciousness, most everyone agrees that animals do, and now, more people are coming to believe that plants do too. This is all explained by quantum physics, but I prefer to see it as a magical world within our physical world. It is a world of energy, or better yet, stardust. I believe it is the world we connect to via divination.

So, if we're all composed of the same stuff, then it stands to reason (for me, anyway) that we are all connected and should be able to communicate with each other if we choose to do so.

Telepathic Animal Communication has no doubt been practiced for eons. While it is typically practiced without cards, relying completely on the communicator's mental and physical impressions, many animal communicators do incorporate cards into their readings (myself included!). Card readers can also choose to include animal readings in their practices and I hope that the information below will help to get you started.

Let's begin with the first steps of connection to source and connection to the animal you'll be reading.

Steps for connecting to animal energies:

1.   1. Relax, center, and ground yourself via earthing, breathing, visualization, or meditation. I always start with earthing followed by focused breathing, a countdown, and visualization. Earthing is an important part of animal communication. Here are some important things to consider:

A. If you want an animal to open up to you, you need to be in the correct state of mind. Level the playing field and place yourself and the animal on equal footing. Discard any condescending attitudes and know that animals are only here for a different purpose – they aren't less evolved or less intelligent in any way. Be open to hearing them and treat them with the same respect you give to the humans you read.

B. While animals are amazing spiritual teachers (horses are considered by many to be spirit guides on earth), for the most part, animals live at a more natural and basic level than humans. For this reason, you will want to slow down your thinking and contain scattered energy. I ground myself by standing on the earth with bare feet. If it's too cold, I put my hands in the soil of my houseplants as well as touching the plants and trees. I also soak my feet in sea salt or Epsom salts with a drop or two of my favorite essential oils.

C. BELIEVE! Trust is the very basis of this work. You have to remain open to any and all impressions that are received. Write them all down as they come. You'll soon discover that even the most far-fetched impressions will be valid.

2. Set your focus on your heart and visualize breathing through it and opening it up or expanding it. I visualize a door opening wide. You will now be "thinking" through your heart rather than your mind.

3. Connect to your source energy. This is optional as I know many readers who don't practice this, but I've never read an animal or human without doing this first. You can connect to God/Source/Universe/Divine energy, your ancestors, your spirit guides, animal guides, angels, or your higher self.

4. Set your intention for the connection and invite the animal to connect with you via your heart (you can picture a bridge, tunnel, or pathways) or invite them into your circle/aura.

5. Greet the animal and invite them to speak to you. Take note here of the impressions you get. Sometimes you'll get a sense that the animal is fearful and needs encouragement and other times the animal will appear bold, confident, and ready to talk! Yes, just as with humans, some animals are more open and communicative than others.

6. Record all the initial impressions that you get – and I mean everything! Feelings, thoughts, pictures, sounds, smells. Yes, some of these things will be your own, but experience will teach you the difference. In the beginning, simply share everything with the animal's human and ask if any of it has significance. You'll be amazed!

7. Focus on your first question as you shuffle or swoosh the pile of cards on the table. The communication begins!

8. At the end of the session, or when you feel the animal is leaving you, express gratitude for their cooperation and ALWAYS disconnect from them, leaving them with a sense of peace and safety.

Why use the cards at all?

- The cards will provide focus and will prompt thoughts, ideas, and knowings.
- I've personally found that using cards saves time and energy in my readings.
- The cards will provide a visual guide for your querent's as to what you're seeing and I've found that in face-to-face readings, the querent's will often study the images and add their own interpretations, which they really enjoy!

While Lenormand is my go-to for animal communication because of its simple images that lend themselves so easily to animal messages, there are a few other card systems I've found useful:

- Tarot – well, is there anything that Tarot can't be used for?
- Kipper – Lots of people and human situations work well for certain questions.
- Gypsy – Perfect for underlying themes.
- Grand Jeu Lenormand – Another system that is perfect for analyzing the human elements that pertain to an animal reading.

Card Steps:

1. 1. Decide upon your questions and write them down along with all the background information that you have been given.

2. 2. I next establish all my significators. This is a very important step as you're going to be dealing with humans as well as animals for these readings. For example, if you're reading for a family who has a husband, wife, children, and several pets, how will you differentiate between them all? You can look through your deck and assign the standard card emblems to the players as well as the court card insets. However, what I've found

through experience is that you will be taking too many cards out of play if you have many players to contend with. What I do instead, is take extra cards from another deck to represent the animal or animals I'm reading so I still have the animal-related card in play.

3. 3. For cold readings, I often start with a physical and personality trait spread to get a general feel for the animal. I'll go on to lay anything from a 3-card fan to a box to a GT to get all the information I need. This will depend on who I'm reading for and why.

4. 4. Lastly, I decide on the decks and spreads I'll be using and get everything ready before I connect to the animal/s.

Tips and Advice:

The best questions are those that are specific. Stay away from purely human concepts. Think more simply and more naturally – as an animal thinks. It's very important to separate questions that are from the owner's point of view and those of the animal. For example, in asking about the welfare and whereabouts of a missing cat, when I ask what the cat is doing now I may get birds, dogs, kids, trees, flowers, stars, sun … all the things in nature that the animal understands and notices. There's no way of telling if they're in danger, dead, or alive (yes - passed animals may show you the same images!). I've had great success in asking the cards specific questions such as: "Describe the current condition of the animal's physical body;" "Show me if the animal is currently lacking food/water/shelter;" "Show me the level of negative stress the animal is currently experiencing;" "Show me the level of joy/peace in the animal's life at this time;" "Show me what animals or humans are currently residing with the animal;" "Show me if the animal is currently residing in a human-built private home, a shelter, or outside;" "Show me the level of freedom the animal currently experiences;" so forth. You can see that these are not questions I'm asking the animal, but questions I'm asking the Universe on the animal's behalf.

Animal Communication Keywords

What you'll find here are some keywords for use with animal readings. Some of them pertain to the animals humans and some to the animals themselves. You'll find many locations listed here for missing animal readings. Add your own as you go!

1. Rider – Exercise, running/moving, fast, opportunities, enthusiastic, athletic, active, fit, energetic or curious personality, horses, something that arrives, agility, sports/competitions, houseguests, delivery person, visitors or visiting, messages from Spirit, a new pet, fast, feedback, legs/knees/ankles/hooves.

2. Clover – Something sudden and unexpected but usually good, herbs, eating grass, catnip, finding something, a gambler/risk-taker, take a chance/grab the opportunity, synchronicity, don't overlook the small things, nature, grab the opportunity, funny/comical, fun, short-term, green, short, small, easy-going, sociable, recovery, vitamins/minerals, a need for greens.

3. Ship – Movement, going further from home, new adventures, adventurous, riding in the car, a long-distance/far, lost while traveling, foreign/overseas, with Rider = Strangers at your home, to navigate, exploring, departure, farewell, Spirit transition to another realm, a wet place, garage, ocean, exotic or exotic looking, motion sickness, liver/spleen/pancreas/gallbladder.

4. House – Home, how safe they feel in their surroundings, those they live with, routine, safety, security, comfort, refuge, traditional, with Mice = Structural problems (for the kennel or barn), local, crate/pen if they love it, in someone's home, (playing card insert = Father), square, solid build/strong constitution.

5. Tree – Climbing trees, health, boredom, stuck (especially in a tree or in the woods), need for shade, a situation that will take a lot of time and energy, something is needed for well-being, forest, nature, houseplants,

physically unfit, grounded personality, a holistic approach taking body, mind, and spirit into account, grounding. (This card commonly shows up in thunderstorm phobia questions.)

6. Clouds – Unpredictable, moody, insecure, the situation is unclear, unstable, bad weather, confused, smoke, avoidance, something's brewing, clearing the air, moody, thunderstorm phobia, can't find their way home, it's there but you can't see it, a humid place, gray or multi-colored, hidden, lungs, breathing, airborne diseases.

7. Snake – Snakes, leashes/lead ropes/chains, ball of yarn, tangled, bloat/colic, intending harm to another, lies, feeling deceived, poison, competition/rival, temptation, elusive, rivalry, bitten or a biter, someplace slimy/slippery, stolen, in the bathroom, wants to be near grounded pipes (thunderstorm phobia), piercing eyes, pet tattoo, smooth movement, pacing/ambling gait, shrewd, will follow whoever has a treat/toy (knows how to get what they want), intestines, digestive issues (especially with the Bear).

8. Coffin – A box, down low, stuck, buried or burying objects, with Whip = a digger, needing sleep/rest, very ill, tired, chronic, loss, depression, crate/pen if they hate it, litter box (especially with Mice), stuck, finished, luggage/backpack (with Rider), tunnel, dark or black, in or near the bed, in a closet/drawer, left behind/forgotten (left for dead), tunnel (with Crossroads), in/down the toilet (with Fish, Anchor, or Ship), learned helplessness, claustrophobia.

9. Bouquet – Rewards, beauty, creativity, Bees/insects, flower garden/flowers, pollen/allergies, homeopathy/flower essences/essential oils/alternative or holistic care, pretty/attractive, polite/nice manners, charming, happy, receiving what they want, appearing innocent, well-groomed/a beautiful coat, preening (with Birds), surprises, a gift, attractive, beautify, being helped, a groomer (especially with Dog and/or Scythe), a celebration, Spring, brightly colored, smells great or needs freshening, recovery.

10. **10.** Scythe – Sharp objects, cuts/broken bones, a shock, sudden aggression, a biter/scratcher, difficult to handle, cautious temperament, break-up/split/rejection, danger, accident, grooming tools with blades/ nail clippers, dental issues (with Tree), verdict, a sudden event, battle wounds/scars, clippers (especially with Stars), shot/injection/vaccines, surgery, bold, impulsive, in the kitchen/workshop/laboratory, farm/ garden tools, in an area that needs mowing.

11. Whip – Discord in the home, repetitive fighting, tension, drama, verbally assertive/growling, discipline/harsh training or a need for discipline, humping or other bad habits, anger, abuse, painful and repetitive exercise, unintentional or repetitive mating, a trouble-maker, competition, OCD, literally a whip, broom, training or cleaning equipment, brushes, grooming tools without blades, sticks, fishing pole, belt, rubber band, near swings, crowded/heavy-traffic areas, the fight in fight-or-flight, throat/voice, hearing, recurring ailments. Shows up a lot in terrier spreads!

12. Birds – Birds, flying, crazy brain/can't settle down, too busy all day, hyper, a barker/whiner/loudly or annoyingly vocal, stressful, small troubles that will pass, distracted, flying/pestering insects, the flight in fight-or-flight, couple/pair/ partnership /littermates, nervous/fidgety, eyes.

13. Child – Play, toys, innocent, playful, young/small, fun, easy, kids, just starting, children, carefree, trusting, novel/new, inexperienced, naive, immature, pregnant (with Stork and/or Tree), amicable, playground, kid's room, youthful appearance, eager to please (typical Golden Retriever!), training by successive approximations (tiny increments repeated over and over until each one is grasped), training needs to be more fun – like play, growing pains (panosteitis).

14. Fox – Foxes and similar wild animals, cats, sneaky, wrongness, competition, distrustful, investigate, trickster, a hunter, use caution, consider what skills you need, outsmart, a trap, in the wrong place, opportunistically taken/moved, hidden, disguised as something else, orange or red,

facial mask, hungry, nose, illness masked by another condition, mange/ fleas/ticks (with Mice).

15. Bear – Overeating/feeding, will eat anything, resource-guarding, possessive, controlling, manage it, hair too long/shedding, with Bouquet = a beautiful thick coat or food allergies (will depend on the question and other cards), jealousy, bossy, a strong leader, territorial, overwhelming, nutrition, overly-protective, mothering, loves children, strong, a need to protect, manage the situation, still in your possession, brown, restaurant, dining room, kitchen, where you store things, stomach.

16. Stars – Night, spreading, future, wishes, computer, networking, sparkly/ shiny things, talents, focused, Spiritual (especially horses), guidance, you're on the right path/heading in the right direction, look beyond the everyday, an animal who's a dreamer/thinker, a positive influence on another, fireworks phobia, electricity, Internet, skin, freckles/spots, issues at night.

17. Stork – Change, moving/relocation, returning home, a new baby, house renovations, restless, needs a change, pregnant (with Child, Tree), advance, fly (playing card insert = mother), graceful, slender, up high/on top of something, stairs, elevator, marshlands, white, a jumper (horses), legs/mobility.

18. Dog – Dogs, loyal, friends, support, dependable, obedient, pet, guardian, trustworthy, clingy/dependent, helper/assistant, devotion, instinctive, brown, a pet area, friend's house, in the guest room, at the kennel/ shelter/training area, alert, mouth/teeth/tongue, veterinarian (with Tree/Scythe)

19. Tower – Apartment, office, legal, long-term, for a long time, tall/up high, boundaries, rules, feeling above others/aloof, animal shelter, dog warden/animal control, authority, large-scale, military, upstairs, monument, isolated, confined, introvert, a loner, likes to be in charge, longevity card – other cards will tell you if this refers to a strong constitution or long-lasting issues in a health reading, spine/long-backed.

20. Garden – Socializing, park, environment, others/friends/parties, outside, fresh air, open spaces, more room, celebrating, network, chat room, advertise (with Letter), in public/wherever people gather, in the country, common area, game room, near holiday items, extrovert/ sociable, openly postures, enjoys physical touch, outgoing, popular, with appropriate cards – veterinary hospital or contagious/zoonotic diseases, garden of Eden – that big park in the sky (often shows up as a final card for pets in Spirit).

21. Mountain – Isolation, big and looming, feeling cold, hard, enemy, obstacles, struggles, delay, feeling rejected, odds are against you, anything that gets in your way, stubborn, limitations, heavy, stuck, high, far away, cold, stone, gray or white, rugged, attic, a cooler, angular features, large head, large or deep-chested, skull.

22. Crossroads – Taking a different route, going for a walk, tough decision, going another way with something, branching out, alternatives, escape route, opportunity, driveway, intersection, hallway, on or near a road, exit, where road/river/rooms meet, sidewalk, indecisive, treatment alternatives, arteries/veins.

23. Mice – Chewing, fleas/ticks/parasites, with Heart = Heartworm, fearful, nervousness, stealing, hiding, litter box issues, soiling in the house, pack mentality, destructive behavior, weight loss, hungry/scavenging, annoying, loss, chaos, mistakes, kitchen, attic, basement or low places, grey, slum/ghetto, gutter, in the little nooks and crannies, dirty places, laboratory (rats/mice), with a "Metal" card = Machinery, stolen, if near and with SC – you'll get it back, squirrels/rodents/vermin, crooked or prominent teeth, nail biter (dogs), hair loss (w/Bear), panic disorder, mange/fleas/ticks (with Fox).

24. Heart – Love, attraction, affection, desire, closeness, emotions, a big heart, a need to open your heart/come out of your shell, sensitivity, contentment, enjoyment, blood, red or pink, warm, a favorite place, the master bedroom, the heart of the home, flirtatious with other animals, heart and circulatory system.

25. Ring – Relationship, spinning/going in circles/chasing tails, commitment, binding, valuable, coming full circle, agreement, contract, promise, jewelry box, dressing table, gold or yellow, metal, where precious objects are kept, where meetings take place/agreements are made, someplace you join, a members-only area, circular, things that cycle, binding objects (handcuffs), a noose, anything with a ring around it, bike/cyclist (with Rider), progressive illnesses, round body shape, wears bling, separation anxiety (followed by Mice).

26. Book – Hidden, secrets, unknown, mysterious, education/training/ learning, actual books, private, teachers/trainers, books, bookshelf, study or library, school, a quiet place, office, shelf, photo album, diary, computer/notebook/tablet, files, filing cabinet, a deck of cards, e-readers, museum, cultural center, a university town, well-trained, brain, undiagnosed health issues.

27. Letter – Records, paper-training, awards, tests, pedigree, proof/evidence, research, confirmation, letters, newspapers, emails, texts, office, desk (where you write), hands and fingers, post office, mailbox, archives, research places, paper, paper money, checks, records or files, pictures, posters or flyers, certificates, bonds, official documents, something sent, a good communicator, toes/paws, angular body, prescriptions.

28. Man – The man of the house, a new man, most important man, or another person in the situation when used as the partner card to the PSC. Masculine, logical, focused, active, proactive, dominant.

29. Woman – The lady of the house, a new woman, most important woman, or another person in the situation. Feminine, sensitive, passive, gentle, receptive, submissive.

30. Lily – Mature, calm, relaxed, satisfaction, family, ancestors (especially when with your spiritual card – mine is Stars though many use Tree),

older, wisdom, patience, retired, forgiveness, planned or intentional mating, white, cold, snowy, freezer or refrigerator, retirement community or nursing home, family room, spa, spiritual place, retreat, any place that uses a fleur-de-lis, grandparent's room, old, restful place, rest in peace (shows up in almost all my readings when asking if an animal is passed), heritage center, male reproductive health, devoted to pack/flock/herd.

31. Sun – Energy, bright, thinker, optimism, day, hot, successful, clarity, ego, dehydration, heat, fire, confidence, pride, sunny area, hot, fireplace, electrical source, heat source, oven, gold or yellow, Palomino, exposed, desert, dry, southern, south, bright, near a window, something growing, light bulb, battery/energy source, under bright lights, tanning booth (Sun + Coffin), in clear view, dehydration, sunburn, dry skin (w/Stars).

32. Moon – Night, howling at the moon, recognizing or honoring them, how they see you, famous, self-esteem, attraction, animals that like to be in the spotlight, dog/horse/cat shows (especially with Bouquet), bedroom, woman's room, silver, white, glimmer or glistening, famous/ renowned place, workplace, in the office, pillows, where the moon shines, round or moon-shaped, movie theatre, nightclub, Broadway, things that rise and set, monthly things, calendars, lens, magnifying glass, glasses (with Birds for eyes), photos or videos – captured images as seen through a lens (usually with Letter or Rider), female reproductive health, craves praise, proud appearance.

33. Key – Finding a solution, opening a door, lock it up, unlock a door, yes, health diagnosis, security, safe place, a safe, locked, security, door, doorway, gate, anything with a lock, diary (Book + Key), metal, silver/ grey/bronze/gold, lockbox, important area, central hub, security system, keys, keychain (with Snake), confident, a leader, problem-solver, tests/ diagnosis.

34. Fish – Fish, swimming, easy-going/go with the flow, expensive, fertility, drinking more liquids, independent, indulgent, market place, busi-

ness, swimming pool, sea, near the coast, near water, lake area, river, shower, bathroom, sink, laundry room, any place wet, kitchen, bar, island, where we keep our money, bank, aquarium, sushi bar, blue, fishing trip, seafood, stock market, where you keep drinks, retail locations, deep, flowing freely, urinary system, hoarding (with inauspicious cards such as Mice and Whip).

35. Anchor – Safety, being centered, not swayed, reaching goals, being secure/anchored, consistent, hopeful of success, hard-working, heavy, base, harbor, port, pier, (near water and/or boats), on the ground, basement, low, heavy, metal-large, blue (along with #34 and #3), something that holds something in place, something that is or was dropped, related to commerce/trade, ocean, naval-related, ball and chain, a hook, weights, paperweight, secure, grounded, happy to stay in its own territory, hips, pelvis.

36. Cross – Burdens, heavy, feeling stuck, pain, suffering, guilt (for humans – not an animal emotion), a difficult period, something that can't be avoided, Church, holy place, sacred place, altar, in a hard-to-reach location, heavy, painful, at an intersection, wood, sacred site, pilgrimage site, cathedral town, place of worship, spiritual retreat center. Thrown away accidentally (you have to live with it – you did it!), serious, burdened, pain, depleted energy, lower back.

MISSING OR LOST OBJECTS, PEOPLE, ANIMALS

The biggest mistake that I used to make when trying to locate a missing object was asking only one question. If I found the missing object after the first question, good for me! But, unfortunately, that's not the way it usually went. What often happened is that I laid the cards and looked at them like I'd never seen them before and wondered what on earth they were trying to say. So, the method I've devised has worked out well for me and I hope it helps you too! I begin by asking these questions:

1. Is it still in my possession?
2. Show me how it went missing.
3. Show me if it is inside or outside.
4. Was it lost/taken/removed by accident?
5. Was it removed due to foul play?
6. If in the house, what floor is it on?
7. Describe the room it's in.
8. Will I get it back?

I then choose a spread.

Spread ideas:

- Lay a box asking for a description of where it is now. I'd do this after determining that it's still in my possession and if it's inside, outside, at work, in the car, etc. All cards would be read as descriptors.

- If you know it's inside the home, lay a box envisioning your house asking in what part of the house it is. Is it high or low? Central or perimeter? Don't forget which cards indicate cardinal directions.

- Lay a PPF box to see how it went missing (past), where it is right now or what you can do now to get it back (present), and will you get it back and how long it will take (future).

- Lay a GT after assigning a card to the missing object. Look for connections to cards and houses such as your own card, House, Stork, Mice, or any cards you've assigned to those whom you think may have borrowed or taken the object.

Some missing object keywords:

1. Rider – Still arriving, in transit, near the entrance, ground level, in the barn, near the bike or motorcycle, on the road, where you exercise.

2. Clover – You overlooked it, out in the open – you walked right by it, in the grass, near herbs, near houseplants, low down, near something green, where you gamble, with the lottery tickets, near charms or trinkets, in a bargain store, flea market, yard sale.

3. Ship – In or around the car, on the plane or ship, garage, far away, near imported objects, in a wet place (bathroom, laundry), near water, lost while traveling.

4. House – Home (see card following to determine which room), small business/office/building, someplace safe, retail business, website, apartment, near anything related to real estate, in a square object.

5. Tree – Health center, medicine cabinet, in the woods, under a tree, at the doctor's office, in a shady spot, near a picture or object with a tree, near a large houseplant, green, wooden.

6. Clouds – Hidden in a closet, pocket, cabinet, mixed in with other things, near smoke, pollution, perfume, incense, humidifier or a humid place, in a grey room or near grey, near your pillows or cushions.

7. Snake – Pipes, wires, tubes, rope, down the drain, with a chain or bracelet, on the shortcut/detour/scenic route, near the river, winding path, on the roller coaster, fell into something, rolled up in something, tangled, dragging behind something, stolen, bathroom, green, slippery, long and curvy, with the dog leashes or horse lead ropes.

8. Coffin – In a box or container with a lid, low place – basement or floor, buried, in or under the bed, in the closet or drawer, luggage, forgotten or left behind (left for dead), in the garbage, in an empty space, the exit, dark place, down the toilet, tunnel, graveyard, near cremated remains.

9. Bouquet – At the beauty salon, near make-up or hair products, with gifts or awards, near flowers, with art and craft supplies, near a mirror, cosmetic drawer, with perfume or essential oils, given to someone, flowering-up or making it look like you're innocent.

10. Scythe – Dropped suddenly, broken, with knives/scissors/sharp objects, in the kitchen, toolbox, workshop, laboratory, with farm equipment/gardening tools, near the lawnmower, needles/razors/letter opener, out in the tall grass (an area that needs mowing).

11. Whip – Where you already looked, where you had an argument, a busy heavy-traffic area, with your kinky sex toys (LOL), at the gym, with the training equipment (horse, dog, etc.), with the cleaning equipment, crowded places, with belts, fishing rods, near the swing, rubber bands.

12. Birds – Near birdseed/feeders, pictures of figurines of birds, small feathers, near the phone or computer, between two things, lost while distracted while running errands, near music players or instruments, with Letter can show your sheet music.

13. Child – In the kid's room, with children's items, child has it, used for some sort of play, (*in a new place you haven't checked*), with something young, small, new, with toys, playground, school.

14. Fox – Hidden, stolen, disguised as something else, in the wrong place, opportunistically moved by (see following card), at the police station, with something red, near the cat or similar animal.

15. Bear – Still in your possession, large room, a hairy spot, dining room, restaurant, kitchen, wallet/safe/purse/a place where you protect your stuff, at the bank (with Fish), in a brown place, with your Teddy bear.

16. Stars – Near the Internet, near electrical items, up high, in the attic, with a lot of small and similar items, spread out, in clear view, against something of the same color, North, in a white area, near electricity, stuck to something with static cling (how I found my missing sock!), with Maps or GPS, near astrology items, with spiritual or divination items, where you look at the stars, with fireworks, with sparkly items, glitter, with crystals (especially with Mountain).

17. Stork – Near infant items/diapers, lost when moving, with your "change" (with Fish or Bear), it's been moved, where you changed your clothes, up high, on top of something, chimney, stairs, elevator, near marshlands, with your pantyhose, someplace white, large feathers.

18. Dog – With the dog's items, a pet area, the dog took it, at your friend's house/car (see following card), with stuffed animals/dog pictures or figurines, where you entertain/socialize, in the guest room, at the kennel/shelter/training area, brown place, someplace where you spend a lot of time, a colleague has it.

19. Tower – At the office, apartment/condo, government building, elevator, escalator, up high, a tall place, attic, school/university, at the mall, at a monument, upper floor, upstairs, town center/capital, high shelf,

balcony, military facility, legal office/building, in a grey place, urban area, isolated.

20. Garden – Outside, at the park, in a common area, near shrubbery, green, plants, where people gather, public areas, golf course, stadium, theaters, suburbs, meeting places, resort, garden center, in the country, in the game room, someplace green, near a window, in the yard, at a party or holiday spot or near such items.

21. Mountain – High, far away, cold, stone, roof, snowy/icy, refrigerator, isolated, a cooler, a rugged place, hilly, grey, stuck somewhere/obstructed, heavy, attic, up against a wall.

22. Crossroads – A path, driveway, intersection, hallway, where two rooms meet, between two rivers, a fork (can be literal), where you make decisions – a voting booth, multiple-choice tests, on the road/highway, at the exit, sidewalk, stairway, near a road.

23. Mice – Kitchen, attic, basement or low places, grey, slum/ghetto, gutter, in the little nooks and crannies, dirty places, laboratory (rats/mice), with a "Metal" card = Machinery, stolen, if near and with SC – you'll get it back.

24. Heart – A favorite place, romantic place, red or pink, near blood, warm, central area, heart of the home, master bedroom.

25. Ring – Jewelry box, dressing table, gold or yellow, metal, where precious objects are kept, where meetings take place/agreements are made, someplace you join, a members-only area, circular, things that cycle, binding objects (handcuffs), a noose, anything with a ring around it.

26. Book – Books, bookshelf, study or library, school, a quiet place, office, shelf, photo album, diary, computer/notebook/tablet, files, filing cabinet, deck of cards, e-readers, museum, cultural center, a university town.

27. Letter – Letters, newspapers, emails, texts, office, desk (where you write), hands and fingers, post office, mailbox, archives, research places, paper,

paper money, checks, records or files, pictures, posters or flyers, certificates, bonds, official documents, something sent.

28. Man – N/A

29. Woman – N/A

30. Lily – White, cold, snowy, freezer or refrigerator, retirement or nursing home, family room, spa, spiritual place, retreat, any place that uses a fleur-de-lis, grandparent's room, old, restful place, heritage center.

31. Sun – Sunny area, hot, fireplace, electrical source, heat source, oven, gold or yellow, exposed, desert, dry, southern, south, bright, near a window, something growing, light bulb, battery/energy source, under bright lights, tanning booth (Sun + Coffin), in clear view, things that rise and set.

32. Moon – Bedroom, woman's room, silver, white, glimmer or glistening, famous/renowned place, workplace, in the office, pillows, where the moon shines, round or moon-shaped, movie theater, nightclub, Broadway, things that rise and set, monthly things, calendars, lens, magnifying glass, glasses (with Birds for eyes).

33. Key – Key, key card, keychain (#7 + #33), lock, password or passcode, safe place, a safe, locked, security, door, doorway, gate, anything with a lock, diary (Book + Key), metal, silver/grey/bronze/gold, lockbox, important area, central hub, security system.

34. Fish – Marketplace, business, swimming pool, sea, near coast, near water, lake area, river, shower, bathroom, sink, laundry room, any place wet, kitchen, bar, island, where we keep our money, bank, aquarium, sushi bar, blue, fishing trip, seafood, stock market, where you keep drinks, retail locations, deep, flowing freely.

35. Anchor – Base, harbor, port, pier, (near water and/or boats), on the ground, basement, low, heavy, metal-large, blue (along with #34 and #3), something that holds something in place, related to commerce/trade, naval-related, ball and chain, a hook, weights, paperweight.

36. Cross – Church, holy place, sacred place, altar, in a hard-to-reach location, something related to your lower back, heavy, painful, at an intersection, wood, sacred site, pilgrimage site, cathedral town, place of worship, spiritual retreat center. Thrown away accidentally (you have to live with it – you did it!).

A fun exercise to try:

Have someone hide an object for you. This can be a friend that will hide it somewhere in their home, somewhere on their property, or in their local vicinity. You can also ask someone in your home to hide an object for you. Here's an example:

I asked my husband to hide one of my crystal angels in the house. So, in this case, I knew the object was still in my possession and somewhere inside my home. I laid a box spread and this is what I read: I saw that the Angel was in the basement (House + Anchor told me inside and low), not clearly visible (Clouds), centrally located and in a warm spot (Heart), with many similar items (Stars), where we change out of our outside cloths (Stork), where the keys (Key), training items (Whip), and leashes (Snake) are kept. My husband watched as I walked right to it! Give it a try. It may take some practice before you get good at it. Practice makes perfect!

BABY STEPS TOWARD GRAND TABLEAU MASTERY

L et's give a Grand Tableau (GT) a try, the easy way! Here are some steps to get you started.

1. Decide on which layout you want to use. The most common is the 8x4+4 but many use the 9x I primarily use the former only because it's what my original teacher, Bjorn Meuris, used. I've now memorized the house positions through repetitive use, so I tend to stick with it. You'll find that you become very comfortable looking at the same layout over and over and a change can upset the apple cart, at least early on in your practice.

2. Be sure that you have enough table space to accommodate the size of the deck you'll be using. I primarily use mini decks for my GT's so that I can easily lay them in small spaces. I can then easily fit one on a folding snack table and place it next to my chair. This way I can type while looking at it so that my concentration isn't broken by taking my eyes off it.

3. Look through your deck first and be sure that you have only 36 cards with one #28 and one #29 that are facing each other. This is important now as so many new decks contain alternate and extra cards. I can't tell you how many times I laid out a GT in a hurry only to discover that I had no people cards and three dogs!

4.   Choose a house layout format. The reading mats that I use can be purchased online and you'll find the information in the appendix. If you're a creative type, you can create your own with some poster board or even taping blank pieces of paper together to give you the right size. Use a pen and ruler to draw the squares and write in the names. Remember that you want the card name and number at the top or the bottom and the squares need to be slightly larger than the cards you'll be using so that you can easily see the name of the house without moving the cards on top. You can also lay out a GT without a house board and simply count. For example, if you lay an 8x4+4, you know that each row is a count of 8, so the first cards are 1, 9, 17, and 25 and the end cards are always 8, 16, 24, and With enough practice, you'll automatically know all the position numbers without much thought. Another option is to use two decks. If one is larger than the other, it's perfect for the houses. Also, any deck that has the card name and number printed at the top or bottom will be perfect for houses. Under the Roses Lenormand by Kendra Hurteau and Katrina Hill is such a deck. Lay out the house deck in order 1-36 as the houses and you'll then lay the drawn cards on top.

5.   If you know that you'll become card-blind by staring at all the cards in front of you, you can use blank pieces of paper or index cards to cover any areas that you aren't looking at the moment. You can also turn cards upside down and only keep those that you're considering face-up.

6.   Start with only one question rather than attempting to read an entire life story. For example, you can simply ask about the progression of a couple's relationship over the next month and then lay a GT where every card presents the possibility of answering that question, and only that question. So, cards that can be used to relate to specific themes such as health or work such as the Ring, Moon, Anchor, Tree, Dog, Child, will only relate to the theme of the relationship.

7.   You can get comfortable with GTs by using them for weekly draws for yourself. In this case, you'll ask the cards for your week ahead and set

your intention to only read the cards touching your card and your line of sight (your row). In this case, you can easily cover or turn over all other cards.

8.   Start practicing with my "How Am I Doing" GT.

9.   Keep in mind that not every card will be read. Because you're using the entire deck, the cards have no choice but to appear. It will be the positions and connections among the relevant cards that will give you your information.

10. Be sure that you know who your people cards will represent before you begin. For example, if you're single and have no significant other person in your life at the moment, the partner card can represent the most significant person impacting any part of your life such as someone at work or even your closest friend, a parent, or even your masculine or feminine side. You may choose to use the partner card in this way for specific questions regardless of whether or not you have a physical partner if you set your intention beforehand to do so.

11. Know your theme cards. Decide which will be your primary work card, family card, sex card, or school card. If you have more than one child or pet, assign cards to them from the list under the theme section or by using the court insets.

12. Decide on a time frame for the spread.

13. PLAY! I LOVE playing with my cards! And, I do mean playing – not asking the cards if your boyfriend is cheating on you! I'm sorry but that's not playing no matter how you phrase the question (unless you don't give a flying fig!). One of my favorite techniques is to lay a general GT for any topic that has nothing to do with me. Something where I will be completely neutral and under no pressure. When I'm playing, I generally snoop on my neighbor's pets, ask about movies I haven't seen yet or books I've yet to read. If you want a topic that will provide immediate feedback, you can search for news stories from the past. I performed

an online search one day for "top news stories of the 20th century" and got some great ideas for practice GTs. All the stories were old enough and famous enough that I could easily verify any information I saw in the cards. I simply chose the stories that I wasn't already familiar with. Another option is to lay GT's for the outcome of upcoming sporting events. Use the people cards to represent the two teams.

14. When you aren't playing but are looking for specific information, have a plan. Don't make the mistake of laying all the cards to just see what jumps out at you as you can do when you are playing. Consider what your purpose is in laying the spread. Do you have a client who's asking about their career, health, and relationship? Then, your plan will be to focus on those three areas by establishing in your mind which cards represent your primary work, health, and relationship cards and then focusing your attention on where they fall in relation to the client's cards and what cards fall around them. You can follow that with chaining, knighting, or any other technique that you want to try such as mirroring or counting rounds. You'll find that with practice you'll quickly be able to determine if a method will be useful or not. For example, I sometimes begin a counting round but immediately see that it isn't going to lead me in the right direction, so I discard it. Are you laying a GT for a mediumship reading? Then, it will be an all-past reading and you can set your intention for the fate line to describe the reason for their passing if that's a question that's being asked or a message from the deceased loved-one. Are you laying the spread to see how a possible career change or a move to another country will play out? That's an all-future spread and all cards will relate to that topic. Is the GT for the progression of a new relationship? You can choose a present into the future spread or a PPF. PPF spreads can be useful if you're concerned about baggage or relationships from either partner's pasts coming into play.

GRAND TABLEAU (GT) STEPS

When I read a GT, I see the general flow of the story as following the house numbers, so it goes from top to bottom, left to right, 1-36. (See Lenormand: The Game of Life.) A Grand Tableau uses the entire deck and as such will touch upon all life areas. Originally, it was used with no single question and was used to show a snapshot of someone's present life and where it was leading. I began using the GT to answer specific questions in 2019 – something I thought I brilliantly invented – but, in reality, I'm quite sure that others were doing it as well. I'm not quite sure why I could find no mention of it anywhere. It's perfect when you have a single area to look at such as a career or a personal relationship as you'll get a complete story with one lay of the cards.

I want you to look at a GT in the same way you look at a roadmap for an entire State or region. You'll see so many roads that your head will spin unless you focus only on where you're starting and where you want to wind up. The GT is no different. Don't be distracted by all the cards in front of you. Simply look for the relevant ones, how they're connected to your PSC, and where they are heading.

So, do you need a specific question for a GT? No.

Can you lay a GT for a specific question? Yes.

Always remember to set some sort of time frame before laying the cards. This can be as general or specific as you'd like. For example, I may simply ask to see how an aspect of someone's life will play out through the year without breaking the spread down into specific months or I may lay a 9x4 for the next 9 months when someone finds out that they're pregnant. In the case of the latter, we can look at each column as a specific month.

Fate Line:

Because I rarely see anything in life as a set-in-stone, the fate line is simply the end of the story as it contains card #33, the Key, for solutions, card #34, the Fish for abundance, card #35, the Anchor for reaching your goals, and card #36, the Cross for the burdens you'll endure and how you'll deal with them. I've already used it as an advice line, but prefer to use oracle cards for advice outside of the GT. On occasion, I view it as a "most likely to happen" type of fate. In other words, this is what will most likely play out unless you make changes that the warning cards will indicate.

I may use it to show things that are already set in motion, which will be difficult but not impossible to change.

Directional Reading:

Some readers choose to read their GTs directionally. This is based on the direction that the PSC faces. So, if the deck you're using has a Woman card facing left, you'd then read the entire spread from right to left. This is a technique I studied and mastered, though I later discarded simply because I don't like to read right to left! I adopted my own method where I always follow the flow of the story from left to right, regardless of the direction the PSC card faces. I do give consideration to the card/cards the PSC is facing and whether or not they are facing the partner card, if applicable, but the flow of the reading is still moving from left to right, top to bottom.

Houses:

It may help you to look at houses as spread placements in Tarot. The houses, just as Tarot spread placements, ask a question and the cards that fall in them answer it. To form the houses for a GT, you simply lay the cards out in order from 1 to 36. The most common configurations are the 9x4 and the 8x4+4. You can also lay the cards in a 6x6 format, if you prefer. There are also Petite Tableaus and you'll find one in my "Signature Spreads" section.

Houses retain the primary meanings of the cards. The only time I don't use them in a GT is when I'm laying a traditional MOD GT. I think the most important thing to know about houses is that they will always be considered as secondary or supporting information to the cards that fall naturally. Consider the fact that the houses are stationary and their positions will never change. Therefore, the Rider will always be in the first position and the Cross will always be the final house. The cards that fall in them will therefore hold the greatest importance and should be considered first and foremost.

So, you'll consider where your drawn cards fall, what groupings or clusters of cards form, and the connections between them before you add the influence of the houses. Not every house will be important just as not every card that's drawn is read.

Now that you know that the cards drawn are primary, you can view the houses as the backdrop of the story. If it helps in your understanding, see the houses as actual houses or locations that you may visit. In this case, the house of the House will be your own home. The card that falls here will show what is currently happening or influencing your home or personal life.

For example: I just drew the Book for a house and the Garden for the random card. How appropriate! We have the card of secrets and being "closed" for a house with the card of openness or "coming out" falling in it. As Book is the house of knowledge and secrets, the Garden falling in it might indicate an opening up of secrets, unknown information about your social group, information about a party you'll be attending, learning about your environment, etc.

What information the houses provide:

- A house may modify the card that falls in it when that card is a theme card. For example, if the Letter falls in the house of Mice, the message will be one of losses or something being gnawed away.
- Cards falling in their own houses are intensified or emphasized, so pay special attention to them. I also pay special attention to what I call criss-crossed houses where a card lands in a house and that house's card lands in the house of the other card. For example, the Rider lands in Clover and Clover lands in Rider. Again, this emphasises or strengthens the message.

- The house may show where the action of the falling card is taking place. So, if Mountain falls in the house of House, the enemy is within your four walls as opposed to the Mountain falling in the house of Garden, which shows that the enemy is still in your environment but not as close as in your own house. Or, if you're planning a wedding and asking where to hold the reception, the Garden card landing in the house of House would suggest having it at home or a private location.

- Houses give us our chains! You can't follow a chain without houses. If the Fox falls in the house of Book, to follow a chain we need to look either at the house of Fox or the house that the Book card lands in.

Chaining:

I perform chaining in every GT. It's the basis for my connect-the-dots method. When you chain, you're connecting a string of cards based on the houses they fall in. Select a starting point. For example, if you're asking about the possibility of moving house, you may select the Stork. You find that it lands in the house of Mountain. You'll now look for the Mountain card and see what house it falls in. It lands in the house of Fish. You then look for the Fish card and find that it falls in the house of Scythe. You're now seeing that finances will be a problem and it's most likely not the right time to consider moving. You'll add this information to that which you receive from reading the cards touching the Stork card. I continue to follow any chain until I feel a break.

Mirroring:

Mirroring is also called reflection and can be done vertically, horizontally, or diagonally. Remembering the flow of energy from left to right and top to bottom, mirroring will give you pairs of cards that reflect each other and give you a cause and effect relationship. To understand which cards to mirror, simply imagine folding the GT in half, either vertically or horizontally, though many also read diagonal mirrors where you'd imagine folding the GT diagonally. In an 8x4+4, looking at the horizontal mirrors, card 8 will mirror card 1. Card 7 will mirror card 2 and so on. In looking at the vertical mirrors, card 25 will mirror 1 and card 32 will mirror 8, and so on. Personally, I don't always mirror – other than the four corners – but if it's something that resonates with you, it may become a favorite technique. I do, however, use the method of "the fours" described below when I just can't get enough information from all the other techniques. It's only through practice that you'll discover which methods you prefer and which you'll forgo.

The Fours:

An additional mirroring technique that I learned from Iris Treppner is called, "the fours". Using this technique, you ignore the center column of the 9x4 or the fate line in the 8x4+4. What you'll notice in mirroring is that from any given card you can mirror it in three directions: Vertically, horizontally, and diagonally. What you wind up with is a group of four cards for each mirroring round. Using a 9x4 as an example, if you mirror card #1 with card #9 horizontally, #1 with #28 vertically, and #1 with #36 diagonally, you have a group of 4 cards to give you a story. When you work through the GT using this technique, you end up with eight groups of four cards that give you an additional story.

Knighting:

Knighting within a GT provides some "around the corner" information relating to any topic or theme cards you're looking at. It's a technique taken from chess, but it holds obvious value in reading a GT when you consider that a tableau is nothing more than a game board that is used as a map or puzzle where we look for paths that lead to answers and fit pieces of information together. You already know that there's a box of cards around any topic card that are all touching it and that these have the greatest impact or influence. If you then move out one layer to the next-bigger box around that topic card, you have influences that are impacting those cards that have the most influence. This is the next tier of consideration. When you knight from any SC, you are revealing the influences and results of that next tier.

How do you knight? You select a topic card and count out two spaces from any SC, and up and down or left and right one. You can do this in all directions. Some readers only consider knighting when it gives them two cards so that they have a pair to work with. I consider all knighted cards regardless of a pair. This is entirely up to you.

What's more important to consider when knighting is the direction you're moving in. Are you knighting in the past? Into the future? Into auspicious or inauspicious cards? Into the influencing cards or into the effect cards?

Counting Rounds:

Counting rounds truly fascinate me. I wish I had some brilliant explanation as to how they work, but I don't. I only know that they work for me every time I use them and as I've said before, I love leaving some element of magic in divination! What I'm referring to is how you can lay out the entire deck, choose a SC, count through the spread by a certain number, and get a group of cards that gives you an accurate story related to that SC. If you have a scientific explanation as to why this works, please keep it to yourself. I prefer some mystery!

According to Andy Boroveshengra, this was a common technique in reading tableaus of any card system prior to the twentieth century. You may choose to only perform a counting round from the PSC at the end of the reading for a final message. When you perform a counting round, you aren't gathering pairs of cards, but a group of cards that gives you a story. I perform counting rounds from any SC that I need more information on. The technique is a simple one. You decide what number you'll count by, start at the SC and count it as one, then move through the GT ending and beginning on the same card. Now, pull out or write down every 3rd, 5th, 7th, 9th, or 13th card. I always count by 7, which in a standard GT of 36 cards gives me a simple line of 5.

For example, if my client is asking about their child, I'll locate the Child card and after reading the cards around it, noting it's house and what falls in the house of Child, examining the connecting cards between the Child and the PSC as well as their distance and who's above or below, knighting from the Child, I can also perform a counting round from the Child card. This is my standard procedure when I want to gather every bit of information that I can from the GT.

My standard steps:

1. Locate the querent's card and partner if there is one.

2. Analyze where they are in relation to each other, directions faced, connecting cards.

3. The first three cards set the theme and tone of the reading. This is where the story begins.

4. Corner cards frame the reading. They tell you what the question or querent is up against. I read them first clockwise and then pair the diagonals.

5. I like to next see what card fell in the house of House. It tells me something about the nature of the querent's personal life. I then look to see where the House card landed. This will tell me what I can expect from this reading regarding what the querent is really looking for. In other words, what they want to bring into their lives or manifest.

6. The center four cards give us the heart of the reading.

7. I next read the box around the querent and partner. Because I naturally follow a flow from 1-36, I will see the card above a person card as an external influence and the card below as what they're bringing to the table or what is supporting them. The card behind is where they're coming from or what's motivating or pushing them. The card in front will show what they're moving toward or their next action. (See the section on "The Box Spread" for more details.)

8. Read the line of sight for the querent. This doesn't refer to the cards the person card is facing (for those decks that show a direction) but the entire row. I give the partner the column for their primary line. In this way, unless they are in the same row or column, they'll always have an intersecting point or points.

9. I now check knighted cards from querent, partner, and any theme cards. This will show me the indirect information related to the players and the themes. Knighting shows influences from above and motives or actions below.

10. I now start chaining houses and cards. For example, if my PSC falls in the house of Birds, what house does the Birds card fall in? What card falls in the house of the PSC? What I'm looking for are connections among these cards and I can take the chain as far as I'm inclined to. You'll sometimes find a crisscross here where the PSC falls in a house and the card of that house falls in the house of the PSC. This is an important correlation.

11. I perform a counting round.

12. I read the fate line. This is the end of the story – the bottom line – the summation – what's already set in motion. Just as with the exit card in the box spread, this shows you where it's all heading unless changes are made.

13. Check the proximity of relevant cards. What is near and what is far?

14. I look to see what is in Anchor and what is in Cross. How is the seeker doing in reaching their goals and what do they have to overcome to reach them?

15. I may check the diagonal lines through any relevant cards to show indirect influences from above and motives or actions below.

16. I may check the mirrored cards. Sometimes I'm drawn to a message from the mirrored cards as they can show cause and effect.

17. Timing: Go through and read each column according to the pre-se-
     lected time scale. Tie key cards into the cards before and after them, so
     spread out the interpretations from the columns themselves.

Consider the Game of Hope:

If you analyze the game, you'll find some helpful parallels that you can use
in your GT.

- What discord will you have? Check the card and house (c/h) of Whip.
  To find how to resolve the discord, check c/h of Child.

- What troubles will you have? Check Clouds c/h for what troubles
  you'll face. Check Clover c/h to find your luck and opportunities to
  deal with those troubles.

- What is driving you crazy? Check Fox c/h. The Fox forces you to hide
  in the forest (house of Tree), but that's where you go to recuperate.
  Check the Tree c/h as this indicates your well-being.

- The trio: Garden, Mountain, Ways. The Garden will show the reason
  for your current issue (it most likely came from outside of you). The
  Mountain shows your current obstacle in dealing with it. The Ways
  shows your options or the result of not making the right choice.

POSITION MEANINGS IN A GRAND TABLEAU

According to Lenormand historians such as Andy Boroveshengra and Bjorn
Meuris, the original GTs were all read for the present and future. Reading for
the past was conceived of later and has its own purposes. Many new readers
love a PPF GT as it's easy to decipher the positions to the left and right of the
PSC. That is, as long as the PSC doesn't fall in the first or last column. But a GT
without the past is just as easy once you know what those positions behind
the person mean. All positions are in relation to the primary significator card.

Cards left and right:

- For a past, present, and future (PPF) spread, all cards to the left of the PSC are the past, the column containing the PSC is the present, and all cards to the right are the future. The further away, the more distant.

- (My usual method) For standard GTs (present into the future), the cards to the left are weakened and the cards to the right are intensified, for good or bad. You can view this as the PSC is moving away from or ignoring the cards to the left while moving toward or putting their focus and energy on the cards to the right. So, the energy is moving from left to right just as it does with a PPF spread, but in this case you're getting more information about what's going on now and what will happen in the future. You can clearly see what will be easier (in front) and what will be harder (behind). You can clearly see what your client is facing head on (in front) and what they're ignoring, avoiding, or will simply take more effort to deal with (behind).

Cards left/behind = Past or inauspicious

Cards right/ahead = Future or auspicious

Cards above and below:

If you're familiar with Tarot and the four elements, you might choose to view the cards above a person card as relating to air and thoughts or ideas. The cards below a person card would then relate to earth and what one creates from the above cards.

I see the cards above as influencing and the cards below as the effects of those influences or what the client is standing on, what they control, what actions they take or intend to take, or what's supporting them. Just think about the weight of the cards above. You want your card to be weighing on others, not being weighed-on. Influences can be external and coming from outside of the SC or internal such as thoughts, ideas, and plans that haven't been put into motion yet or aren't yet finalized. The effects can be actions (intentional) or reactions (responses).

You can set an intention to view the above cards as conscious motivations and the cards below as unconscious motivations as you'd do in a smaller spread with vertical interactions. You can choose to see the above cards as thoughts and the below cards as feelings. As with any spread, you're the one who decides how it will be read which may vary depending on your purpose for laying those cards. I may do this if I'm laying a quick GT to see what's going on with someone. You can look at the cards above as exerting an impact, whereas the cards below receive that impact, counter it, or do something because of it. Cards above can be external forces and the cards below can be internal forces. Cards above can be what is controlling you and below is what you have control over.

Above = Influencing and weighing down. Thoughts/intentions.

Below = Supporting or under control. Actions/reactions. Feelings.

Diagonal Lines:

Checking the diagonals is perfect when you want to look at life out of the corners of your eyes to see it from a different perspective. Because the entire flow of energy in a GT is moving from left to right and from top to bottom, you need to follow the story in those directions. Cards in the same row (also called the line of sight) are the general themes of the forward movement of the story. The cards above are influencing or affecting that theme and the cards below show what effect or consequence results from those influences. It's the diagonals that give you bigger chunks – bigger leaps forward in the story as they skip many spaces. Diagonals are showing the major progression or development of the story. Remember what the cards above and below mean and what the cards behind and in front mean, and the diagonals then, will give you a broader perspective on what's happening.

Diagonals give great insight into what's influencing the seeker (what's coming toward them from above) and what those influences will lead to or what actions the seeker will take (the diagonal cards below). Note if your

PSC's diagonal line leads into the fate line as that will indicate that the seeker will influence this line.

As always the case, you want the PSC to fall as high as possible in the spread and in one of the first few columns. In reference to diagonals, fewer cards above equals fewer influences and more cards below equals more actions. Fewer cards behind equals fewer difficulties and more cards in front equals a greater number of easy/doable actions.

Diagonals = Influences from above hitting the SC and moving into consequences of those influences below.

The Fate Line:

This is a very interesting topic for me as it truly confused the hell out of me when I was a novice reader. What on earth is this line supposed to mean, anyway? Well, as I say for everything you do with cards, it is whatever you want it to be!

How do you view the idea of fate? Personally, I do believe that some things are fated but there's always a reason and when things happen to us that are beyond our control, they're always for our highest good, though it certainly may not seem that way at the moment. I do, however, feel that we have some element of control. Think of it this way, if you believe that something is fated and you do nothing, you may have missed an opportunity to make a change that would've proven that the situation wasn't meant to play out as it did. This reminds me of the story of the person who drowns in a flood because they did nothing but sit and pray to be saved. They missed several opportunities to accept help because they thought God was going to send them a miracle. When they got to heaven and asked God why he didn't save them, he said, "Well, I sent you help several times and you didn't take it!" So, whether or not I view something as fate, I'm not going to sit by passively unless I'm completely satisfied with where it's heading without my intervention.

I truly believe that we have so much more control over our lives than we realize. All of today's actions shape our tomorrows. Of course, there's an element of timing to consider here. Sometimes maybe we're too late to change the immediate future. (If this isn't a great reason to receive frequent card readings, I don't know what is!) When someone gets a reading and doesn't like what the outcome shows, they simply have to make changes now which will send the future in another direction. This is one of the reasons why not all predictions come to pass. Predictions show the most likely future according to the current trajectory. If anything changes along the way, the outcome will most likely change.

Why is there a fate line in an 8x4+4? If we consider that the earliest parlour sibyl decks contained only 32 cards, and the Lenormand deck was designed as a game to be played using a pair of dice – which doesn't work with a 32-space game board – the deck was given 36 cards. (Anthony Louis). The original game was laid out in a 6x6 format but cartomantic tableaus of 32 cards were laid out in an 8x4 pattern. With 36 cards, this was adjusted to an 8x4+4 or later, a 9x4.

Does a 9x4 contain a fate line? It does if you want it to! My research indicated that everyone who uses a 9x4 format chooses the center column of four as the fate line.

Ways to read a fate line:

- The fate line can be viewed as important events or situations that need to be focused on.
- Things that are set to happen, as in already set in motion, and will therefore be more difficult, but not impossible, to alter.
- It can show what will be out of the seeker's control. It's the bottom line and therefore everything is weighing down on it making these cards the heaviest or most difficult to manage.
- You can use this as an advice line. (See the section on extended tableaus for more ideas on this subject.)

- You can read it as the bottom line of the story or the last word. In this case, it isn't showing anything fated, simply what's important.
- You can simply read this line as the bottom row – nothing different. This is still the bottom row and will have all the other cards weighing down on it for better or worse (which is my go-to method).

All of these have to be determined before you lay the cards so that the cards will fall as they should.

Timing:

While all GT's should be given a general time frame, such as, the entire spread represents the next month or eight weeks, or eight months, you may want to break it into specific time periods. In this case, you'll break the columns into days, weeks, or most commonly, months. You'll begin by reading the entire GT as you would normally, and you'll finish the reading by analyzing the columns according to the time frame you decided upon.

HOUSE MEANINGS

1. Rider – Thoughts, messages/news, or people coming to you.

2. Clover – Sudden and short-term luck or opportunities.

3. Ship – Movement toward goals, travel, change. What is distant? Where are you heading?

4. House – Personal and inner life, home, family, and security.

5. Tree – Health and well-being. What is needed to thrive? How is the environment affecting your health or the situation? How is your health impacting the situation or how is the situation impacting your well-being? What needs help/time to grow?

6. Clouds – Troubles. What aren't you seeing clearly? Where are your fears and insecurities? What is creating confusion or uncertainty?

7. Snake – Complications, betrayal. Where are the complications? Who or what is betraying you? Where are the difficulties that may require a detour?

8. Coffin – Endings. This house often shows the greatest problem the seeker faces. What needs to die or is dying? What have you been or need to be suppressing/burying?

9. Bouquet – Happiness, beauty, surprises. What's blossoming or being offered?

10. Scythe – Danger and separation. Where is the danger? What is or needs to be cut out?

11. Whip – Discord, conflict, repetition, and intensity. Where are you struggling? Who's stirring up trouble?

12. Birds – Restlessness, chatter, gossip. What's upsetting you?

13. Child – What's fresh, new, or wondrous? What's small and just starting? Where do you need to trust/lighten-up? What's new? Children.

14. Fox – Falsehood and caution. What lands here is wrong or a call for action due to something being wrong.

15. Bear – Power, protection, strength. Who's in control or what are you in control of? How are you protecting what you have? Where is your power/strength?

16. Stars – Spirituality/divine guidance. What is taking shape/forming/spreading? What potential are you realizing? Where are you meant to go? Where will you find inspiration?

17. Stork – Change. Pregnancy, if applicable. What is or needs to be changed, relocated or improved?

18. Dog – Loyalty and devotion. Friends/supporters. What are you devoted to or who's devoted to you?

19. Tower – Anything related to government, associations, organizations, laws, all things official. What separates you from what you want? What is restricting you?

20. Garden/Park – Publicness and outer life. What's going on in your social life? How are others around you or your environment affecting the situation? In what way should you be connecting with others or opening up?

21. Mountain – Obstacles and challenges. What obstacles are in your way? What is being delayed? What enemies (literal or figurative) are causing adversity?

22. Ways/Crossroads – Decisions, choices, and altering your direction. The card that lands here will tell you about your decisions or describe your options.

23. Mice – Loss, erosion, nagging worries. What is decaying/eroding? What is causing you underlying anxiety? What is lost/missing/stolen?

24. Heart – Passions, desires, emotions, love. What brings your heart joy? Where is your desire? What or who do you love or desire?

25. Ring – Relationships, commitments, continuous cycles. What are you committed to? What continues? What's going on with your relationships/partnerships? What do you agree with?

26. Book – Knowledge and secrets. What is unknown? What are you about to or need to learn/find out? What is being hidden?

27. Letter – Communication, correspondence, words. What is or needs to be communicated? What correspondence is being sent or received? What is or should be put in writing?

28. Man – Male client or the other person. Masculinity can be chosen.

29. Woman – Female client or other person. Femininity can be chosen.

30. Lily – Satisfaction, zen, wisdom, experience, sexuality. What is or will bring satisfaction? Where can you find peace/what do you need for peace? What about your family harmony or sex life?

31. Sun – Energy, growth, confidence, success. Where should you put your energy? What will grow and flourish? What victories or successes can you expect regarding this situation?

32. Moon – Career, recognition, reputation, social success. What about your career? How are you being viewed? How are you viewing the situation?

33. Key – Solutions, answers. What's important and certain? Where can you find the solution? What's certain? What needs to be opened up in order to move forward?

34. Fish – Finances, plentitude/abundance, deep and flowing. How is and what is affecting your income? What freedom do you have to bring abundance into your life?

35. Anchor – Goals. Where do you drop your anchor? Stability, perseverance. What are your goals or what's affecting them? What gives you stability? Where are you placing your hopes for security or what is giving you hope for security?

36. Cross – Burdens, pain, religion. What hardships/trials/challenges will you face? What burdens must you endure?

MOD/METHOD OF DISTANCE/ NEAR-FAR STEPS

Bjorn Meuris' Volume 2 is devoted entirely to the Method of Distance and if you'd like an in-depth analysis, I recommend his book highly. With this method, the entire spread is read based on the proximity of cards to the PSC, each other and the clusters of cards that fall. MOD GT's are laid for a single timeframe, typically from the current moment into the future. You can also lay an all past MOD GT. You don't use houses in this method. Whether or not you intend to read MOD GT's, it's valuable to understand the impact that proximity plays in a GT regardless of your method of interpretation.

General steps.

1. Locate the Significator Card (SC).

   - Near top – You'll handle everything.

   - Near bottom – Everything is weighing down on you.

   - Middle – You're surrounded, for better or worse.

   - Left – Everything is ahead and you're ready, if PPF you're overly focused on the

   - future or want to forget the past.

   - Right – If reading for PPF, no future cards. May be starting a new chapter in life

   - that is uncertain (good or bad). Otherwise, you have all inauspicious cards showing that the time period of the spread will require more effort.

2. If in a relationship, locate the partner card and note their distance. Are they facing each other? What cards are between them or connect them?

3. Read the cards around the SC.

4. Knight all cards from SC.

5. If counting, do it now by 7s.

6. Read the corners and combine them across, up and down, and diagonally.

7. Read the fate line.

8. Locate the Clouds and the Scythe. They are the cards that show the biggest troubles and danger.

9. Locate the GOM or gang of misery (7, 14, 21, 23, CC); Close Circle (13, 18, 20); Travel Cluster (3, 12); Cards of Providence (9, 30); Sea Cluster (finances - 3, 34, 35); Love Cluster (24, 25, 35); Health Cluster (5, 8, 11, 6, 19); Luminaries (16, 31, 32). You want to see how these cards are clustered together and their distance from the SC.

10. Check the position of the House card. You don't want it in the middle of the GT and under the SC. This would tell you that there are a lot of things around it – a lot of people or events can disturb your private life. You want to see it near the SC and surrounded by beneficial cards.

My Life-Area/Theme Cards:

Love = Heart

Relationships = Ring

Home life = House

Extended Family = Lily

Children = Child

Friendships = Dog

Environment/Social = Garden

Career = Moon

Education = Book

Health = Tree

Travel = Ship

Finances = Fish

Distance Rules For Individual Cards:

In MOD, you can read around all life-area cards. Note their proximity to each other and the cards between them and the PSC. You can knight all of them. Consider which cards are in the comfort zone and which are in the "line of sight" (SC's row and column as well as the partner).

Distance rules for the individual cards:

Rider – Nearby references news/visitor coming from close by. Far and the news/visitor is from a distance.

Clover– As it references opportunities and luck, you want it by your side! Far away and you won't see it and can't pick it, and it is fragile and short-lived so if you miss it, it's gone.

Ship – Near indicates a journey but also extra money coming in. Far shows no journey and no extra money.

House – As it's considered a positive card on its own, having it near and with favorable cards shows that your personal life is going well or that things will improve. Traditionally, you didn't want it to appear in the center grouping in a GT. The center cards give you the heart of the story and therefore the House appearing here gives an indication that something is amiss regarding private matters.

Tree – When it falls close to the PSC it brings attention to health. This is confusing to many readers as it's the card of health and well-being, but consider that it wouldn't fall close by or in a small spread just to say that everything is fine. It's trying to bring the reader's attention to the health of the client or the situation they're asking about. Therefore, you want the card far and surrounded by favorable cards.

Clouds – Considered the most troublesome of the unfavorable cards, the Clouds will worsen the influence of other negative cards and lessen or even eliminate the effect of positive cards. Wherever they appear, they cause trouble, so we always want them far. The best you can hope for is to have the light or clearing side toward any other cards of interest.

Snake – Whenever it is near it brings adversity and tension. The cards touching the Snake may show what it's hiding. You never want it within reach to be struck with its venom or strangled.

Coffin – As the card of endings and loss, you will always want it far. When it refers to loss, it's a loss that leaves one with bad feelings and a sense of powerlessness. If close in a health reading, it indicates an illness severe enough to send you to bed. In comparing it to the Tree, the Coffin sucks the life out of other cards while the Tree sucks the energy out of the other cards. This certainly makes the Coffin a worse card. When the Coffin follows any life-area card, always look to see what follows the Coffin to see what will come after the ending.

Bouquet – Nearby it adds its beauty and fragrance to any situation. Because it references receiving something extra, it has no negative meaning when far, but will bring pleasantness to whatever cards it surrounds.

Scythe – As a card that threatens the safety and security of the client, you want to see it far from the PSC. It brings risk into the story and the direction can show where it's directed. The danger of the Scythe can be eliminated or lessened when surrounded by favorable cards as well as favorable cards surrounding the PSC that offer protection. It can be lessened to fear, uncertainty, or a narrow escape when favorably positioned. In the far position, the swinging blade can't reach you but it will have a negative impact on any cards it touches. Consider that the handle side will still deliver a blow, though not as severe as the cut of the blade side.

Whip – As the card of battle, if it's near, you can expect disagreements or a need to defend yourself. You don't want it near any life-area cards and if it's near the PSC, it indicates a disruption of harmony in their personal life.

Birds – When near, the Birds bring stress, annoyance, and chaotic situations. This will cause a lot of chatter about the annoying state, which will be described by the surrounding cards. In the earliest traditional near/far instructions for a grand tableau, the Birds falling very far from the PSC suggested a short trip was to take place (as opposed to the Ship, which needed to be near and referred to a distant journey).

Child – The Child, along with the Dog and the Garden cards relate to how you interact with others and on their own, they are all rather positive cards. When near, the Child indicates that the PSC is in good company and is interacting with others in a positive way. In the near position when describing the PSC, they will be seen as good-natured and amiable as well as retaining a sense of child-like wonder. This can describe a fun and spontaneous person. In the far position, you'd see the opposite of all or any of the aforementioned.

Fox – You don't want this shady character nearby as it's better to avoid his attention. When near, it recommends that you be on guard and protect yourself from those who may be out to trick you or manipulate a situation to their benefit. When far, you are not on his immediate radar but should check the cards that are touching to see what he's trying to manipulate.

Bear – The good fortune that the Bear represents comes with a price. The more one has, the more one attracts attention from those who don't have. When near, it tells you that the PSC has resources and a need to protect them rather than flaunt them. It may also show that you are being protected and supported, depending on the surrounding cards. When far, there's no good fortune coming your way, no power or control over matters, and no assistance in protecting yourself.

Stars – As one of the three luminaries in the deck (Sun and Moon are the others), you want this card near to bask in its light, and having it above you is best. When the Stars card is near, you have hope for success in your endeavors. You know that you're heading in the right direction. If it's near and the other near cards are all favorable, success is guaranteed! When far, your goals may currently be out of reach. Look at the surrounding cards to see where the light is shining.

Stork – When near, this card always represents a significant change in the PSC's life. The flanking cards will determine whether this is a favorable change or not or will relay what the change is about. When far, any changes won't be significant but check the cards it touches to see what changes it may bring to those areas. When it falls in the same vertical column as the PSC, changes are already taking place.

Dog – When the Dog falls near the PSC, it shows support from friends, colleagues, or alliances. An alliance isn't necessarily a person, but may reference anything you've aligned yourself with and are loyal to. When far, the PSC won't be able to count on those he trusts or may experience disappointment with regards to his or her alliances. When the Clouds falls near the Dog it's a warning not to trust those you're unsure of and even your closest friendships may be at risk.

Tower – The instructions only mention health, but what we get from this is that the card relates to something long-term and sturdy when near and surrounded by favorable cards, but that does a complete 180 if unfavorable cards such as the clouds are near. This isn't the card of a long life, but a card of life expectancy. Therefore, it is completely dependent on the surrounding cards and distance from the PSC when asking about health. It's a card you want close to the PSC and surrounded by favorable cards in a GT or small spread for health.

Garden – The original deck referred to this card as the Park and the image on the card was always a well-manicured park where people went to see and be seen by others. Hence, the near/far reference is linked to your social standing. When near, it promises respect and alliances with others that will help you get ahead. Being socially active equated with success. When far, you could see this as people shunning you or turning their backs to you. You're not being seen, noticed, assisted, or appreciated by others.

Mountain – When near, this card represents an enemy or some other sort of obstacle or challenge for the seeker. The severity of which will be explained by the surrounding cards. It may represent anything from a minor setback or delay to a need to defend yourself from a mighty opponent. When far, it won't create any issues directly but as always, look at the cards it's touching to see where it may pose a problem.

Ways/Crossroads – The closer this card falls to the PSC, the more clear the choices will be and the seeker will have more control over them. Bjorn Meuris calls the card in the near position "a way out" as long as the surrounding cards support that. The Clouds card is one you certainly don't want near the Ways when near the PSC. If the other cards are favorable, you may only experience confusion and/or doubts regarding your options, but if all the cards are unfavorable, you're in for problems. At worst, you may hit a brick wall regarding the choices you're considering. When far, your choices and options are out of reach. What we want to see in a GT is this card near the PSC and surrounded by favorable cards.

Mice – This is one of the two negative cards that is considered better to have close by (the other is the Cross). Near, the mice will still bring anxiety but the loss may be recovered or recouped. In the far position, the damage is done and there's no chance of recovery. In order to understand this concept, consider that the Mice card when far and if surrounded by any cards of concern will show a loss that is permanent, at least for the timeframe of the spread if you established one. You can view this as the Mice are already safely back in their holes and out of your reach. Always check the surrounding cards to see if they are favorable or not as this may bring some relief.

Heart – When it refers to a relationship, this is one of the three cards in the MOD that need to be favorably placed. The other two are the Ring for commitment and the Anchor for stability and loyalty. When the Heart is near, it always shows passion and desire, but it requires the other cards in the right positions to show more than that. When near in a reading for a single person, it will show romantic feelings and/or desire. In a reading for a couple, it will show love and passion. When far, we can see this as a cold heart. For a single person, there's no love or it's not there yet. For a couple, it can show deterioration of love and passion. When the reading doesn't refer specifically to a relationship, the Heart near will show some sort of passion or strong feelings for something. The surrounding cards will indicate what it refers to. If far, you need to examine the surrounding cards to see what it refers to, but being far from the PSC, passion isn't at the forefront of the reading.

Ring – This is the one card whose meaning is determined not only by its proximity, but even more so by which side of the PSC it falls on. If it falls to the right (in front of the client's card), there is a connection, union, or agreement. The closer it falls, the more significant this connection is in the reading. This is reversed should it fall to the left. In this case you want it close, as further away shows the worst case scenario. Either way, to the left it represents a possible separation. If it falls in the same vertical column it indicates a shift is taking place. Having it below will at least give the client a little more control.

Book – The primary meaning is that of unknown information, so we can say that the closer it falls, the more important this is. Unknown information isn't always a bad thing, so don't jump to conclusions until you have all the facts. Check all surrounding cards for the type of information. If far, the Book will still refer to secrets or knowledge to be revealed, but it won't have as strong an impact on the client. You'll still check the surrounding cards to see what it refers to. (*Some directional readers choose to differentiate between which side of the book is facing the PSC. If the spine side is facing the PSC, the information will remain unknown.) If you choose to read the Book in this manner, set that intention and be consistent for consistent results.

Letter – The Letter refers to news, messages, or information regardless of proximity. The surrounding cards will determine the details. It was traditionally seen as communication that wasn't delivered in person unless it fell with the Rider. If it fell near the PSC, the news was coming from your local environment or we could say that it was personal news. If far, it was coming from a distance or the news was of an official nature. You'll know which by the context of your question.

Man – The cards that fall the closest are the most significant.

Lady – The cards that fall the closest are the most significant.

Lily – Traditionally seen as one of the three cards of providence or divine guidance (the other two are the Bouquet and Child), this is a card that you want nearby as long as it falls above the PSC. Falling directly below infers that the client is doing something morally questionable or will be in for an unhappy or difficult period. Because the Child card represents innocence and goodness, finding it next to the Lily when below the PSC will greatly neutralize its meaning. You could then say that the client may be doing something wrong, but it's unintentional. In the far position, it will bestow its virtuous meaning upon the card below it but will be too far from the PSC for your client to smell its sweet fragrance.

Sun – As the most intense card of the three luminaries, the Sun is a card that you always want to see close by, particularly above, up in the sky where it can shine its light down. The cards surrounding it will receive light, warmth, and positive energy. When far, you may have no success, no courage, or no energy. You'll still check the flanking cards to see where the positive energy is going. I think the most important thing to realize is that this is an extremely positive card, so it's energy will intensify the beneficial effects of all positive cards near it and it will lessen the negativity of any surrounding unfavorable cards. For example, if it sits above the Clover, the Clover's small luck becomes huge luck and will be lasting. Sitting above the Tree when near the PSC, it doesn't increase the negativity of that card (as it pertains to health), but instead, shows that you will have the energy to deal with whatever illness the Tree is indicating.

Moon – As the last of the three luminaries, my description of the other two (Stars and Sun) holds true for the Moon also. You want this card near and preferably above. When it's close to the PSC, they're being recognized, noticed, appreciated, respected, or at least seen. When near, it can also indicate the tangible rewards of being honored. With the Fish or Ship, you may be in for a pay raise, increased business, or a company car! When far, it's possible that you're being overlooked. If far from the PSC, and the PSC is surrounded by unfavorable cards, this was traditionally seen as a risk to one's reputation. In a relationship reading, finding this card far shows that they just don't "get" you.

Key – Falling near, it shows that ventures will go well and success is within reach through the efforts of the seeker who has access to the Key. When far, especially when accompanied by unfavorable cards, it can indicate failure of your ventures or dreams as is the case when you lose or simply don't have a key.

Fish – The closer this card falls to the PSC, the more stable their financial situation will be. If it's near but surrounded by challenging cards, your attention is required to sort out the issues, but this is still considered a better placement than far away. A far placement indicates lean times, financial losses, unforeseen expenses, poor financial planning, or financial difficulties that will be explained further by the surrounding cards.

Anchor – The nearer to the PSC, the stronger its meaning of stability is, so you want to see it surrounded by favorable cards. Because it traditionally refers to both business and love, when this card is in the near position and is favorably surrounded then your personal or business endeavors are secure and sound. It shows that you have a good grip on the situation. When near but accompanied by challenging cards, you may have dropped your Anchor in the wrong place or too soon. Look at those other cards to see what they're telling you. In the far position, the stability of the Anchor is out of your reach or you may have a long way to go before reaching your goals.

Cross – Another challenging card that is more favorable in the near position (the other is Mice) because you at least have some control over the situation and it shouldn't last long. As a card of misfortune, grief, and suffering, this made no sense to me initially. Why would I want it near my card? I wondered. But in giving it a lot of thought, I realized that no matter what, our lives contain both joy and sorrow. Being able to deal with that sorrow effectively makes all the difference. You can view this as the burdens are more like daily troubles of a short-term nature or the client is being tested in some way when this card falls near. Other than near, you also want it to fall under the seeker's card so that it isn't weighing down on their heads. In the far position, the problems that the Cross brings are out of our control and of a more lasting nature. Check which cards are around the Cross and especially directly underneath as these will receive the worst the Cross has to offer. When I lay a GT, the best placement I can think of for the Cross is not very near, but near and below, while the PSC is surrounded by favorable cards.

A MOD Example:

This was a reading I performed over a year ago for a woman whose marriage was in serious trouble. She also wanted to know how her young daughter was doing as well as her health. To kill all three birds with one stone, I laid a quick MOD GT with the intention to read for those three areas. I set a general timeframe for the next six months.

1. Her position was fitting as she's quite near the bottom showing that she had the weight of the world on her shoulders and felt quite powerless at the time of the reading. She's also at the end of the spread, which told me that she was about to start a new chapter of her life but still had to sort a lot out. She and her husband are far and facing away from each other. Their connecting cards (my own technique and not part of traditional MOD, but it works in every instance) are the Ring and Mice showing the erosion of their union. All the cards between them showed me all that I needed to know! The House sits above the Coffin, the Lily sits above the Snake, and the Clouds sit above the Anchor. Complications had taken hold and their once happy home was clouded in uncertainty.

2. The corner cards showed the dissension in the marriage (Whip and Ring) as well as the unhealthy communication that was taking place between them (Letter and Tree). The first three cards indicated that she was beating herself up a bit about luck and opportunities for her daughter. The center four cards (Book, Mountain, Mice, and Clouds) painted a rather dismal picture of unknown obstacles, losses, and confusion.

3. I was immediately able to provide her with some uplifting news as she had mostly favorable cards in her comfort zone. While the Coffin is at her heel to show that there will be an ending, her home card has the Sun shining on it telling me that her private life would still flourish. She has the Bouquet above her head that told me she'd still have joy and happiness in her life. The Ring falling directly below her showed the shift in

her relationship but also told me that she had some control. Her line of sight showed all that was most important to her at the moment. She was anxious about financial losses and concerned about being deceived. She was also uncertain about family harmony. She knighted to the Cross and Snake and I asked her if she suspected infidelity but she assured me that wasn't the issue. She was simply burdened by how her marriage had turned out and felt deceived by the loss of love and stability.

4. Her husband was facing a difficult decision regarding the stability of the marriage. He still had feelings for his wife because the Heart is near, but the Ways above it and Clouds diagonally above showed confusion and a split. He knew that losses were about to ride into his life and he was stressing over where his loyalties were placed. I was happy to see that the Lily was near and above him, which told me that he wanted to do the right thing. His line of sight showed his primary concerns of making the right choices, the complications of ending a marriage, and having to face the slow-moving and probably expensive venture out into the world to find someone new. (Notice that I'm connecting the cards above to the cards in his row.) He knighted to Stork and Mountain that suggested that the divorce was her idea, which she confirmed.

5. I'd normally read around the Anchor, Heart, and Ring cards, but because they all fell within the comfort zones of the two significators, that was already done.

6. Next, I searched for the Child to see how their daughter was fairing, and she sat all the way at the top telling me that she felt in control and safe. She stands on change, which is coming on suddenly and bringing the danger of the unknown into her life, but she has the Clover and Key on either side to show that she isn't too concerned and knows she still holds the key to new opportunities. I noticed that the cards connecting her to her daughter showed some tense communication and I suggested that she speak openly and lovingly to her to let her know that everything would be alright. The cards connecting the daughter to the father told

me that even though they will be split apart, his door would always be open to her and he'd still be a significant part of her life.

7. She also asked about her health, so I found the Tree card. Luckily, it couldn't be any further from her, which reassured her. It fell far from the Coffin, so she wasn't looking at anything that would make her bedridden. But the Fox's nose was pointing to it, which told me that she did indeed have something wrong. The Fish and Garden suggested that she'd been going out a lot and drinking more alcohol than usual, which she confirmed. I then looked at the cards above and saw that she may be having pain in the urinary tract from repetitive overindulgence and suggested a trip to the doctor.

8. Lastly, I always check the fate line for the bottom line of the story, and in this case, it didn't look bad at all. While her life was about to change in a big way, she'd have new love and new friends coming her way as well as a continuing, rather "soft" relationship with her husband.

HOW AM I DOING? GT

I developed this early in my studies as a way to get comfortable with the grand tableau. Everything that I was reading was telling me that I shouldn't lay a GT for myself too often because much of the information would be redundant. That made no sense to me at all. If I could lay a daily small spread for myself, why on earth couldn't I do the same with a GT? Why did I have to read every card? Why couldn't I lay a GT as a map or puzzle to find the answers to single questions? I couldn't understand why it was common practice to lay a GT only for an all-encompassing reading for a long timeframe. It was at that moment that I began to lay GT's for single questions, daily draws, and almost everything in between! The following GT became my monthly practice. I hope you find it useful!

The concept:

This is a spread to check on how you're doing in life. Are you moving in the right direction? Are you focusing your energy in the right place? Do you have your heart set on the right things? The idea is that you will have certain cards to focus on so that you don't become lost in this big spread. You may choose to only look at a couple of the possibilities that I mention below. It is also valuable for reinforcing your card meanings and learning about the connections between cards as well as the influence of the houses in that you'll lay the spread often and for yourself, so you'll be sure to receive feedback.

You can lay this spread monthly. If you're currently experiencing a lot of changes in your life, you may want to lay it weekly.

The procedure:

Read through all the steps first so that you have an idea of what this is all about and what cards you'll be looking for and what they represent. Set your intention to check how you're doing in life and choose your time period (such as for the next month). Shuffle and lay out your 9x4 or 8x4+4. It's important to remember that you're only going to read this spread for the intention you set. You're going to only look at specific cards and their houses. You'll then look at the connections between them and other specific cards as well as looking at the cards that fall around them (touching them). You aren't going to look at any other cards. It's an excellent exercise to teach you to focus on answering only the question you asked amongst all those cards! It will help you to not get lost whenever you lay a GT for someone else, too.

Follow these steps:

- As always, I start by seeing where my card falls. Am I in one of the houses that I intended to look at? Do I have any of the cards touching me that I was planning to search for? These would be of the utmost importance.

- Look for the Anchor card and to see how well you're doing in achieving your goals. Check the intersection of Anchor and Mountain to see what challenges you'll face and check the intersection of Cross to see what's holding you back. Check the intersection between Anchor and Ship and/or Stars to see if you're heading in the right direction.

- Check the card and house of Clouds to see what you're confused about, what you're not seeing clearly, and what general troubles you can expect. See how these intersect with Stars for focus and the correct way to go, Clover for what luck and opportunities you can find to deal with this, and Sun to see what will lead to clarity and the energy to overcome.

- Look for the card and house of Bear to see what you're in control of, how strong you are, and where your power lies. See how this connects with Mice to see where there may be weakness or losses.

- Look for the Sun card and the card in its house. This will represent where you are putting your energy and what is growing. Check the connection with Fish for the flow of abundance and the House card/ house for your personal security and success. As Sun is the card of big success (as opposed to Clover for small success), see how it connects to any life area cards you're concerned with.

- Look to the Heart card/house to check on your emotions and what you're passionate about. Look at the relationship of these two with the house/card of the Rider to see what new energy/people/news is coming in related to your desires.

- Locate the Ring card/house to see how your commitments/contracts/relationships are doing. See how this connects with Anchor for stability, faithfulness, and safety. Depending on what connection you're looking at Ring for, you can also connect it to Heart for a love relationship or Moon for a work relationship, etc.

- Check the card and house of Fox to see what is wrong or driving you crazy at the moment. Connect it to Ways to see what your options are, Bear to see how to take charge and overcome, or Key to find a solution.

- Check the card and house of Coffin to see what is or needs to end right now or what you need to bury. See how it connects to Child for new beginnings or Stork for changes.

- Look at the card and house of Whip to see what the discord is and where it lies, or what you have to fight through or for.

An Example. Jean's Reading:

Jean is a twenty-eight-year-old single mother whose boyfriend moved in with her nine months prior to this reading. She had no specific question but simply wanted to know if her life was heading in the right direction. I began her session as I generally do, with a GT to get a thorough overview of her life at the moment. This is a recap of the session:

The fact that she and her man showed up back to back in the fate line with no shared cards between them gave an immediate impression of a problem. I said nothing and began to search for clues. I could see that she's got her heart in the right place as it lands in her house directly above him. It's also touching her card and Ways lands in its house telling me that she's making decisions based on her heart rather than her head. The cards surrounding the Heart indicate that she's set her heart on movement and change regarding her career and relationship. She's thinking about a more peaceful and satisfying relationship and searching for a career that she'll enjoy and will bring her to retirement. I see that she's facing the Tree with the Key above. The Tree is also in the house of Key. She informs me that she finally chose to work in the healthcare field where most of her family works. Still keeping the relationship bit to myself, I look at some other cards.

How is she doing in reaching her goals? I see that her man is in Anchor and Anchor is in Birds next to the Birds card which is in his column. Because Birds is the card of everyday stresses and it connects to Man, a problem is becoming more apparent. The Birds card is in the house of Child. She tells me that she invited him to move in with her because he was out of work and she needed a babysitter. He stays home and watches her child (from another father) while she works. She speaks of convenience but doesn't sound like a woman in love. Hmmm. She's in Fish and is currently focused on making money and getting out of debt. He lands in Anchor telling me that her goal is to have a man in her life – maybe any man. Moon is above her head in the house of Man. Is she seeing him clearly? I then checked the house of Moon. Clouds sits there. I think not. I say nothing. She's facing the Tree and I see that Child sits in the house of Tree. I ask her about the relationship between this man and her child and she begins to get a little agitated and tells me that because she's had to work two jobs to support her child, she hasn't been able to go out and meet someone new. I look to the Garden card which confirms this with Scythe above and flanked by Mountain and Tower and House below. She's remained loyal to the current relationship but there's a part of her that knows it will end (Dog in Ring and Ring in Coffin). The Cross contains the Letter which is touching Man and she confirms that the relationship has been strained and they don't speak openly. He's got Heart above but it's next to Rider which is facing Clover and Clouds. He's also in Anchor and Anchor is in Birds. I ask her if she thinks he's speaking to other women and she says yes, and that she discovered that he connects with another woman daily via the Internet from the house while she's at work (Stars is in House and Cross is in Stars). The House lands in Book, Book in Snake, and Snake in Rider. Rider is in Lily and Lily is in Garden. It appears that she's correct and he's actively pursuing someone secretly through social media. I look to the Bear to see what control she has and it lands in Ship. Ship is facing Stork which lands in the Ways and Ways falls in Heart. Coffin lands in Bear and Ring is in Coffin. She has the power to end this relationship but with Ship in Mountain and Mountain in Stork, she's been stalling. Scythe in its own house tells me that she needs to pick it up and swing it. Make it swift and clean! I then look for Whip and find it in the house of Bouquet with Fish in Whip's house. She now tells me that they fight over money and the happiness he initially brought into her life has suddenly ended. Fox in its own house doubles the wrongness of her current life situation. The Fox is facing the Birds which lands in Child with Child above in Tree. I ask her if she's confident in the care he provides for her young child and she says yes, then no, then a troubled look comes over her face. The Key to finding a solution here is communication, as hard as that will be (Key in Letter and Letter in Cross). Around the Key we can see that she needs to rise above the everyday concerns and take a higher view of the situation (Tower in Tower). She needs to open-up (Garden) and recognize (Moon) the long-term unhealthy (Tree) effects (Tower and Lily) of keeping him around as a convenient housemate and babysitter (House and Dog). Looking above the Tower to see where she can gain clarity, we have the Bear and Fish. I tell her she needs to take control of her finances and her freedom. Because he's not contributing any money to the household and her new job offers daycare, the Scythe in its own house is telling her that the time is now to cut him loose.

Looking at the Sun to see where she's putting her energy, we find it in the house of Clouds. Clover lands in Sun next to Clouds in Moon, and Moon connects to the Man via his house. The cards around the Sun are mostly unfavorable. The energy she puts into her child leads to the Stars and Bear so there's no problem there. The relationship appears to be the primary issue as the Book leads to the Ring in Coffin with Coffin and Cross below. Fox under the Sun in its own house facing Birds leading to Anchor and, well, we know who sits in Anchor! She seems to sense this is right and true and doesn't argue at all. She seems almost relieved to hear it from someone else. Apparently, it's been gnawing away at her (Mice in its own house with all the surrounding cards showing a difficult decision to change).

And there it is. A snapshot of someone's life at the present moment.

A QUICK HOW AM I DOING GT BASED ON CHAINING HOUSES

This is a fun way to get comfy with a GT without the worry of becoming "card-blind". The idea is that you'll decide what information you desire and the houses that you'll look at to extract that information. You'll ignore all the other cards. If you think about it, this is no different than laying a small spread where you leave all the other cards in the deck. The beauty of this method is that you can take it as far as you want, turning over as many cards as you're led to.

Steps:

1. Decide on the information you seek..
2. Decide which houses will represent the themes or players regarding your question.

3. Begin by turning over the card that landed in one of the houses that you'll be looking at.

4. The card that lands there will lead you to your next house.

You don't have to chain every house and you may not check every house that you initially decided on. The object is to follow the flow of the story until you receive your answer or until you loop back to a house that's already been revealed.

Example:

I laid this GT when I was trying to decide on a publisher for my first book. I wanted to focus on the following houses:

- Rider - what news/information would be coming to me?
- Clouds - what was I not seeing clearly?
- Man - I chose this house to represent the publishing company that was reviewing my manuscript.
- Lady - I chose my house to represent self-publishing.

This is what I saw:

I tuned over Rider first to see what was coming my way and found the Stork. I knew something was about to change.

I then checked the house of Stork and found Man. The change would be with the publishing company. I then checked the house of Man and found the Scythe. It appeared that I'd be making a final decision to remove them, but the Scythe is also my editing card, so I didn't stop there. What was the Scythe referring to? I looked at its house and found the Ring. It then appeared that I'd make the decision to end my relationship with them. I looked at the house of Ring and found Mice. As a card of loss, it was confirming that I'd end the relationship with this company. I didn't feel I needed to take the chain regarding the publishing company any further and decided to check on the house I'd assigned to self-publishing. There I found the Book! It certainly appeared that I'd be self-publishing, but I wanted to check the house of Book and there was my card. I call this a criss-cross and it confirmed the answer. Lastly, I checked the house of Clouds to see what I wasn't seeing clearly and found the Garden. This told me that I'd spent enough time waiting for the publishing company and needed to get the book out to the public. I looked at the house of Garden and found the Key. This was the solution. I went to the house of Key and found the Star. This was the direction I was meant to follow. I then checked the house of Star and found the Rider. It was time to make this happen! The Rider was the stopping point because it led me back in a loop to the first house that I checked. I found the solution and answered my question. I'd be self-publishing my book.

Unforgettable Lenormand by Teri Smith

LET'S PLAY CONNECT THE DOTS!

A READING EXAMPLE

Some refer to GT's as maps. It truly is a map of 36 locations and you're look-ing for the roads that connect the locations, which locations are in close proximity, or examining the routes between the locations to see if it will be an easy or a difficult journey to get from one to another.

If you prefer, you can look at a GT as a puzzle. Not a jigsaw puzzle, where you have a pile of pieces that you need to connect, but a connect-the-dots puzzle. Looking at it in this way, imagine searching for connections among theme groups rather than simply examining the locations and cards surrounding a single theme card. Think about looking for cards of a particular theme group and drawing a line to connect them and then examining the cards that you drew the lines through.

Here's an example from a GT reading I performed recently based on a single question that illustrates this technique.

A young married man came to me in a quandary. He had intended on returning to school for yet another Master's Degree, but a new opportunity had just arisen to take a job as a script writer, which, according to him, was something he'd dreamed of doing for most of his adult life.

The first thing I did was choose two theme cards for each option so that I could see where they fall and how they connect to each other and to the client. I chose Book and Tower for attending the University and Moon and Letter for the writing job. This is what I saw:

Straight away, the first three cards indicated acting on a new opportunity. Ship landed in its own house and was heading toward a change. The center four told me that he'd be expanding his world and putting a lot of energy and effort into something. The corners told me that he had news of a new opportunity and because Clover fell in Rider and Rider is diagonally placed in Moon, it was already apparent to me that the writing job was the way to go. But I of course, didn't stop there. Tower fell in Coffin and was diagonally matched with Ways, telling me that he'd go another way and bury the school plan. He fell in the house of change and he and his wife were seeing eye to eye regarding his decision. She fell in the house of loyalty. With Birds above her, I could see that she was a little nervous about things. He had the contract on his mind. Looking at the cards that fell in their houses, I could see that she was worried about a possible erosion of her current lifestyle and he was worried about making the wrong decision. I searched for the two school cards and saw that they fell in difficult houses and had only the Tree between them which confirmed for me that this was a dead option. I found the Letter and Moon next and saw that they were in favorable houses and connected by the Sun in the house of Child for starting something new. The job just kept looking better! Heart landed in its own house, indicating that he should follow his heart. Letter fell in the house of goals and his only burden was going to be finding the strength to take the job. With Lily in the house of Letter linking to Clouds in the house of Lily, I could tell that he was uncertain of his abilities in making this job a success. Because I always look to the Stars card and house for the way to go, it was clear that grabbing this job opportunity was written in the stars. I then looked for the Key and found it safely in its own house, which told me that this was a sure thing. Lastly, the fate line couldn't have been more clear. The key was to drop his Anchor at the new job where he'll prosper. This was another happy ending reading and I can't get enough of them! They more than make up for the difficult ones.

Unforgettable Lenormand by Teri Smith

TIPS AND STEPS FOR USING EXTRA CARDS

Many decks include extra cards and you can certainly include them in a GT. There are other instances when you might want to add extra significator cards such as when you have several people or animals in the story but don't want to assign them to any of the original 36 cards as this tends to take them out of play. Because I began by reading for animals, I added extra animal cards to my GT's on a regular basis and simply assumed that others did the same. If you consider that every card in a GT has a house, then adding extra cards requires you to add extra houses. You'll treat this in the same manner as any other house. For example, if you are a woman, then #29 is your card and house #29 is your house. The same applies to any extra card. If you're including the extra card from a deck such as the Maybe Lenormand, the houses will retain the meaning of the cards as with any other house.

Here are some tips:

- After careful consideration of exactly what information you're seeking, decide on your question, your spread, and what extra cards you need.
- Decide and write down who the original #28 and #29 will represent.
- Always write down who or what the extra cards will represent while you're writing down your question and any other background information you may need.
- Choosing the extra cards from another deck (of the same size for shuffling purposes) helps them to stand out in the spread so you can easily spot them. I've found it to be much less confusing than using the extra cards from the same deck.
- Create a house for each extra card based on that card's meaning. You can use cards from another deck or make your own from index cards.

- In choosing cards for the extra houses, make them slightly bigger than the cards you're using for the reading so that you can clearly see the house name without having to move the cards on top.

- You can also buy blank cards in every size at a good price from https://www.makeplayingcards.com/promotional/plain-blank-flash-cards.html

- If you're the type of person who likes to use only one deck (is there such a person?), then buy 2 or 3 of them so you have the extra cards you need.

- I always add an even number of extra cards. This is something I started doing simply because odd numbers seemed off to me some-how and I wanted to keep the same flow as a traditional 36-card GT – which of course, is an even number.

- You may choose to add an entire row or more to your GT (if you want to use the full Maybe Lenormand deck for example) or you may want to add an extra fate line for advice or a spiritual message or blessing.

- For those of you who love counting rounds (as I do), there's no law that says you have to wind up back at the card you started with. You simply need to decide how many cards you want to wind up with and divide the number of cards you laid by that number to get your counting number. So, if I have a 40 card GT and want to wind up with 5 cards for my summary, I divide 40 by 5 and get 8. When the division gives me an exact number, I count from each card, not the next card. For example, in the extended family GT example, I counted by 8's starting at the new woman's child, and started each counting round on the same card as you do in a 36-card GT. This gave me 16, 31, 27, 4, 14. For the 38-card animal GT, dividing by 5 gave me a non-exact number – 7.6. In this case, I count by subsequent cards rather than the cards I land on. This brings me back to the nearest space before the card I started on without passing it. In counting for dog #2, I got 11, 7, 16, 18, and 33.

- You can use mixed systems for extended GTs. You might choose tarot, oracle, Grand Jeu Lenormand, or gypsy cards for an additional advice line or for extra houses. Play around with it using fun questions and see how it works out for you.

Extra card GT example:

Here's an example of a GT reading using extra cards. This was for a divorced female client. She has one daughter from her marriage and is living with a new man. Her ex is living with a new woman, who also has one daughter. She came to me for a reading to see how her daughter feels about the new woman and the new woman's daughter as well as how they both feel about her daughter. She wanted to check on the overall dynamic involving everyone.

Question asked: How do all members of this newly-extended family feel about each other?

Procedure:

Because the client is in a relationship, I chose #28 to represent her new man, #29 is the client, and the Child card from deck number 1 is her own daughter. I then took another #28 to represent her ex, another #29 to represent his new woman, and another Child card to represent the new woman's daughter. Because I like to keep the GT's at an even number of cards, I chose the Owls card from the second deck to represent wisdom or a couple.

While deck #1 contained the necessary extra cards for this reading, I like to use another deck so that the extra cards are easy to spot. When they're all from the same deck, it gets very confusing. Also note the hand-made house placements for the extra cards.

Reading synopsis:

The first thing I noticed was the ex in his own child's house next to the new child, who lands in the house of Fox and the Tower lands in her house. He's separated from his own child by the Stork, the card of change. His own child lands in the house of Whip. You can already see the dynamic at play here. His own daughter feels some discord and is putting energy into it and getting away with quite a bit, too (Whip in Sun). The new daughter is being sneaky and balking at authority. She also has Snake above her head Moon below, telling me that she's not showing her true colors. With the Tower in her house down in the corner with Sun, her mother, and Bear, she's protected and getting away with a lot. The client's daughter has House above and Heart below, so she's still feeling secure and loved, though you can see the Scythe cutting into her dreams (Stars). She's a bit nervous about the changes (Birds and Stork) and is feeling burdened by the new relationships (Cross and Ring). The Client landed all the way at the bottom and in her ex's house with Mice in Anchor with Key above and Mountain in Cross with Coffin above and facing the Dog in the house of wisdom/couple. She's still burdened by the ending of her marriage, feeling a loss of security, but she'd be wise to see that her husband is still loyal to their daughter and her security. Look at the new woman right in the client's house! Right in her face! She now has the ex's heart and feels empowered. With the Bear in her house, I could see a bit of a power struggle going on. I then saw that the new woman faces Bouquet in Lily, her own daughter lands in Fox and Fox lands in the house of Bouquet. Her daughter is bringing some wrongness/sneakiness into the family dynamic while making herself look good at the same time (flowering-up with the Bouquet and Lily is in the house of Clouds). The client's new man is in the house of Change with Rider at his back, facing Stars, with Tree over his head. He rode into this relationship with stars in his eyes, but is now feeling that it's a bit unhealthy. He's discovering some buried secrets (Book and Coffin).

Ok, while this spread was showing a lot of issues, nothing was dire. When the client returned four months later for another unrelated reading, her personal life was getting back on track and all the players were still in the picture.

Whisper Lenormand by Teri Smith

ALL GOOD THINGS
COME TO AN END

A nd, so, my friends, I say goodbye for now. I hope this book has both helped and inspired you. You just joined me on a daily journey that spanned over a year of my life where I set my pendulum and oracle cards aside, and committed to mastering the language of the Lenormand oracle by using it as my primary method for prediction and divination. I've begun working on videos, and online courses, so this really isn't goodbye. Please look for me on Youtube and my new website. I think I'll go have a well-deserved beer. Ciao for now!

ABOUT THE AUTHOR

Lisa Young-Sutton is a professional card reader, animal communicator, dog trainer and groomer, and journalist from the US. She's known for her amazingly detailed and specific readings that she delivers with sensitivity and care. She's a Pro-level endorsed Lenormand reader with the World Divination Association. When she's not writing, working with dogs and horses, or reading cards, she enjoys hiking, traveling, gardening, cooking, and baking.

https://lisaloveslenormand.com/
https://www.instagram.com/lisaloveslenormand/
https://www.linkedin.com/in/lisa-young-sutton-a0a962164/
https://www.facebook.com/LenormandLisa
https://www.youtube.com/channel/UCoJ0s12JU99ex7zasppO9Hw

CREDITS

Special thanks to Ciro Marchetti for allowing me to use his Gilded Reverie Lenormand and Sui Generis Lenormand decks.

Teri Smith of Divine Walks on Etsy for her Whisper Lenormand, Unforgettable Lenormand, and Her Legacy Lenormand decks.

Loreen Muzik of Divination Apothecary on Etsy for her amazing Grand Tableau mats.